From Duck Country

Ducks Unlimited

Golden Retreat

Terry Redlin

CROCK•POT CASSOULET

1 cup chopped carrots
1/2 cup chopped onion
1/3 cup water
1   8 ounce can tomato
        sauce
1/2 cup dry red wine
1 teaspoon garlic powder
1/2 teaspoon thyme
1/8 teaspoon cloves
2 bay leaves
1   15-ounce can navy
    beans, drained
4 duck breast filets
8 ounces Polish sausage,
        sliced

Bring carrots, onion and water to a boil in saucepan; reduce heat. Simmer, covered, for 5 minutes. Place in 3¹/2 to 4-quart Crock•Pot. Stir in tomato sauce, wine, seasonings and beans. Place duck breasts and sausage on top of bean mixture. Cook on Low for 9 to 10 hours or on High for 5¹/2 to 6 hours or until duck breasts are tender. Remove bay leaves. Yield: 4 servings.

From Duck Country

Ducks Unlimited

Credits

From Duck Country

A compedium of favorite recipes of the readers of
Ducks Unlimited magazine.

by Billy Joe Cross

*Billy Joe Cross is an award-winning wild game chef and cooking columnist from **Ducks Unlimited** magazine. He has authored or edited six books on how to cook wild game and fish.*

From Duck Country

A Ducks Unlimited Book

Harry D. Knight, President
Matthew B. Connolly, Jr., Executive Vice President
Charlotte Rush, Director of Communications
Editorial Assistance: Gary Cox, Steve Kerr and Shari Zalewski, Graphics
Mike Beno, Text

Ducks Unlimited, Inc.
One Waterfowl Way
Long Grove, Illinois 60047
Library of Congress Catalog Number: 89-11625
ISBN: 0-87197-251-4

Dedication

To all those who know the tug on a line, the rustle and crack of a buck's approach, and the sibilant whisper of wings before the dawn, this book is dedicated. The preparation, sharing and enjoyment of nature's gifts is no less than the consummation of your seasonal experiences. May your hours in the kitchen be as warm as your moments outdoors.

Billy Joe Cross

Preface

A Tribute to Terry Redlin

THE COVER: *"Golden Retreat,"* by Terry Redlin, is the most successful conservation print in Ducks Unlimited history. Chosen as DU's 50th anniversary painting, Redlin's work raised nearly $3 million for the cause of North American waterfowl conservation. Since 1980, on a national level, four of his print editions raised some $7 million.

An illustrator and graphic designer for most of his career, Redlin made the break to become a fulltime wildlife painter in 1979. Within four years he had won three state conservation stamp design competitions and placed his work on six covers of national magazines. In the ensuing years, the popularity of Redlin's work has grown, as has the demand.

"Today, I've backed away from all contests and most art shows," Redlin says, "with the exception of the annual show in my hometown of Watertown, South Dakota. I guess I just prefer to stick close to my studio by the lake and paint."

Popularity has put Redlin in the position to paint whatever he chooses. Today the work coming from his studio/home on the wooded shore of Lake Minnetonka, west of Minneapolis, includes landscapes, rural Americana and Christmas scenes. "I still do wildlife paintings, but I've diversified my work," Redlin says.

"I did it for pure fun. I now have a variety of directions to go in."

So has the world seen its last Terry Redlin waterfowl painting? "Not a chance," he says. While Redlin will not render as many duck paintings as he once did, he says he'll never quit. After all, Redlin says, he grew up hunting waterfowl in South Dakota pothole country, "and you can't quit something that's part of you."

Contents

Foreword

Harry D. Knight, President

Any outdoor sperson will tell you that hunting and eating go together. On the primal level, the latter act is simply the natural culmination of the first. But on the modern level, I'd have to say eating is more *celebration* than culmination. After all, a wild game dinner with family or friends is the warmest way in which to share an evening.

I've never known a hunter who didn't love to eat—and I've been doing both for a long time. But not long enough, where waterfowl hunting is concerned. Thank goodness I had the luck to meet Joe Biggins.

Joe was City Manager in Newport News, Virginia, back in 1964. He was also my boss. At age 65 or so, he'd hunted the Atlantic coast during the days of the sinkbox, so it was an honor when this veteran invited me, a raw rookie, to his shore blind on the Atlantic Flyway's legendary shooting grounds of Back Bay, Virginia.

Teal, widgeon, pintails and black ducks swirled over our blind on the grassy bay that day, and I didn't hit many. In fact, you might even say that I was hit harder than the ducks were. The raw salt air, decoying ducks and the companionship of a hunting partner converted me for life, and 25 years later, I can't get enough.

Today, things have changed at Back Bay. The marsh grasses are gone, and most of the ducks have gone elsewhere. Old Joe and I hunted for 14 years before his death at age 79, and I'm thankful for all the things he taught me. Were it not for him, there might never have been a roast duck on my dinner table.

I hope there is an Old Joe in your life and that you have special memories of a place where the ducks flew every morning. As conservationists, we must work hard to make sure that places like this, and the people who love them, remain forever in our future. May your mornings on the marsh be many, and may your evenings at the table be filled with much laughter and many friends.

Introduction

Ducks Unlimited

Today Ducks Unlimited is the largest conserver of waterfowl wetlands in the world. But in 1936 it was little more than an ambitious dream in the minds of some concerned sportsmen.

The historic drought of the duckless Thirties had baked dry the ancestral waterfowl nesting grounds of North America. The ducks faced crisis, and everyone knew it. But it took a special group of sportsmen—the More Game Birds in America Foundation—to do something about it.

Ducks Unlimited was formed by the Foundation in 1937. It was built on one premise: that habitat development on North America's primary waterfowl breeding range was the best way to conserve ducks and geese. Over a half-century later, DU remains committed to that precept.

It is a long road from the simple earthen dams that DU constructed in prairie Canada in 1938 to the computer and satellite technology with which Ducks Unlimited today maps and evaluates critical waterfowl habitats. But the purpose remains the same: conservation of wild places for wildlife. As today's vernal and autumnal migrations of ducks and geese cross the continent, they find breeding, resting and nesting habitat on DU projects, for Ducks Unlimited is everywhere the ducks are. DU's 5.1 million acres of wetlands and uplands gives hatching ducks a start on life, migrating ducks a place to rest and refuel and wintering ducks a place to wait out the cold, form pair bonds and begin the cycle anew. And beyond the ducks and geese, over 600 wild birds and mammals—many of the endangered or threatened species—find life on Ducks Unlimited habitat projects.

Nutritional Analysis Guidelines

The editors have attempted to present these Ducks Unlimited family recipes in a form that allows approximate nutritional values to be computed. Persons with dietary or health problems or whose diets require close monitoring should not rely solely on the nutritional information provided. They should consult their physicians or a registered dietitian for specific information.

Abbreviations for Nutritional Analysis

Cal — Calories   Chol — Cholesterol   Potas — Potassium
Prot — Protein   Carbo — Carbohydrates   g — gram
T Fat — Total Fat   Sod — Sodium   mg — milligram

Nutritional information for recipes is computed from values furnished by the United States Department of Agriculture Handbook. Many specialty items and new products now available on the market are not included in this handbook. However, producers of new products frequently publish nutritional information on each product's packaging and that information may be added, as applicable, for a more complete analysis. If the nutritional analysis notes the exclusion of a particular ingredient, check the package information.

Unless otherwise specified, the nutritional analysis of these recipes is based on the following guidelines:

- All measurements are level.
- Artificial sweeteners vary in use and strength so should be used "to taste," using the recipe ingredients as a guideline.
- Artificial sweeteners using aspartame (NutraSweet and Equal) should not be used as a sweetener in recipes involving prolonged heating which reduces the sweet taste. For further information on the use of these sweeteners, refer to package information.
- Alcoholic ingredients have been analyzed for the basic ingredients, although cooking causes the evaporation of alcohol thus decreasing caloric content.
- Buttermilk, sour cream, and yogurt are the types available commercially.
- Chicken, cooked for boning and chopping, has been roasted; this method yields the lowest caloric values.
- Cottage cheese is cream-style with 4.2% creaming mixture. Dry-curd cottage cheese has no creaming mixture.
- Eggs are all large.
- Flour is unsifted all-purpose flour.
- Garnishes, serving suggestions and other optional additions and variations are not included in the analysis.
- Margarine and butter are regular, not whipped or presoftened.
- Milk is whole milk, 3.5% butterfat. Lowfat milk is 1% butterfat. Evaporated milk is produced by removing 60% of the water from whole milk.
- Oil is any type of vegetable cooking oil. Shortening is hydrogenated vegetable shortening.
- Salt to taste as noted in the method has not been included in the nutritional analysis.
- If a choice of ingredients has been given, the nutritional analysis reflects the first option.

The Best of Times

Menus and Memories

Winging In–Mallards

Eldridge Hardie

HARDIE'S DUCK BREAST

Breasts from 4 large ducks
1 cup all-purpose flour
1 teaspoon sage
Dash of salt and pepper
1/2 cup butter
1 cup chopped fresh
    mushrooms
1 cup chopped white
    onion
1 cup chopped celery
3 slices bacon, crisp-fried,
    crumbled
1/2 teaspoon thyme
1/4 teaspoon garlic salt
1/4 cup butter

Cut duck breasts into thin strips. Roll in mixture of flour, sage, salt and pepper. Brown in 1/2 cup butter in iron skillet over low heat. Remove and set aside. Add mushrooms, onion and celery. Cook until tender. Add duck, crumbled bacon, thyme, garlic salt and remaining 1/4 cup butter. Simmer for 30 minutes, stirring frequently. Serve over rice. Yield: 6 servings.

Ann Hardie

NANCY
GRIFFEN

Dinner At Home

Harry Knight: President, Ducks Unlimited

The abundance of game and fish in Virginia makes me a fortunate fellow. From the coast to the mountains, bountiful bags await the lucky sportsman. For this reason I would guess that my family enjoys more wild game dinners than most. This is no boast, but an expression of gratitude from a man who's drawn both physical and spiritual sustenance from wild places. Ducks, geese, turkeys, quail and grouse grace our table regularly. And as the seasons change, so will our meals. Crabs, shrimp and many types of finfish make for festive, flavorful dinners. Combine this variety of wild game with some traditional domestic fare, and you've got a very special meal indeed.

The following dinner is a favorite at our house, and I pass it along to you in the hope that it brings some enjoyment to your home as well. Prepare it for your family and savor the smiles.

Always remember, cold days in the field mean warm evenings around the table.

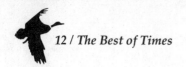

Favorite Family Dinner

Crab Louis Appetizer
Roast Canada Goose and Smithfield Ham
Baked Sweet Potatoes
Hot Curried Fruit
Buttered Spinach
Golden Popovers with Butter
Sweet Potato Pie

CRAB LOUIS APPETIZER

1 head lettuce, shredded
1 pound crab meat
Juice of 1 large lemon
3/4 cup mayonnaise
3 to 4 tablespoons chili sauce

Make bed of lettuce on individual serving plates. Top with crab meat. Sprinkle with lemon juice. Combine mayonnaise and chili sauce in small small bowl; beat well. Spoon over crab meat.

ROAST CANADA GOOSE

1 oven-ready goose
2 tablespoons Burgundy
or Claret
2 cups water
1 tablespoon salt
1 teaspoon pepper
1 tablespoon celery salt
1 cup chopped celery
1 cup chopped onion

Wash goose; pat dry inside and out. Place in large roasting pan with cover. Pour Burgundy and water around goose. Sprinkle goose with salt, pepper and celery salt. Sprinkle celery and onion over goose. Roast at 500 degrees for 20 minutes or until brown. Reduce temperature to 350 degrees. Roast, covered, for 2½ to 3 hours or until goose is tender.

SMITHFIELD HAM

1 Smithfield ham
Whole cloves
Honey
Fine dry bread crumbs
Brown sugar

Place ham with enough water to cover in deep roasting pan. Let stand overnight. Remove, drain and wash ham. Return to pan with enough water to cover. Simmer for 3 to 4 hours or until tender. Cool ham in liquid. Remove skin. Score fat; stud with whole cloves. Place in shallow baking pan. Brush with honey. Pat mixture of dry bread crumbs and brown sugar over surface. Bake at 425 degrees for 20 minutes or until brown. Slice very thinly to serve.

The distinctive flavor of this ham comes from the unique method of curing which includes hanging and smoking. Hams must be aged for six months before selling. The authentic ham comes from Smithfield, Virginia.

BAKED SWEET POTATOES

Sweet Potatoes
Butter

Scrub potatoes well. Place on baking sheet. Bake at 425 degrees for 45 minutes or until potatoes are soft. Cut down center of each potato. Fill with pats of butter. Serve hot.

HOT CURRIED FRUIT

1   16-ounce can peach halves
1   16-ounce can pear halves
1   15-ounce can pineapple
chunks
1 tablespoon cornstarch
2 tablespoons brown sugar
1 teaspoon curry powder
1   16-ounce jar spiced
apple rings

Drain peaches, pears and pineapple, reserving juice. Pour juice into saucepan. Stir in mixture of cornstarch, brown sugar and curry powder. Cook over medium heat until thickened, stirring constantly. Add all fruit. Cook until heated through. Serve hot.
Yield: 8 to 12 servings.

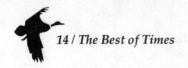
BUTTERED SPINACH

Spinach
Butter
Salt and pepper to taste

Wash spinach thoroughly, removing any discolored leaves. Cook, tightly covered, in steamer or in saucepan with a very small amount of water just until barely tender. Drain. Chop finely. Add butter and salt and pepper to taste.

GOLDEN POPOVERS

1¹/2 cups all-purpose flour
1¹/2 cups milk
3 eggs, slightly beaten
¹/2 teaspoon salt

Combine flour, milk, eggs and salt in mixer bowl. Beat at medium speed just until smooth. Preheat well-greased muffin cups in 450-degree oven for 3 minutes. Remove from oven. Fill ²/3 full with batter. Bake at 450 degrees for 30 minutes. Reduce temperature to 300 degrees. Bake for 10 to 15 minutes or until golden brown. Serve immediately. Yield: 1 dozen.

SWEET POTATO PIE

2 cups mashed cooked
sweet potatoes
1 egg, slightly beaten
¹/4 cup sugar
¹/2 cup milk
2 tablespoons melted butter
1 teaspoon cinnamon
1 unbaked 9-inch pie shell

Combine sweet potatoes, egg, sugar, milk, butter and cinnamon in mixer bowl. Beat at medium speed until well blended. Spoon into pie shell. Bake at 425 degrees for 35 minutes or until knife inserted halfway between edge and center comes out clean. Cool before serving. Yield: 6 to 8 servings.

Thanksgiving at Ashepoo

Gaylord Donnelley: Past President, Ducks Unlimited

Thanksgiving Day is a very special and eventful day at Ashepoo Plantation. The day begins with breakfast at 5 a.m., followed by a duck hunt on the Plantation ponds. After the hunt, the hunters gather in the kitchen for refreshments and to tell of their morning hunt.

The grandchildren are ready for a ride on the hunting wagon pulled by a team of mules.

A dove hunt takes place in the afternoon for those who want to participate. Meanwhile, the grandchildren are busy making place cards and decorations for the Thanksgiving table. Before dinner, the grandchildren present a talent show for the evening entertainment.

Family and friends sit down to a bountiful Thanksgiving dinner and then, to end a busy, fun-filled day, the grandchildren roast marshmallows at the outdoor fireplace while the rest of the family sit by the fire and recall the events of the day.

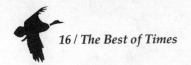

Bountiful Thanksgiving Dinner

Ashepoo Wild Turkey with Giblet Gravy
Fresh Cranberry Sauce
Relishes
Oyster Stuffing
Candied Sweet Potatoes
Dilly Green Beans
Hot French Rolls
Pumpkin Pie and Mincement Pie

ASHEPOO WILD TURKEY

1 *8 to 10-pound wild turkey*
Salt to taste
Vegetable oil
Pepper to taste
2 to 3 stalks celery
2 medium onions, cut into
quarters
2 cups water

Clean turkey thoroughly; wipe dry inside and out. Sprinkle cavity with salt. Rub turkey with oil. Sprinkle with pepper. Place in roasting pan. Place celery and onions inside and around turkey. Pour water around turkey. Roast, covered with foil or lid, at 325 degrees for 2¹/₂ to 3 hours, basting with pan juices every 30 minutes. Roast, uncovered, for 30 minutes longer or until brown.

FRESH CRANBERRY SAUCE

4 cups fresh cranberries
2 cups sugar
2 cups water
2 teaspoons rum flavoring

Wash cranberries; drain. Combine cranberries, sugar and water in saucepan. Bring to a boil. Cook until cranberry skins pop. Stir in rum flavoring. Mash berries slightly. Cool.

OYSTER STUFFING

1/2 cup chopped celery
1/2 cup chopped onion
1/4 cup butter or margarine
6 cups dry bread crumbs
3 cups oysters
Salt and pepper to taste
1 teaspoon poultry seasoning
2 eggs, beaten
1 1/2 cups oyster liquor
Milk

Sauté celery and onion in butter in skillet until tender. Add bread crumbs; mix well. Add oysters, seasonings and eggs; mix well. Add enough oyster liquor and milk to moisten. Spoon into turkey cavity or into casserole. Bake casserole at 325 degrees for 1 hour or until brown.

CANDIED SWEET POTATOES

6 sweet potatoes
1/2 cup melted butter or margarine
1/4 cup packed brown sugar
1 1/2 tablespoons orange juice
Marshmallows

Peel sweet potatoes. Cut into halves lengthwise. Place in heavy casserole. Pour mixture of butter, brown sugar and orange juice over top. Bake at 325 degrees for 1 hour. Top with marshmallows. Bake just until marshmallows are brown.

DILLY GREEN BEANS

4 slices bacon
1/2 cup chopped green onions
6 cups cooked green beans
1 teaspoon salt
Dash of pepper
1 tablespoon dillweed

Sauté bacon until crisp. Drain, reserving 1 tablespoon drippings. Sauté onions in reserved drippings in skillet until tender. Add green beans, salt, pepper, bacon and dillweed. Cook until heated through.

Dutch Oven Dinners

Bud and Carlina Phelps

Dutch oven cooking has been used for hundreds of years. It moved west with the pioneers. Many of the ovens used today have been around for numerous decades. The following recipes will use the method of cooking with coals on the ground. This type of cooking is fun and generally fairly easy. See pages 201 to 202 for expert information on using the Dutch oven for cooking outdoors.

Down-Home Dinner

Bud's Good Ole Chicken or
Stuffing-Topped Chicken
Von's Mother's Swedish Stew
Potatoes, Onions and Stuff
Celery-Bean Bake
Easy Drop Biscuits
Pineapple Upside-Down Cake with Lemon Sauce

BUD'S GOOD OLE CHICKEN

1/2 cup butter
1/4 cup oil
8 chicken breast halves, skinned
4 thighs
4 drumsticks
All-purpose flour
2 10-ounce cans cream of chicken soup
2 soup cans beer
1 teaspoon tarragon flakes
2 tablespoons dried parsley flakes
Salt and pepper to taste
Dash of paprika

Use 12-inch Dutch oven with 8 to 10 coals under and 12 to 14 coals on top. Melt butter in Dutch oven over hot coals. Add oil. Coat chicken with flour. Brown in butter mixture. Add soup, beer, tarragon, parsley, salt and pepper and paprika. Cover with lid and coals. Cook for 45 minutes to 1 hour or until chicken is tender. Yield: 8 to 10 servings.

Chicken adapts well to Dutch oven cooking in many variations. You can use any of the soups, herbs and vegetable combinations, rice, noodles, dumplings, etc.

STUFFING-TOPPED CHICKEN

1 miniature bottle of Cognac
8 chicken breast halves, skinned
8 slices Swiss cheese
2 10-ounce cans mushroom soup
1 cup sour cream
6 tablespoons white wine
2 packages cornmeal stuffing mix with herb seasonings
1/4 cup chopped parsley
Melted butter

Use 12-inch Dutch oven with 8 to 10 coals under and 12 to 14 coals on top. Preheat Dutch oven over hot coals. Pour Cognac in heated oven; ignite. Let flame subside. Place chicken breasts in oven. Place 1 slice cheese on each chicken breast. Combine soup, sour cream and wine in bowl; mix well. Pour over chicken. Sprinkle stuffing mix and herb seasonings over top. Sprinkle with parsley. Drizzle with butter. Cover with lid and coals. Bake for 1 hour. This recipe appeared in the *Salt Lake Tribune* by Ager and Jones and is a delicious dish. Yield: 8 servings.

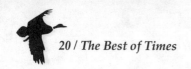

VON'S MOTHER'S SWEDISH STEW

1 turnip, peeled, cut into
chunks
4 potatoes, peeled, cut into
chunks
6 carrots, peeled, cut into
chunks
2 pounds link sausage
8 peppercorns
1 head cabbage, cut into
wedges

Use 12-inch Dutch oven over fire. Place turnip, potatoes, carrots, sausage and peppercorns in cast-iron Dutch oven. Add enough water to cover. Place on hanger over fire or directly on coals. Bring mixture to a boil. Cook for 30 minutes or until carrots are tender. Add cabbage. Cook for 15 minutes longer or until cabbage is tender. Yield: 6 servi ngs.

POTATOES, ONIONS AND STUFF

10 large Irish potatoes
5 medium onions
12 ounces sliced bacon
1/4 cup oil
Salt and pepper to taste
1/2 cup beer
Paprika to taste

Use 12-inch Dutch oven with 10 coals under and 15 coals on top. Peel and slice potatoes and onions. Chop bacon into small pieces. Brown bacon in Dutch oven over hot coals. Add oil, potatoes and onions. Season with salt and pepper. Cover with lid and coals. Cook for 15 minutes; turn potatoes. Cook for 5 minutes. Add beer. Cook until brown, turning occasionally. Sprinkle with paprika. May add mushrooms, bell peppers, pimento or Italian sausage if desired. Yield: 10 servings.

CELERY-BEAN BAKE

2 cups water
3   10-ounce packages frozen
green beans, thawed
3 cups 1-inch slices celery
3 tablespoons butter
1/2 teaspoon dillweed
Salt and pepper to taste

Use 12-inch Dutch oven with 8 coals under and 15 coals on top. Bring water to a boil in Dutch oven over hot coals. Combine green beans, celery, butter, dillweed and salt and pepper in bowl; mix well. Add to boiling water. Cover with lid and coals. Cook for 20 minutes or until vegetables are tender. Yield: 10 servings.

EASY DROP BISCUITS

Butter
4¹/2 cups Bisquick
1¹/3 cups warm beer

Use 12-inch Dutch oven with 8 coals under and 12 to 14 coals on top. Preheat Dutch oven and lid over hot coals. Melt butter in Dutch oven. Combine Bisquick and beer in bowl; mix well. Drop by spoonfuls into butter. Cover with lid and coals. Bake for 10 to 20 minutes, checking frequently to prevent burning. Yield: 20 biscuits.

PINEAPPLE UPSIDE-DOWN CAKE

1 cup butter
1 cup packed brown sugar
9 slices pineapple, drained
9 maraschino cherries
1 8-ounce can crushed pineapple, drained
1¹/2 packages yellow cake mix

Use 12-inch Dutch oven with 8 coals under and 14 coals on top. Line Dutch oven with foil, leaving edges so cake can be lifted out and inverted. Melt butter in Dutch oven over hot coals. Stir in brown sugar. Arrange pineapple slices over brown sugar mixture. Place maraschino cherry in center of each slice. Spoon crushed pineapple around pineapple slices. Prepare cake mix using package directions. Pour over pineapple. Cover with lid and coals. Bake for 30 to 35 minutes or until cake is golden and tests done, checking after 15 minutes. Lift cake out; invert onto serving plate. Serve with Lemon Sauce.
Yield: 15 to 20 servings.

LEMON SAUCE

¹/2 cup sugar
1 tablespoon cornstarch
1 cup water
2 tablespoons butter
¹/2 teaspoon grated lemon rind
1¹/2 tablespoons lemon juice

Combine sugar and cornstarch in saucepan. Stir in water. Cook until thickened, stirring constantly. Remove from heat. Stir in butter, lemon rind and juice. Make this at home and take with you. Yield: 2¹/2 cups.

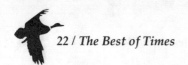

Elegant Outdoor Dinner

*Ruby Glazed Cornish Game Hens or
Pork Chops and Sauerkraut
Veggie Medley
Sourdough French Bread with Pine Nuts
Pear Gingerbread Upside-Down Cake
Fruit Cobbler*

RUBY GLAZED CORNISH HENS

*8 Cornish game hens, split,
flattened
3 cups apricot-pineapple jam
3 cups Rosé or red wine
Salt to taste*

Use 12-inch Dutch oven with 8 coals under and 12 to 14 coals on top. Preheat Dutch oven over hot coals. Place 4 Cornish hens on bottom of oven. Combine jam and wine in bowl; mix well. Pour half the mixture over Cornish hens. Arrange remaining Cornish hens on top. Pour remaining jam mixture over top. Sprinkle with salt. Cover with lid and coals. Bake for 45 minutes, turning Cornish hens occasionally. Yield: 8 servings.

PORK CHOPS AND SAUERKRAUT

*1/2 cup butter
8 pork chops
1 32-ounce can sauerkraut,
drained
1 12-ounce can beer
1 cup sour cream
Salt and pepper to taste
2 or 3 large tart apples, cut
into 1/4-inch slices
1/3 to 1/2 cup packed
brown sugar
Cinnamon to taste
Paprika to taste*

Use 12-inch Dutch oven with 8 to 10 coals under and 14 to 16 coals on top. Preheat Dutch oven over hot coals. Melt butter in oven. Add pork chops. Cook until brown. Remove pork chops. Add sauerkraut. Stir-fry for several minutes. Add beer and sour cream; mix well. Remove half the sauerkraut mixture. Place 4 pork chops over remaining sauerkraut. Season with salt and pepper. Cover with half the apple slices. Sprinkle with half the brown sugar and cinnamon. Repeat layers Sprinkle with paprika. Cover with lid and coals. Bake for 45 minutes or until pork chops are tender. Yield: 6 to 8 servings.

VEGGIE MEDLEY

6 small zucchini, sliced
6 carrots, sliced
2 cups broccoli flowerets
24 mushrooms, sliced
1/2 teaspoon rosemary
1/8 teaspoon thyme
1 cup water
1/4 cup butter
1/2 cup beer (optional)
1/2 cup sunflower seed
Salt and pepper to taste

Use 12-inch Dutch oven with 10 coals under and 15 coals on top. Combine zucchini, carrots, broccoli and mushrooms with rosemary and thyme in bowl; toss to coat vegetables. Place water and butter in Dutch oven over hot coals. Add vegetables and beer. Cover with lid and coals. Cook for 20 minutes or until vegetables are tender-crisp. Sprinkle with sunflower seed and salt and pepper.
Yield: 12 servings.

SOURDOUGH FRENCH BREAD

1 package dry yeast
1 12-ounce can warm (110-degree) Coors beer
2 cups all-purpose flour
1 cup sourdough starter, at room temperature
3 tablespoons sugar
2 tablespoons butter or margarine, softened
2 teaspoons salt
1 cup all-purpose flour
1/2 teaspoon soda
1/3 cup pine nuts
2 to 21/2 cups all-purpose flour
Yellow cornmeal

Use 12 to 14-inch Dutch oven with 10 coals under and 14 to 16 coals on top. Dissolve yeast in warm beer in bowl. Combine 2 cups flour, sourdough starter, sugar, butter and salt in bowl; mix well. Add mixture of 1 cup flour and soda. Add pine nuts and enough remaining 2 to 21/2 cups flour to make stiff dough. Knead in remaining flour for 5 minutes or until smooth and elastic. Place in greased bowl, turning to grease surface. Let rise, covered, until doubled in bulk. Punch dough down; divide in half. Let rest for 10 minutes. Shape into 2 oblong loaves. Place in greased Dutch oven sprinkled with cornmeal. Let rise, covered, for 1 hour. Make diagonal slashes across top of loaves. Sprinkle with water. Place on hot coals. Cover with lid and coals. Bake for 40 to 50 minutes or until loaves test done, checking every 20 minutes to prevent over baking. Remove several coals during baking if bread is baking too fast. Dough may also be shaped into rolls, dipped in melted butter, and baked as above for 15 minutes. May make cinnamon rolls by rolling dough into 2 oblongs, spreading with melted butter, sprinkling with sugar, cinnamon, nuts and raisins, and rolling and cutting into 11/2-inch slices. Bake as above for 15 to 30 minutes.
Yield: 2 loaves.

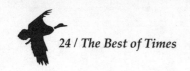

GINGER PEAR UPSIDE-DOWN CAKE

1 cup butter
1 cup packed brown sugar
1/2 cup chopped pecans or
walnuts
1 28-ounce can pears halves,
drained
2 packages gingerbread mix

Use 12-inch Dutch oven with 8 coals under and 14 to 16 coals on top. Line Dutch oven with large pieces of foil, leaving edges so cake can be lifted out and inverted. Melt butter in Dutch oven over hot coals. Add brown sugar and pecans. Arrange pear halves on top. Prepare gingerbread mix using package directions. Pour over pears. Cover with lid and coals. Be sure oven is level. Bake for 25 minutes. Lift cake out; invert onto serving plate. Yield: 10 to 12 servings.

FRUIT COBBLER

2 quarts fresh fruit or
3 28-ounce cans fruit,
drained or 4 6-ounce
packages dried fruit
1 to 1 1/2 cups sugar
Dash of cinnamon
2 tablespoons cornstarch
1 2-layer package yellow
cake mix

Use 12-inch Dutch oven with 8 coals on bottom and 14 coals on top. Preheat Dutch oven and lid over hot level coals. Combine fruit, sugar, cinnamon and cornstarch in Dutch oven. Prepare cake mix according to package directions using no eggs and increasing water by 1/4 cup. Pour over fruit. Cover with lid and coals. Bake for 30 to 45 minutes or until cake is golden brown and tests done. Fruit cobblers can be made with any fruit such as dried, canned or fresh peaches, apples, cherries, blueberries and apricots.
Yield: 10 to 12 servings.

Wining and Dining

Wine Guide

The pairing of good food with fine wine is one of the great pleasures of life. The rule that you drink white wine only with fish and fowl and red wine with meat no longer applies—just let your own taste and personal preference be the guide. Remember to serve light wines with lighter foods and full-bodied wines with rich foods so the food and wine will complement rather than over-power each other.

Food and Wine Pairings

Semidry White Wines
Dove, quail, fish or shellfish in cream sauce
Roast turkey, duck or goose
Seafood pasta or salad
Fish in herbed butter sauce

Dry White Wines
Roast young game birds and waterfowl
Shellfish
Fried and grilled fish

Light Red Wines
Mild game sausage
Fowl with highly seasoned stuffings
Soups and stews
Hare
Creole foods

Hearty Red Wines
Duck and goose
Gamebirds
Venison, wild boar and hare
Game soups and pies

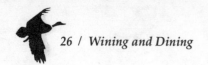

Semidry White Wine

These wines have a fresh fruity taste and are best served young and slightly chilled.

- Johannisberg Riesling –
  (Yo-hann-is-burg Rees-ling)
- Frascati – *(Fras-cah-tee)*
- Gewurztraminer –
  (Ge-vert-tram-me-ner)
- Bernkasteler – *(Barn-kahst-ler)*
- Sylvaner Riesling –
  (Sil-vah-nur Rees-ling)
- Est! Est! Est!
- Fendant – *(Fahn-dawn)*
- Dienheimer – *(Deen-heim-er)*
- Krauznacher – *(Kroytz-nock)*

Dry White Wines

These wines have a crisp, refreshing taste and are best served young and slightly chilled.

- Vouvray – *(Voo-vray)*
- Chablis – *(Shab-lee)*
- Chardonnay – *(Shar-doh-nay)*
- Pinot Blanc – *(Pee-no Blawn)*
- Chenin Blanc – *(Shay-nan Blawn)*
- Pouilly Fuisse –
  (Pwee-yee-Fwee-say)
- Orvieto Secco – *(Orv-yay-toe Sek-o)*
- Piesporter Trocken – *(Peez-porter)*
- Meursault – *(Mere-so)*
- Hermitage Blanc –
  (Air-me-tahz Blawn)
- Pinot Grigio – *(Pee-no Gree-jo)*
- Verdicchio – *(Ver-deek-ee-o)*
- Sancerre – *(Sahn-sehr)*
- Soave – *(So-ah-veh)*

Light Red Wines

These wines have a light taste and are best served young at cool room temperature.

- Beaujolais – *(Bo-sho-lay)*
- Bardolino – *(Bar-do-leen-o)*
- Valpolicella – *(Val-po-lee-chel-la)*
- Moulin-A-Vent Beaujolais –
  (Moo-lon-ah-vahn)
- Barbera – *(Bar-bear-ah)*
- Lambrusco – *(Lom-bruce-co)*
- Lirac – *(Lee-rack)*
- Nuits-Saint Georges "Villages" –
  (Nwee San Zhorzh)
- Gamay Beaujolais –
  (Ga-mai Bo-sho-lay)
- Santa Maddalena –
  (Santa Mad-lay-nah)
- Merlo di Ticino –
  (Mair-lo dee Tee-chee-no)

Hearty Red Wines

These wines have a heavier taste, improve with age, and are best opened thirty minutes before serving.

- Barbaresco – *(Bar-bah-rez-coe)*
- Barolo – *(Bah-ro-lo)*
- Zinfandel – *(Zin-fan-dell)*
- Chianti Riserva –
  (Key-ahn-tee Ree-sairv-ah)
- Cote Rotie – *(Coat Ro-tee)*
- Hermitage – *(Air-me-tahz)*
- Taurasi – *(Tah-rah-see)*
- Merlot – *(Mair-lo)*
- Syrah – *(Sir-rah)*
- Chateauneuf-Du-Pape –
  (Shot-toe-nuff dew Pop)
- Petite Sirah – *(Puh-teet Seer-rah)*
- Cote de Beaune – *(Coat duh Bone)*
  Cabernet Sauvignon –
  (Cab-air-nay So-vin-yawn)

Early Flights

Appetizers, Soups and Salads

Morning Flight

Jim Killen

DOVE SUPREME

12 dove breasts
All-purpose flour
1 cup oil
2 cans beef consommé
1 carrot, minced
3 stalks celery, chopped
1 onion, minced
1/4 cup cooking Sherry

Coat dove with flour. Brown in hot oil in skillet. Drain well. Pour consommé into 2-quart casserole. Stir in carrot, celery, onion and Sherry. Add enough flour to thicken to consistency of gravy; avoid getting too thick. Cook until thickened, stirring constantly. Place doves in mixture. Bake at 325 degrees for 1 hour. Serve with brown rice and mushrooms. Yield: 4 servings.

Karen Killen

BARBECUED GAME CUBES

2 pounds venison round steak
1/4 cup oil
2 cups spicy barbecue sauce
1 ounce blackberry Brandy

Cut steak into 1-inch cubes. Brown on all sides in hot oil in skillet. Combine with barbecue sauce in Crock•Pot. Cook on Low for 3 hours. Add blackberry Brandy. Cook for 1 hour longer. Serve hot as appetizer. Yield: 8 servings.

Approx Per Serving: Cal 274; Prot 34.4 g; T Fat 10.8 g; Chol 73.7 mg; Carbo 7.3 g; Sod 589 mg; Potas 490 mg.

Bernie Szczesniak
Rosemount, Minnesota

CHAR SUI BARBECUED PORK

3/4 cup soy sauce
1/2 cup lemon juice
1 1/2 cups sugar
1 small onion, sliced
2 to 3 large cloves of garlic, crushed
3/4 teaspoon ginger
2 tablespoons red food coloring
1 teaspoon smoked salt
1 teaspoon salt
1 4-pound pork tenderloin

Combine soy sauce, lemon juice, sugar, onion, garlic, ginger, food coloring, smoked salt and salt in zip-lock plastic bag. Add pork; seal well. Marinate in refrigerator for 24 hours or longer. Place pork in roasting pan lined with foil. Pour sauce over top. Insert meat thermometer. Bake at 300 degrees until pork reaches 185 degrees on meat thermometer, basting often with marinade. Remove pork to serving platter. Slice thin. Serve as appetizer with hot mustard and sesame seed. Yield: 16 servings.

Approx Per Serving: Cal 392; Prot 38.1 g; T Fat 16.6 g; Chol 120 mg; Carbo 20.7 g; Sod 1125 mg; Potas 513 mg.

Sharron Wasser
Fairbanks, Alaska

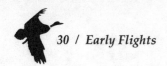
CRUNCHY CHICKEN WINGS

10 chicken wings
1¹/₂ cups Parmesan cheese
2 cups crushed potato chips
1 teaspoon garlic powder
2 eggs, beaten

Cut each wing into 3 portions; discard tip portions. Combine cheese, potato chip crumbs and garlic powder in bowl; mix well. Dip wings into egg; roll in cheese mixture, coating well. Place in baking pan. Chill overnight if desired. Bake at 350 degrees for 1 hour; wings do not need to be turned. Yield: 20 appetizers.

Approx Per Appetizer: Cal 204; Prot 8.9 g; T Fat 13.8 g; Chol 46.6 mg; Carbo 12.1 g; Sod 240 mg; Potas 340 mg.

Judy Nugent
Waupun, Wisconsin

BUFFALO STYLE DOVE BREASTS

20 dove breasts, split, boned
1¹/₂ cups unsweetened pineapple juice
1 pound butter
1 12-ounce bottle of Texas Pete hot sauce
Oil for deep frying

Wash dove breasts and pat dry. Combine dove breasts with pineapple juice in bowl. Marinate in refrigerator for 2 hours. Drain, discarding pineapple juice. Combine butter and hot sauce in saucepan. Cook until butter is melted; mix well. Combine with dove breasts in bowl. Marinate in refrigerator overnight. Drain, reserving sauce. Deep-fry dove a few at a time in hot oil for 2 minutes. Combine with reserved sauce in serving bowl. Season to taste. Serve as appetizers. Yield: 6 servings.

Approx Per Serving: Cal 716; Prot 24.1 g; T Fat 63.1 g; Chol 256 mg; Carbo 9.8 g; Sod 766 mg; Potas 137 mg. Nutritional information does not include oil for deep frying.

John Mason
Cairo, Georgia

BUTTER'S ARTICHOKE DIP

2 16-ounce cans water-pack
artichoke hearts
1 4-ounce can chopped
green, chilies
1/2 4-ounce can chopped
jalapeño peppers
1 clove of garlic, minced
1 cup Parmesan cheese
1 cup mayonnaise

Drain and chop artichoke hearts. Combine with green chilies, jalapeño peppers, garlic, cheese and mayonnaise in bowl; mix well. Spoon into 1½-quart baking dish. Bake at 350 degrees for 20 minutes or until bubbly and heated through. Serve with tortilla chips or crackers. Yield: 8 servings.

Approx Per Serving: Cal 301; Prot 7.5 g; T Fat 25.2 g; Chol 24.1 mg; Carbo 14.6 g; Sod 524 mg; Potas 378 mg.

Judy Hoffman
Twin Bridges, Montana

CLEVE'S DUCK DIP

12 duck breast filets
1/8 teaspoon pepper
1/8 teaspoon red pepper
1/4 teaspoon salt
2 bay leaves
1 stalk celery, finely chopped
2 onions, finely chopped
2 hard-cooked eggs, chopped
1 teaspoon chili powder
2 cups mayonnaise

Wash duck breasts and pat dry. Combine with pepper, red pepper, salt and bay leaves in water to cover in saucepan. Cook until tender. Drain, discarding cooking liquid. Bone duck breasts. Process in food processor container until finely chopped. Combine with celery, onions, eggs, chili powder and mayonnaise in bowl; mix well. Serve as appetizer with crackers or as sandwich spread. Yield: 6 servings.

Approx Per Serving: Cal 1039; Prot 42.6 g; T Fat 94.8 g; Chol 316 mg; Carbo 3.6 g; Sod 664 mg; Potas 656 mg.

Joan Marsh
Humboldt, Tennessee

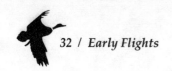

HALIBUT DIP

2 cups flaked cooked halibut
1 teaspoon sweet hot mustard
1/2 teaspoon celery seed
2 tablespoons minced
green onion
2 cloves of garlic, minced
2 teaspoons Worcestershire
sauce
1/2 teaspoon lemon juice
1/8 teaspoon white pepper
Dash of Tabasco sauce
1/8 teaspoon nutmeg
1/2 c. mayonnaise
1/2 (about) cup sour cream

Combine halibut with mustard, celery seed, green onion, garlic, Worcestershire sauce, lemon juice, white pepper, Tabasco sauce and nutmeg in bowl; mix well. Add mayonnaise and sour cream; mix well. Chill for 1 hour or longer. Serve with vegetables, chips, crackers or toast strips. Yield: 8 servings.

Approx Per Serving: Cal 196; Prot 12.6 g; T Fat 15.3 g; Chol 32.6 mg; Carbo 1.8 g; Sod 137 mg; Potas 301 mg.

Barbara Springer
Fairbanks, Alaska

SHRIMP DIP

4 ounces cream cheese, softened
3 tablespoons mayonnaise
8 drops of hot sauce
8 drops of Worcestershire sauce
1 teaspoon red pepper
1/8 teaspoon pepper
1/2 teaspoon Creole seasoning
1 tablespoon chopped parsley
2 stalks celery, chopped
2 green onions, chopped
11/2 cups chopped
cooked shrimp

Blend cream cheese and mayonnaise in bowl. Add hot sauce, Worcestershire sauce, red pepper, pepper, Creole seasoning, parsley, celery and green onions; mix well. Mix in shrimp. Chill in refrigerator. Serve with crackers.
Yield: 6 servings.

Approx Per Serving: Cal 157; Prot 9 g; T Fat 12.7 g; Chol 80.2 mg; Carbo 1.7 g; Sod 169 mg; Potas 141 mg.

Becky Fore
Wiggins, Mississippi

GOOSE BREAST APPETIZER

6 goose breast filets
1 cup dry mustard
1 cup malt vinegar
1 cup sugar
3 eggs

Wash goose breasts and pat dry. Combine with water to cover in large saucepan. Bring to a boil; reduce heat. Simmer for 12 hours; drain. Chill in refrigerator. Blend mustard and vinegar in bowl. Let stand overnight. Combine with sugar and eggs in double boiler; mix well. Cook over simmering water for 30 minutes or until thickened, stirring constantly. Chill. Slice goose breasts into thin slices. Serve with mustard and crackers. Yield: 8 servings.

Approx Per Serving: Cal 284; Prot 31.2 g; T Fat 6.7 g; Chol 284 mg; Carbo 26.9 g; Sod 26.7 mg; Potas 55.2 mg.

Susan Bambara
West Yellowstone, Montana

LOBSTER HORS D'OEUVRES

25 slices white bread
1 6-ounce can lobster
8 ounces Velveeta cheese, finely chopped
1 cup butter, softened
1/2 cup melted butter
1/2 cup sesame seed

Trim crusts from bread. Roll slices flat with rolling pin. Combine lobster, cheese and softened butter in bowl; mix well. Spread on flattened bread. Roll up bread to enclose filling. Chill for several hours to overnight. Cut each roll into 5 pieces. Dip in melted butter; roll in sesame seed. Place on baking sheet. Bake at 375 degrees for 20 minutes. Serve immediately. Yield: 125 appetizers.

Approx Per Appetizer: Cal 46; Prot 1.3 g; T Fat 3.3 g; Chol 8.7 mg; Carbo 2.9 g; Sod 78.5 mg; Potas 17.2 mg.

Barbara Ludwig
Reno, Nevada

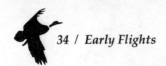

AUNTY LAURA'S STUFFED MUSHROOMS

1 pound large mushrooms
1 medium onion, finely chopped
1/3 cup butter
11/4 cups bread crumbs
1 tablespoon catsup
1 tablespoon lemon juice
1/2 teaspoon salt
1/4 teaspoon pepper
10 slices bacon
1/4 cup half and half

Remove and chop mushroom stems. Sauté stems and onion in butter in skillet. Stir in bread crumbs, catsup, lemon juice, salt and pepper. Mixture will be very stiff. Spoon into mushroom caps. Place in shallow baking pan. Slice bacon into long 1/8-inch wide strips. Arrange bacon in cross on each stuffed cap. Drizzle lightly with half and half. Bake at 400 degrees for 20 minutes. Serve as appetizer or side dish.
Yield: 20 appetizers.

Approx Per Appetizer: Cal 73.5; Prot 2.1 g; T Fat 5.3 g; Chol 12 mg; Carbo 4.8 g; Sod 172 mg; Potas 122 mg.

Laura Lee Puls
Barrington, Illinois

STUFFED MUSHROOM CAPS

1 pound mushrooms
Lemon juice
3 small hot Italian sausages
1 medium onion, chopped
3 small cloves of garlic, chopped
1/4 cup bread crumbs
11/2 tablespoons Romano cheese
1 teaspoon parsley
3/4 teaspoon salt
1/8 teaspoon pepper

Combine mushrooms with salted water to cover in saucepan. Add desired amount of lemon juice. Cook until tender; drain. Repeat process if strong aroma remains. Remove and grind stems; set aside caps and stems. Remove sausages from casings. Cook in skillet, stirring until crumbly. Remove with slotted spoon. Add onion. Sauté until almost tender. Add garlic. Cook for several minutes longer. Stir in sausage, bread crumbs, cheese, mushroom stems, parsley and seasonings. Spoon into mushroom caps. Place on baking sheet. Bake at 350 degrees for 15 minutes.
Yield: 20 appetizers.

Approx Per Appetizer: Cal 50; Prot 3.7 g; T Fat 3.1 g; Chol 10.4 mg; Carbo 1.9 g; Sod 208 mg; Potas 113 mg.

Jim and Marsha Greto
Braintree, Massachusetts

WILD ALASKA DUCK LIVER PÂTÉ

8 ounces wild duck livers
1/2 cup butter, softened
1/2 small onion, chopped
2 cloves of garlic, minced
1 teaspoon dry mustard
1/4 teaspoon nutmeg
1/8 teaspoon cloves
1 teaspoon salt
1/8 teaspoon cayenne pepper
2 tablespoons Brandy

Combine livers with enough water to just cover in saucepan. Bring to a boil; reduce heat. Simmer for 15 minutes. Drain and chop livers. Combine with butter, onion, garlic, seasonings and Brandy in food processor or blender container. Process until smooth. Spoon into serving bowl. Chill until serving time. Yield: 6 servings.

Approx Per Serving: Cal 210; Prot 9.5 g; T Fat 17.4 g; Chol 280 mg; Carbo 2.9 g; Sod 504 mg; Potas 72.9 mg.

Nancy Murkowski
Fairbanks, Alaska

TERIYAKI DUCK

Duck breasts
Teriyaki sauce
Toothpicks
Bacon

Cut duck breasts into 3/4-inch cubes. Combine with teriyaki sauce in large bowl. Marinate in refrigerator overnight. Drain well and pat dry. Soak toothpicks in water for several hours. Wrap a small piece of bacon around each cube of duck; secure with toothpick. Place on broiling pan. Broil until bacon is crisp.

Nutritional information for this recipe is not available.

D. W. Sinclair
Aylmer, Ontario, Canada

Henry Trione of Santa Rosa, California, uses duck livers in canapès. Sauté 1/2 pound of minced duck livers in 3 tablespoons butter. Add 2 tablespoons of minced parsley, 1 minced clove of garlic, 2 mashed anchovies, 1/2 teaspoon of salt, 1/4 teaspoon of freshly ground pepper and 2 tablespoons of Geyser Peak wine. Serve warm on thin slices of French bread sautéed in butter.

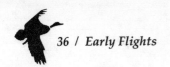

PHEASANT STRIPS

2 pheasant
1/2 cup cornstarch
3 tablespoons butter
1/2 cup white wine
1/2 cup water
1/4 teaspoon tarragon
1/4 teaspoon parsley
1/8 teaspoon paprika
1/8 teaspoon pepper

Wash pheasant and pat dry. Bone pheasant, discarding lower legs. Cut into strips. Roll strips in cornstarch, coating well. Brown in butter in skillet. Stir in wine, water and seasonings. Simmer for 15 minutes or until liquid is absorbed. Serve hot as appetizer.
Yield: 8 servings.

Approx Per Serving: Cal 269; Prot 24.2 g; T Fat 14.3 g; Chol 91.4 mg; Carbo 7.2 g; Sod 80.2 mg; Potas 272 mg.

Carlena Phelps
Salt Lake City, Utah

RUMAKI

2 pounds bacon
5 cans whole water chestnuts, drained
1 cup catsup
1 tablespoon Worcestershire sauce
1 cup packed brown sugar
1/4 teaspoon garlic salt
1/4 teaspoon salt
1/8 teaspoon pepper

Cut each bacon slice into 3 pieces. Wrap 1 piece bacon around each water chestnut; secure with toothpick. Place in shallow baking pan. Bake at 350 degrees for 1 hour; drain well. Combine catsup, Worcestershire sauce, brown sugar and seasonings in saucepan. Simmer for 10 minutes. Combine with water chestnuts in chafing dish.
Yield: 50 appetizers.

Approx Per Appetizer: Cal 157; Prot 6 g; T Fat 9 g; Chol 15.3 mg; Carbo 12.5 g; Sod 377 mg; Potas 291 mg.

Laura Lee Puls
Barrington, Illinois

Lee Silha of Bowman, North Dakota, stuffs fresh mushroom caps with a mixture of 8 ounces softened cream cheese and 1 pound browned hot sausage. Sprinkle with paprika and bake at 400 degrees for 10 minutes.

SALMON NACHOS

4 cups tortilla chips
1¹/2 cups shredded Monterey
Jack cheese
1¹/2 cups shredded Cheddar
cheese
¹/4 to ¹/2 cup chopped
green chilies
4 green onions, chopped
8 ounces salmon, cooked,
flaked
¹/4 cup sliced black olives
¹/2 cup salsa

Arrange tortilla chips in 2 round 12-inch pans. Combine cheeses, green chilies and green onions in bowl; mix well. Sprinkle ¹/4 of the cheese mixture over chips in each pan. Top with salmon, olives, remaining cheese mixture and salsa. Broil 4 to 5 inches from heat source for 2 minutes or until cheese is melted. Substitute crab meat or halibut for salmon if desired.
Yield: 20 servings.

Approx Per Serving: Cal 361; Prot 13.3 g; T Fat 22.3 g; Chol 35.6 mg; Carbo 29 g; Sod 410 mg; Potas 162 mg.

Karen Lane
North Pole, Alaska

SWEET POTATO PUFFS

¹/3 cup milk
²/3 cup water
¹/2 cup unsalted butter
¹/2 teaspoon freshly
grated nutmeg
1¹/4 teaspoons salt
Freshly ground pepper to taste
1 cup all-purpose flour
4 eggs
2 tablespoons cold milk
1 cup shredded cooked
sweet potatoes
2 scallions, minced
1 tablespoon minced parsley
1 egg, beaten

Combine ¹/3 cup milk, water, butter, nutmeg, 1¹/4 teaspoons salt and pepper in saucepan. Heat until butter is melted; remove from heat. Add flour all at once, stirring until mixture leaves side of saucepan. Return to heat for 2 minutes longer. Place in mixer bowl. Add 4 eggs 1 at a time, beating until smooth after each addition. Blend in 2 tablespoons cold milk. Add sweet potatoes, scallions and parsley; mix well. Pipe into mounds on buttered baking sheets. Brush with beaten egg. Bake at 400 degrees on center rack of oven for 20 to 25 minutes or until brown. Remove to wire rack to cool. To reheat, place in cold oven and set temperature at 300 degrees. Heat for 10 minutes. Yield: 40 appetizers.

Approx Per Appetizer: Cal 51; Prot 1.4 g; T Fat 3.3 g; Chol 47.7 mg; Carbo 3.9 g; Sod 178 mg; Potas 29.5 mg.

Ellen Olson
DePere, Wisconsin

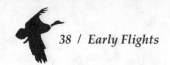

TACO DIP HORS D'OEUVRES

8 ounces cream cheese,
softened
8 ounces sour cream
1/8 teaspoon garlic salt
1/2 head lettuce, shredded
2/3 cup chopped onion
1/4 cup chopped green
bell pepper
2 tomatoes, chopped
1 cup shredded Cheddar
cheese
2 teaspoons chopped
black olives
Taco sauce
Taco chips

Combine cream cheese, sour cream and garlic salt in bowl; mix well. Spread on shallow plate. Place in refrigerator for 15 minutes. Sprinkle lettuce, onion, green pepper and tomatoes over the cheese mixture. Sprinkle cheese and olives over top. Dot with taco sauce just before serving. Serve with taco chips for dipping.
Yield: 8 servings.

Nutritional information for this recipe is not available.

Margie Knoblauch
Minnetonke, Minnesota

VAMPIRE BITES

4 ounces lean beef, finely
chopped
2 tablespoons finely chopped
onion
Juice of 1/2 fresh lime
Several dashes of Tabasco
sauce
1/2 teaspoon garlic salt
1/4 teaspoon pepper

Combine beef, onion, lime juice, Tabasco sauce, garlic salt and pepper in serving bowl; mix well. Chill until serving time. Serve with thin dry toast or crackers. Yield: 4 servings.

Approx Per Serving: Cal 59; Prot 8.2 g; T Fat 2.3 g; Chol 23.3 mg; Carbo 1 g; Sod 285 mg; Potas 134 mg.

Ben Moise
Charleston, South Carolina

KEEFER'S PINK BEAN SOUP

3 slices bacon, chopped
2 6-ounce onions, chopped
6 ounces chopped celery
6 ounces chopped carrots
1 pound dried pink beans
1 medium tomato, peeled,
seeded, chopped
2 cloves of garlic, chopped
2 quarts beef stock
1 teaspoon Italian seasoning
1/2 cup red wine
1/4 teaspoon salt
1/8 teaspoon pepper

Sauté bacon in skillet until partially cooked. Add onions, celery and carrots. Cook until vegetables are tender. Combine with beans, tomato, garlic, stock and Italian seasoning in stockpot. Simmer for 3 hours or until beans are tender, skimming several times. Place half the beans in blender or food processor container. Process until smooth. Return to soup. Add wine; mix well. Bring to a simmer. Add salt, pepper and additional water if needed. Serve hot. Yield: 4 servings.

Approx Per Serving: Cal 521; Prot 35.8 g; T Fat 4.8 g; Chol 5.2 mg; Carbo 82.4 g; Sod 1992 mg; Potas 2370 mg.

Fare Thee Well—Dolley

CRAB SOUP

1/2 cup chopped green onions
1/2 cup butter
2 cans cream of mushroom soup
2 soup cans milk
2 cups half and half
1 pound crab meat
2 teaspoons liquid crab boil

Sauté green onions in butter in saucepan. Add soup, milk, half and half, crab meat and crab boil; mix well. Bring to a boil; reduce heat. Simmer for 20 minutes. Season with salt and pepper to taste. Ladle into soup bowls. Yield: 8 servings.

Approx Per Serving: Cal 354; Prot 17.1 g; T Fat 26.9 g; Chol 114 mg; Carbo 11.5 g; Sod 914 mg; Potas 452 mg.

W. N. Day
Norco, Louisiana

AUTUMN GAME SOUP

1/2 5-pound goose 1 gallon water 1 carrot, split 4 stalks celery with leaves 1 large onion 1 white turnip 1 medium carrot 1/2 leek 3 tablespoons butter 1 cup shredded cabbage 1 cup fresh cranberries 2 cups Port	Remove skin from goose. Combine goose with water, 1 carrot, celery and onion in stockpot. Simmer until goose is tender and stock has been reduced to 1 quart. Remove goose from stock. Bone and cool goose. Strain and chill stock. Cut goose meat, turnip, 1 carrot and leek into julienne strips. Sauté turnip, carrot and leek in butter in skillet until tender-crisp. Remove congealed grease from top of stock. Bring stock to a medium boil in stockpot. Add sautéed vegetables and goose meat. Cook for 5 minutes. Add cabbage and cranberries. Cook for 2 minutes. Stir in wine and salt and pepper to taste. Simmer for 2 minutes longer. Ladle into soup bowls. Yield: 6 servings.

Approx Per Serving: Cal 198; Prot 10.1 g; T Fat 7.4 g; Chol 69.2 mg; Carbo 11.9 g; Sod 103 mg; Potas 381 mg.

Barbara Kamman
Old Lyme, Connecticut

BOOYAH BELGIAN SOUP

1 3 1/2-pound chicken 1 beef bone 3 quarts water 1 8-ounce can tomato sauce 1/2 cup chopped onion 1/2 cup chopped carrot 1/2 cup chopped celery 3 cups shredded cabbage 3 cups chopped potatoes 1 16-ounce can whole tomatoes 1 8-ounce can peas	Combine chicken and beef bone with water in large saucepan. Simmer until chicken is tender. Remove and bone chicken. Return boned chicken to broth. Add tomato sauce and fresh vegetables. Crush canned tomatoes. Add to soup. Simmer for 2 hours. Stir in peas and salt and pepper to taste just before serving. Yield: 10 servings.

Approx Per Serving: Cal 59; Prot 3.8 g; T Fat 0.7 g; Chol 4.4 mg; Carbo 10.6 g; Sod 276 mg; Potas 362 mg.

Lorraine Beno
Green Bay, Wisconsin

ARIZONA RED SOUP

2 cans condensed beef bouillon
2 cans tomato soup
1/3 cup thinly sliced onion
1 tablespoon lemon juice
1/4 teaspoon nutmeg
4 whole peppercorns
1/2 teaspoon salt
1 cup water
1/2 cup Sherry

Combine bouillon, tomato soup, onion, lemon juice, nutmeg, peppercorns and salt in saucepan. Stir in water. Bring to a boil; reduce heat. Simmer, covered, for 30 minutes. Strain soup, discarding onion and peppercorns. Return soup to saucepan. Stir in Sherry. Heat to serving temperature. Ladle into mugs to serve. Yield: 6 servings.

Approx Per Serving: Cal 59; Prot 1.6 g; T Fat 1 g; Chol 0.2 mg; Carbo 6.1 g; Sod 698 mg; Potas 150 mg.

Gaeel Beaham
Tucson, Arizona

BAREFIELD'S CHOWDER

12 medium new potatoes
2 1/2 cups milk
2 cans Campbell's creamy natural potato soup
Several drops of hot sauce
6 slices bacon
1 large onion, chopped
2 cloves of garlic, minced
3 8-ounce fish fillets
Garlic powder to taste
1 8-ounce bottle of clam juice
1 6 1/2-ounce can minced clams
1/4 cup butter

Cut unpeeled potatoes into halves. Combine with milk in saucepan. Simmer until potatoes are tender. Stir in soup. Simmer for several minutes. Add hot sauce; set aside. Fry bacon in saucepan until crisp. Drain on paper towel. Sauté onion and garlic in drippings in saucepan. Cut fish into 1-inch pieces. Season with garlic powder and salt and pepper to taste. Add fish and clam juice to sautéed onion. Simmer, covered, just until fish flakes easily; do not over-cook. Remove from heat. Stir in clams, potato mixture and butter. Add crumbled bacon. Heat to serving tempera- ture. Ladle into serving bowls. Garnish with green onion tops and freshly ground black pepper. Yield: 6 servings.

Approx Per Serving: Cal 683; Prot 49.2 g; T Fat 23.4 g; Chol 125 mg; Carbo 68.3 g; Sod 872 mg; Potas 1814 mg.

Paul Barefield
Lafayette, Louisiana

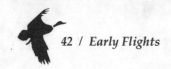

MAINE INDIAN FISH CHOWDER

2 tablespoons chopped
salt pork
1/2 cup butter
3 cloves of garlic, crushed
1 cup chopped celery
1 cup chopped green bell pepper
1 cup chopped onion
1 teaspoon sweet basil
1/4 teaspoon oregano
1/2 teaspoon fennel seed
1/8 teaspoon rosemary
1 teaspoon salt
1 teaspoon pepper
1 1/2 cups water
8 medium potatoes, chopped
2 pounds haddock
1 quart half and half
1 medium tomato, crushed
1/4 cup butter

Brown salt pork in stockpot; remove with slotted spoon. Add 1/2 cup butter and garlic. Sauté garlic until light brown. Add celery, green pepper, onion and seasonings. Sauté for 20 minutes. Stir in 1 1/2 cups water. Simmer for 10 minutes. Add potatoes and enough additional water to just cover. Simmer until potatoes are tender. Cut fish into 1-inch cubes. Add to soup. Simmer, covered, for 10 minutes or just until fish flakes easily; do not overcook. Cool for 15 minutes. Add half and half, tomato and 1/4 cup butter. Heat just to serving temperature; do not boil. Ladle into soup bowls. Garnish with salt pork if desired.
Yield: 8 servings.

*Approx Per Serving: Cal 642; Prot 31 g; T Fat 32.7 g;
Chol 157 mg; Carbo 59.9 g; Sod 595 mg; Potas 1500 mg.*

William Shaw
Prides Crossing, Massachusetts

DUCK SOUP GRANDMA

1 can pea soup
1 can tomato soup
1 can consommé
3/4 cup chopped parboiled
wild duck
1/2 cup Sherry

Combine undiluted soups in saucepan; mix until smooth. Bring to a simmer. Add duck. Simmer for 30 minutes. Stir in Sherry. Ladle into small cups. Duck for this soup should be parboiled for 15 minutes, boned and chopped in food processor container with steel blade.
Yield: 12 servings.

*Approx Per Serving: Cal 77; Prot 4.3 g; T Fat 1.9 g;
Chol 7.9 mg; Carbo 8 g; Sod 425 mg; Potas 126 mg.*

D. C. Rebhun, Jr.
Cincinnati, Ohio

FRENCH ONION SOUP

4 onions, sliced into rings
1/3 cup bacon drippings
1 tablespoon all-purpose flour
3 cans beef consommé
2 consommé cans water
1/2 teaspoon salt
1/4 teaspoon pepper
1/3 cup Sherry
6 slices French bread
1 cup shredded Swiss cheese
1/2 cup Parmesan cheese

Sauté onions in bacon drippings in saucepan. Stir in flour. Cook until flour is brown, stirring constantly. Stir in consommé, water, salt and pepper. Simmer for 30 minutes. Stir in Sherry. Sprinkle bread with cheeses. Ladle soup into oven-proof bowls; top with bread. Broil until cheese is melted. Yield: 6 servings.

Approx Per Serving: Cal 426; Prot 25.8 g; T Fat 23.7 g; Chol 99.5 mg; Carbo 23 g; Sod 4591 mg; Potas 780 mg.

Teresa Shank
Brighton, Illinois

WILD RICE AND PHEASANT SOUP

1 bunch scallions with
stems, chopped
2 tablespoons butter
1/4 cup all-purpose flour
4 cups chicken broth
2 cups cooked wild rice
1 pheasant, cooked, chopped
1 teaspoon salt
1 cup heavy cream
2 tablespoons dry Sherry

Sauté scallions in butter in 3-quart saucepan until tender. Add flour. Cook for 1 minute, stirring constantly. Stir in broth gradually. Cook over medium heat until thickened, stirring constantly. Stir in rice, pheasant and salt. Simmer for 5 minutes. Stir in cream and Sherry. Cook until heated through; do not boil. Ladle into soup bowls. Yield: 6 servings.

Approx Per Serving: Cal 382; Prot 24.1 g; T Fat 22.2 g; Chol 115 mg; Carbo 19.4 g; Sod 949 mg; Potas 445 mg.

Linda Heineke
Madison, Wisconsin

JOAN'S STEAK SOUP

1 pound ground venison
1/2 cup butter
1 cup all-purpose flour
8 cups water
1 cup chopped onion
1 cup chopped celery
1 cup chopped carrots
1   10-ounce package frozen
mixed vegetables
1 tablespoon Accent
2 tablespoons Kitchen Bouquet
1 tablespoon pepper

Brown ground venison in skillet, stirring until crumbly; drain. Melt butter in large saucepan. Stir in flour. Add water. Cook for 5 to 10 minutes or until thickened, stirring constantly. Add venison, vegetables and seasonings. Bring to a boil. Boil for 5 to 10 minutes; reduce heat. Simmer for 5 to 6 hours. Ladle into soup bowls. Yield: 8 servings.

Approx Per Serving: Cal 273; Prot 19.9 g; T Fat 13 g; Chol 67.9 mg; Carbo 19 g; Sod 1775 mg; Potas 386 mg.

Joan Peabody
Alexandria, Minnesota

WINTER WARMER

1 can tomato soup
1 can beef bouillon
1 1/2 soup cans water
Cinnamon to taste

Combine all ingredients in saucepan; mix well. Bring to a boil. Pour into preheated thermos. Take along on a cold fall or winter day. Yield: 4 servings.

Approx Per Serving: Cal 30; Prot 1.4 g; T Fat 1 g; Chol 0.2 mg; Carbo 4.9 g; Sod 487 mg; Potas 115 mg.

Tom Kantos
International Falls, Minnesota

CREAM OF TUNA SOUP

1/4 cup chopped onion
1/4 cup margarine
1/4 cup all-purpose flour
1 teaspoon dry mustard
1 1/2 teaspoons salt
1/4 teaspoon white pepper
3 cups milk
2 cups half and half
2 7-ounce cans water-pack tuna, drained
2 tablespoons finely chopped pimento
3/4 cup cooked chopped potato

Sauté onion in margarine in large heavy saucepan for 5 minutes or until tender. Remove from heat. Stir in flour, dry mustard, salt and pepper. Cook over low heat until smooth and bubbly, stirring constantly. Remove from heat. Stir in milk and half and half gradually. Bring to a boil, stirring constantly. Cook for 1 minute, stirring constantly. Add tuna, pimento and potato. Heat to serving temperature. Ladle into soup bowls. Yield: 8 servings.

Approx Per Serving: Cal 286; Prot 20.4 g; T Fat 16.1 g; Chol 62.6 mg; Carbo 14.7 g; Sod 717 mg; Potas 441 mg.

Miriam Burchell

VENISON CABBAGE SOUP

5 pounds venison
3 onions, chopped
3 tablespoons oil
4 16-ounce cans tomatoes
3 cans beef consommé
1 consommé can water
10 carrots, chopped
1 head cabbage, chopped

Cut venison into 1-inch cubes. Brown with onions in oil in skillet for 5 minutes. Combine with undrained tomatoes, consommé and water in large stockpot. Cook for 30 minutes. Add carrots and cabbage. Cook for 1 hour longer. Ladle into soup bowls. Yield: 10 servings.

Approx Per Serving: Cal 431; Prot 69.9 g; T Fat 9.7 g; Chol 148 mg; Carbo 13.5 g; Sod 543 mg; Potas 1290 mg.

Dale and Julie Thornburg
Beatrice, Nebraska

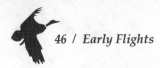

CHEESE AND POTATO WILD RICE SOUP

1/2 cup wild rice
11/2 cups water
8 ounces bacon, chopped
1/2 cup chopped onion
2 cans cream of potato soup
1/2 cup milk
1/2 cup water
4 cups milk
21/2 cups shredded American
cheese

Combine wild rice and water in saucepan. Cook over low heat for 45 minutes; drain. Sauté bacon and onion in skillet until bacon is crisp. Drain on paper towel. Combine soup, 1/2 cup milk and water in large saucepan; mix well. Stir in 4 cups milk, bacon mixture, cheese and rice. Heat until cheese is melted. Ladle into soup bowls. Garnish with carrot curls. Yield: 10 servings.

Approx Per Serving: Cal 368; Prot 19.3 g; T Fat 25.2 g; Chol 65.9 mg; Carbo 15.9 g; Sod 1056 mg; Potas 406 mg.

Joan Peabody
Alexandria, Minnesota

MINNESOTA WILD RICE CHOWDER

1/2 cup wild rice
5 slices bacon, chopped
1 medium onion, chopped
1/2 cup finely chopped green
bell pepper
1 can cream of potato soup
3 cups milk
1 cup shredded Velveeta cheese

Cook wild rice in boiling salted water in saucepan until tender. Drain and rinse. Sauté bacon with onion and green pepper in saucepan. Stir in soup and milk. Add rice and cheese. Heat until cheese is melted, stirring occasionally. Ladle into soup bowls. Yield: 6 servings.

Approx Per Serving: Cal 260; Prot 13.4 g; T Fat 14.3 g; Chol 45 mg; Carbo 19.7 g; Sod 455 mg; Potas 323 mg.

Judy Clarke
Virginia, Minnesota

WILD RICE SOUP

1/2 cup chopped celery
1/2 cup chopped onion
1/2 cup chopped carrot
3 tablespoons butter
3 slices bacon, chopped
4 cups chicken broth
2/3 cup wild rice
1 tablespoon all-purpose flour
1/2 cup chicken broth
1 1/2 cups cream
1/2 teaspoon salt
1/2 teaspoon pepper

Sauté celery, onion and carrot in butter in saucepan. Add bacon. Cook until bacon is almost crisp. Add 4 cups broth and wild rice. Blend flour with 1/2 cup broth in small bowl. Stir into soup. Cook on medium-low heat for 2 to 3 hours. Stir in cream, salt and pepper 30 minutes before serving. Yield: 6 servings.

Approx Per Serving: Cal 380; Prot 8.8 g; T Fat 30.6 g; Chol 100 mg; Carbo 18.3 g; Sod 894 mg; Potas 336 mg.

Benita Coughlin
Aberdeen, South Dakota

ZUCCHINI SOUP

3 cups chopped zucchini
1/2 cup water
1 chicken bouillon cube
1 medium onion, chopped
1 tablespoon parsley flakes
3/4 tablespoon Accent
3/4 tablespoon seasoned salt
1 tablespoon butter
2 tablespoons all-purpose flour
2 cups milk
1/8 teaspoon pepper

Combine zucchini, water, bouillon cube, onion, parsley flakes, Accent and seasoned salt in saucepan. Cook until zucchini is tender. Place in blender container. Process until smooth. Purée may be frozen if desired. Blend butter and flour in saucepan. Stir in milk and pepper. Cook until thickened, stirring constantly. Stir in zucchini mixture. Heat to serving temperature. Ladle into soup bowls. Yield: 4 servings.

Approx Per Serving: Cal 135; Prot 5.9 g; T Fat 7.2 g; Chol 24.5 mg; Carbo 12.5 g; Sod 3887 mg; Potas 437 mg.

Wylma Colehour
Mt. Carroll, Illinois

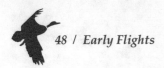

WILD RICE CHICKEN SALAD

3 cups chopped cooked chicken
3 cups cooked wild rice
1/3 cup sliced green onions
1 7-ounce can sliced water
chestnuts, drained
1/2 teaspoon salt
1/4 teaspoon pepper
2/3 cup mayonnaise
1/3 cup milk
2 tablespoons lemon juice
1 cup seedless grape halves
3/4 cup salted cashews

Combine chicken, wild rice, green onions, water chestnuts, salt and pepper in bowl; mix well. Mix mayonnaise, milk and lemon juice in small bowl. Add to chicken mixture; mix well. Chill, covered, for 2 to 3 hours. Fold in grapes and cashews at serving time. Yield: 8 servings.

Approx Per Serving: Cal 474; Prot 32.2 g; T Fat 24.9 g; Chol 98.7 mg; Carbo 30.9 g; Sod 425 mg; Potas 629 mg.

Deborah A. Kleven
Fergus Falls, Minnesota

PINK CHAMPAGNE SALAD

8 ounces cream cheese, softened
3/4 cup sugar
9 ounces whipped topping
1 16-ounce can crushed
pineapple
1 10-ounce package frozen
strawberries, thawed
3 bananas, chopped
1/4 cup chopped walnuts

Blend cream cheese and sugar in mixer bowl until light and fluffy. Mix in whipped topping. Add undrained pineapple, strawberries, bananas and walnuts; mix well. Spoon into 8x8-inch glass dish. Freeze overnight. Let stand at room temperature for 20 to 30 minutes before serving. May be stored in freezer for several weeks if desired. Yield: 9 servings.

Approx Per Serving: Cal 349; Prot 3.4 g; T Fat 18.3 g; Chol 27.5 mg; Carbo 46.4 g; Sod 84 mg; Potas 302 mg.

Ann M. Schaffer
Aberdeen, South Dakota

FRESH FRUIT À LA MEXICO

1 medium cantaloupe
1 medium honeydew melon
2 large mangos
2 cups 1-inch papaya cubes
3 cups 1-inch watermelon cubes
1 large banana, sliced
2 medium apples, sliced
1/2 cup cherry juice
2 cups cottage cheese

Peel cantaloupe, honeydew melon and mangos. Cut into 1-inch cubes. Combine with papaya and watermelon in large bowl. Chill until serving time if desired. Add banana and apples at serving time; mix well. Spoon into serving bowls. Drizzle with cherry juice. Serve with dollop of cottage cheese. Yield: 5 servings.

Approx Per Serving: Cal 390; Prot 14.4 g; T Fat 5.2 g; Chol 12.4 mg; Carbo 78.9 g; Sod 384 mg; Potas 1632 mg.

Dr. Eric W. Gustafson
Monterrey, Nuevo León, Mexico

PASTA HOUSE COMPANY SALAD

1 pound iceberg lettuce
1 pound leaf lettuce
1 cup Parmesan cheese
1 cup chopped canned artichoke hearts
1 cup sliced red onion
1/4 cup chopped pimento
3/4 cup olive oil
1/4 cup red wine vinegar

Tear lettuce into bite-sized pieces. Combine lettuce, cheese, artichoke hearts, onion and pimento in salad bowl; mix gently. Combine olive oil and wine vinegar with salt and pepper to taste in small bowl; mix well. Pour over salad; toss to coat well. Yield: 8 servings.

Approx Per Serving: Cal 261; Prot 6.3 g; T Fat 23.7 g; Chol 7.9 mg; Carbo 8 g; Sod 213 mg; Potas 344 mg.

Charlene Nold
Waterloo, Illinois

CONFETTI SLAW

2 cups shredded cabbage
1 medium red Delicious
    apple, chopped
1/2 medium green bell
    pepper, chopped
1/3 cup mayonnaise
2 tablespoons sugar
1 1/2 tablespoons lemon juice
1 teaspoon poppy seed

Combine cabbage, apple and green pepper in salad bowl; mix well. Mix mayonnaise, sugar, lemon juice and poppy seed in small bowl. Add to cabbage mixture at serving time; mix well. Yield: 6 servings.

Approx Per Serving: Cal 126; Prot 1 g; T Fat 10 g; Chol 7.2 mg; Carbo 9.8 g; Sod 74.1 mg; Potas 104 mg.

Carlena Phelps
Salt Lake City, Utah

HOG ROAST SLAW

2 heads cabbage, chopped
2 large green bell peppers,
    chopped
1 large onion, chopped
1 cup cider vinegar
3/4 cup olive oil
1 tablespoon dry mustard
1 teaspoon celery seed
1 tablespoon salt

Combine cabbage, green peppers and onion in large airtight container. Chill in refrigerator. Combine vinegar, oil, dry mustard, celery seed and salt in saucepan; mix well. Bring to a boil, stirring to mix well. Pour over cabbage; toss to coat well. Refrigerate for 24 hours or longer, turning frequently. Yield: 16 servings.

Approx Per Serving: Cal 108; Prot 1 g; T Fat 10.3 g; Chol 0 mg; Carbo 4.7 g; Sod 410 mg; Potas 176 mg.

Ben Moise
Charleston, South Carolina

Joan Marsh of Humboldt, Tennessee, makes a colorful slaw by mixing 1/2 head shredded red cabbage, 1/2 cup chopped onions, 1 chopped green bell pepper, 1/4 cup mayonnaise, 2 teaspoons sesame seed, 1/2 teaspoon salt and 1/4 teaspoon pepper.

SLAW WITH CLASS

4 large carrots, grated
1 medium cabbage, shredded
1 cup mayonnaise
1/4 cup vinegar
3/4 cup sugar
1 egg
3/4 cup water
2 tablespoons dry mustard
1 teaspoon celery seed
1 teaspoon salt
1/2 teaspoon pepper

Combine carrots, cabbage and mayonnaise in bowl; mix well. Combine vinegar, sugar, egg, water, dry mustard, celery seed, salt and pepper in saucepan; mix until smooth. Cook over medium heat for 10 minutes or until thickened, stirring constantly. Pour over cabbage mixture; mix well. Refrigerate for 4 hours to 1 week. Yield: 8 servings.

Approx Per Serving: Cal 310; Prot 2.2 g; T Fat 22.8 g; Chol 50.5 mg; Carbo 26.8 g; Sod 455 mg; Potas 287 mg.

William G. Quarles
Gastonia, North Carolina

FRESH SPINACH SALAD

2 pounds fresh spinach
8 ounces fresh mushrooms, sliced
1 small onion, sliced into rings
8 slices bacon, crisp-fried, crumbled
3 hard-cooked eggs, chopped

Combine spinach, mushrooms, onion, bacon and eggs in salad bowl; mix gently. Serve with Sweet and Sour Dressing. Yield: 4 servings.

Approx Per Serving: Cal 198; Prot 16.2 g; T Fat 11.5 g; Chol 216 mg; Carbo 11.6 g; Sod 431 mg; Potas 1595 mg.

Sweet and Sour Dressing

1/4 cup vinegar
2 teaspoons onion-flavored bouillon
1/2 cup oil
1/2 cup sugar
1/3 cup catsup
1 tablespoon Worcestershire sauce

Combine vinegar and bouillon in small saucepan. Cook until bouillon is dissolved, stirring constantly. Stir in oil, sugar, catsup and Worcestershire sauce. Cool. Store in airtight container in refrigerator. Yield: 20 tablespoons.

Approx Per Tablespoon: Cal 73; Prot 0.1 g; T Fat 5.5 g; Chol 0 mg; Carbo 6.4 g; Sod 56.6 mg; Potas 25.8 mg.

Joanne Goodell
Cedar Rapids, Iowa

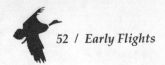

LA GRULLA CLUB SALAD DRESSING

2 cups sour cream
1 cup mayonnaise
1/2 cup (about) milk
1/2 envelope dry onion soup mix
1 clove of garlic, crushed
1 teaspoon pepper

Combine sour cream, mayonnaise, milk, dry soup mix, garlic and pepper in covered jar; shake to mix well. Store in refrigerator. Use over salad of chilled fresh greens.
Yield: 56 tablespoons.

Approx Per Tablespoon: Cal 48; Prot 0.4 g; T Fat 4.9 g; Chol 6.3 mg; Carbo 0.6 g; Sod 33.3 mg; Potas 17.2 mg.

Fare Thee Well—Dolley

DRESSING FOR TOMATOES

2 tablespoons vinegar
2 tablespoons sugar
2 tablespoons salad oil
1 teaspoon salt

Combine vinegar, sugar, oil and salt in small bowl; mix well. Use over peeled and quartered tomatoes; marinate for 30 minutes before serving. Yield: 4 tablespoons.

Approx Per Tablespoon: Cal 85; Prot 0 g; T Fat 6.8 g; Chol 0 mg; Carbo 6.7 g; Sod 533 mg; Potas 7.8 mg.

Barbara Ludwig
Reno, Nevada

ROQUEFORT CHEESE DRESSING

1   12-ounce can evaporated milk
4 cups mayonnaise
3 cloves of garlic, minced
1/2 cup lemon juice
2 teaspoons Worcestershire sauce
2 to 3 drops Tabasco sauce
8 ounces Roquefort cheese, crumbled

Beat evaporated milk and mayonnaise in mixer bowl until smooth. Add garlic, lemon juice, Worcestershire sauce and Tabasco sauce; mix well. Stir in cheese. Store in airtight container in refrigerator. Yield: 86 tablespoons.

Approx Per Tablespoon: Cal 89; Prot 1 g; T Fat 9.3 g; Chol 9.6 mg; Carbo 0.9 g; Sod 111 mg; Potas 20.8 mg.

Marilyn Tuttle
Homer, Alaska

Main Flights

Ducks and Geese

Snows At Dawn

John P. Cowan

COWAN STUFFED WILD GOOSE

1   4 to 6-pound goose
Salt and pepper to taste
1/2 cup chopped onion
11/2 cups diced peeled
apples
1/2 cup margarine
31/2 cups soft bread cubes
1/2 cup raisins
1/4 teaspoon sage
8 slices bacon
1 cup orange juice
2 tablespoons margarine

Season goose inside and out with salt and pepper. Sauté onion and apples in 1/2 cup margarine in skillet until tender. Add bread cubes, raisins, sage and salt and pepper to taste; mix well. Stuff goose with mixture. Cover drumsticks with bacon. Place in roasting pan. Roast at 325 degrees for 2 to 21/2 hours or until tender, basting with mixture of orange juice and remaining 2 tablespoons margarine. Yield: 4 servings.

BAVARIAN DUCK À LA MOORE HAVEN

(Compliments Baron Von Blue)

4 ducks
2 16-ounce containers sauerkraut
1 bottle of Port
1¹/2 cups dark rum
¹/4 cup packed brown sugar

Rinse ducks inside and out; pat dry. Brown ducks on all sides in a small amount of hot oil and margarine in skillet to seal skin. Place half the sauerkraut in roasting pan. Arrange ducks on bed of sauerkraut. Add enough wine and rum to cover ducks. Cover with remaining sauerkraut; sprinkle with brown sugar. Bake at 250 degrees for 5 to 5¹/2 hours. Serve with brown bread and cold beer. Yield: 8 servings.

Approx Per Serving: Cal 583; Prot 30.9 g; T Fat 26 g; Chol 136 mg; Carbo 13.5 g; Sod 855 mg; Potas 767 mg.

Eugene M. Jones
Ft. Lauderdale, Florida

CAJUN DUCKS

4 ducks
4 onions, chopped
2 bunches green onions, chopped
2 stalks celery
¹/2 bunch parsley, chopped
2 sticks butter, sliced
2 4-ounce cans mushrooms
2 cans golden mushroom soup
1 pint oysters
¹/2 cup red wine

Rinse ducks inside and out; pat dry. Place breast side down in large roasting pan. Place onions, green onions and ¹/2 stalk celery on ducks. Add layers of remaining ingredients except oysters and wine. Bake, covered, at 350 degrees for 2¹/2 to 3 hours. Remove ducks from sauce; place breast side up in baking pan. Bake until brown. Place roaster on stove-top over medium heat. Add oysters. Cook until edges curl. Add wine. Let stand for 5 minutes. Garnish with additional chopped parsley and green onions. Serve sauce over rice with ducks. Yield: 8 servings.

Approx Per Serving: Cal 613; Prot 36.6 g; T Fat 44.4 g; Chol 202 mg; Carbo 13.6 g; Sod 968 mg; Potas 812 mg.

Markel R. Wyatt
Mobile, Alabama

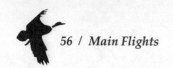

CROCKED DUCKS

3 or 4 ducks
3 large potatoes, peeled
3 large carrots
3 large stalks celery
1 cup red vermouth
Pepper or Poultry Magic
Cajun Spices to taste
Allspice to taste
1 large onion, chopped
1 large apple, thinly sliced

Rinse ducks inside and out; pat dry. Cut potatoes into thick slices; place in Crock•Pot. Cut carrots and celery into large pieces; place in duck cavities. Place ducks breast side up on potatoes. Add vermouth and seasonings. Layer onion and apple over top. Cook on Low for 8 hours or until ducks are tender. Thicken pan juices if desired. May use orange instead of apple. Yield: 8 servings.

Approx Per Serving: Cal 476; Prot 31.2 g; T Fat 26.1 g; Chol 136 mg; Carbo 20.5 g; Sod 126 mg; Potas 793 mg.

Dr. J.T. "Puldoo" Dibble
Vienna, Virginia

CROCK • POT DUCKS

2 small ducks
1 cup Sherry or white wine
1 tablespoon Worcestershire sauce
1 onion, cut into quarters
8 ounces fresh mushrooms
1 green bell pepper, sliced
2 carrots, cut into 1-inch strips
2 stalks celery, finely chopped
1 bay leaf
1 small turnip, chopped
2 potatoes, peeled, sliced

Rinse ducks inside and out; pat dry. Place in Crock•Pot. Add wine, Worcestershire sauce, onion, mushrooms, green pepper, carrots, celery, bay leaf, turnip and potatoes. Cook on Low for 5 to 6 hours or until ducks are tender. Remove bay leaf. Yield: 4 servings.

Approx Per Serving: Cal 356; Prot 18.1 g; T Fat 13.4 g; Chol 68 mg; Carbo 24.8 g; Sod 371 mg; Potas 826 mg.

Joe Bosco
Bay St. Louis, Mississippi

Donna Pittenger of Lake Zurich, Illinois, makes a mustard sauce of 1 tablespoon of butter, 1 teaspoon of Worcestershire sauce, 1 teaspoon of catsup, 2 teaspoons of mustard and 2 tablespoons of water simmered until smooth. Brush on duck breast filet and broil or grill to desired degree of doneness.

DUCK WITH COYOTE SAUCE

6 ducks
1 8-ounce bottle of Italian
salad dressing
1 8-ounce bottle of
A-1 sauce
1 8-ounce bottle of
Heinz 57 sauce
Juice of 1 lemon
1 teaspoon Worcestershire
sauce
1 teaspoon soy sauce
3 tablespoons dry mustard

Rinse ducks inside and out; pat dry. Combine salad dressing, steak sauces, lemon juice, Worcestershire sauce, soy sauce and dry mustard in large bowl; mix well. Marinate ducks in mixture for 2 hours or longer. Remove ducks; reserve marinade. Season ducks with salt and pepper to taste. Cook ducks by favorite barbecue method until rare. Heat reserved marinade to serving temperature. Serve with ducks. Yield: 6 servings.

Approx Per Serving: Cal 973; Prot 61.6 g; T Fat 74.3 g; Chol 272 mg; Carbo 17.9 g; Sod 442 mg; Potas 864 mg.

Wylie "Coyote" Griffeth
Denver, Colorado

DUCK À L'ORANGE

1 3-pound (or larger) duck
1/2 orange
1/2 white onion
Curry powder to taste
Fruited Sauce

Rinse duck inside and out; pat dry. Cut orange and onion into wedges; place in duck cavity. Rub with mixture of curry powder and salt and pepper to taste. Prepare kettle-type charcoal grill with charcoal banked on side. Place duck on grill. Cook for 30 minutes. Baste with Fruited Sauce. Cook until tender, basting every 10 to 15 minutes with Fruited Sauce. Yield: 2 servings.

Approx Per Serving: Cal 902; Prot 30.5 g; T Fat 26.2 g; Chol 136 mg; Carbo 124 g; Sod 250 mg; Potas 664 mg.

Fruited Sauce

1 cup apricot preserves
1/4 cup dry white wine
2 tablespoons fresh lemon juice
1 teaspoon teriyaki sauce
Cayenne pepper to taste
1 tablespoon honey
21/2 tablespoons Curaçao or
Triple Sec

Combine preserves, wine, lemon juice, teriyaki sauce and cayenne pepper in saucepan. Cook over medium heat until mixture is reduced to 11/2 cups, stirring frequently. Add honey and Curaçao; blend well.

Nutritional information for Fruited Sauce is included in Duck À L'Orange recipe.

David Knapp
Sitka, Alaska

ORANGE-SAUCED DUCK

1 large wild duck
1 envelope brown gravy mix
1/4 cup all-purpose flour
1 teaspoon salt
2 tablespoons sugar
2 tablespoons orange or
    plum jam
1 6-ounce can frozen orange
juice concentrate, thawed
1 cup hot water

Rinse duck inside and out; pat dry. Combine gravy mix, flour, salt and sugar in oven-cooking bag; mix well. Add jam, orange juice concentrate and water in bag; mix well. Place duck in bag; seal using manufacturer's instructions. Place in roasting pan. Cut slits in top of bag. Bake at 350 degrees for 2 hours. Place duck on serving plate. Pour sauce into gravy boat. Yield: 2 servings.

Approx Per Serving: Cal 687; Prot 34.5 g; T Fat 27.1 g; Chol 137 mg; Carbo 75.9 g; Sod 1779 mg; Potas 1060 mg.

Margo Ellard
Tuscaloosa, Alabama

KETTLE-GRILL ROAST WOOD DUCK WITH SAUSAGE AND APPLE STUFFING

4 undrawn wood ducks
1/2 pound pork sausage
2 large apples, peeled, chopped
1 medium onion, chopped
1/2 cup chopped celery
2 cups bread crumbs
1 egg
1 teaspoon salt
1 teaspoon poultry seasoning
1 peppercorn, crushed
11/2 cups water
1/2 cup white wine
1/2 cup melted butter

Hang wood ducks upside down at temperature below 45 degrees for 2 days. Pluck and clean ducks; rinse and pat dry. Cook sausage in skillet until brown and crumbly; drain, reserving 1/4 cup drippings. Sauté apples, onion and celery in reserved drippings for 10 minutes or until tender. Combine with sausage, crumbs, egg and seasonings in bowl; mix well. Stuff neck and body cavities of ducks; truss. Prepare kettle-grill in usual fashion. Arrange hot briquettes around outer edge; top with 10 to 12 fresh briquetes. Place ducks in foil pan in center of grill. Add water and wine to pan. Cook ducks in closed kettle for 1 to 11/2 hours or until ducks are tender, basting with mixture of butter and drippings every 15 minutes. Serve with wild rice. Yield: 4 servings.

Approx Per Serving: Cal 1097; Prot 59.6 g; T Fat 82 g; Chol 383 mg; Carbo 23.4 g; Sod 1760 mg; Potas 1054 mg.

Colonel Eiten
Troy Grove, Illinois

BILL'S ROAST DUCK

1 duck
1 onion, cut into quarters
8 mushrooms
2 tablespoons margarine
1 teaspoon lemon juice
4 slices bacon

Rinse duck inside and out; pat dry. Stuff cavity with onion and mushrooms. Place margarine and lemon juice in center of large piece heavy-duty foil. Place duck breast side down on foil; arrange bacon over duck. Fold foil over duck; seal tightly. Place duck breast side down over open campfire or on barbecue grill. Bake for 30 to 45 minutes or until tender. Yield: 2 servings.

Approx Per Serving: Cal 502; Prot 34.4 g; T Fat 38 g; Chol 147 mg; Carbo 4 g; Sod 376 mg; Potas 617 mg.

Bill Eibner
Ashland, Oregon

ROAST DUCK

1 duck
1/2 orange
1/2 apple
1/2 onion
1/2 envelope dry onion soup mix

Rinse duck inside and out; pat dry. Place orange, apple and onion in duck cavity. Place in roasting pan. Sprinkle soup mix over duck. Add enough water to cover bottom of roaster. Bake, covered, at 350 degrees for 2 to 2½ hours or until duck is tender. Yield: 2 servings.

Approx Per Serving: Cal 424; Prot 30.7 g; T Fat 26.3 g; Chol 136 mg; Carbo 15.8 g; Sod 254 mg; Potas 617 mg.

Dianne Schram
Vittoria, Ontario, Canada

DUCK AND SAUERKRAUT

3 or 4 ducks
1½ quarts undrained sauerkraut
1/2 cup wild rice
3/4 cup rice
1 pound pork sausage, crumbled
4 cups water

Rinse ducks inside and out; pat dry. Combine sauerkraut, rices, sausage and water in large roaster; mix well. Mixture will be very sloppy. Place ducks in roaster; cover with sauerkraut mixture. Bake, covered, at 350 degrees for 2½ to 3 hours or until ducks are tender. Serve with garlic bread and cranberries. Yield: 6 servings.

Approx Per Serving: Cal 939; Prot 52.4 g; T Fat 65.2 g; Chol 233 mg; Carbo 32.1 g; Sod 1139 mg; Potas 896 mg.

Mrs. Tom Gilmaster
Wisconsin Rapids, Wisconsin

ROAST TEAL

4 teal
2 tangerines, peeled
3/4 cup red Port
1 1/2 tablespoons lemon juice
1 cup red currant jelly
1 1/2 teaspoons all-purpose flour
2 tablespoons water

Rinse ducks inside and out; pat dry. Separate tangerines into halves; pierce with fork. Insert tangerines into duck cavities. Place in large roaster. Heat wine and lemon juice in saucepan. Add jelly; stir until melted. Pour over ducks. Bake, uncovered, at 400 to 425 degrees for 20 to 30 minutes or until cooked through, basting several times. Remove ducks to serving platter; slice as desired. Blend flour with water. Stir into pan drippings. Cook over medium heat until thickened, stirring constantly. Yield: 4 servings.

Approx Per Serving: Cal 864; Prot 31.7 g; T Fat 27.1 g; Chol 136 mg; Carbo 106 g; Sod 188 mg; Potas 881 mg.

Carol Allen
Wabasha, Minnesota

SAUSAGE-STUFFED TEAL

4 teal
1 pound hot pork sausage
Tony Chachere's creole seasoning

Pluck duck; do not skin. Rinse inside and out; pat dry. Stuff duck cavities with sausage. Rub ducks with seasoning. Place ducks 18 inches above hot coals in smoker. Cook for 45 minutes or until sausage is cooked through. Yield: 4 servings.

Approx Per Serving: Cal 833; Prot 42.9 g; T Fat 71.6 g; Chol 214 mg; Carbo 1.2 g; Sod 852 mg; Potas 654 mg.

Greg Tschida
Metairie, Louisiana

Kathy Toms of Cameron Park, California, marinates ducks for 24 hours in 2 ounces of Brandy, 2 ounces of soy sauce, 1 ounce of sesame oil and 1 ounce of oyster sauce. Add 3 crushed cloves of garlic and pressed fresh ginger to taste. Baste with marinade during baking or grilling as well.

DUCK AND SPAGHETTI

1 quart Old Crow Bourbon
whiskey
4 wild ducks
4 onions
1 gallon cooked spaghetti
2 28-ounce cans tomatoes
2 pounds American cheese,
thinly sliced
1 28-ounce bottle of catsup
8 slices bacon

Pour snifter of Old Crow for each guest and the cook. Refill glasses as necessary; enhance with favorite duck-hunting stories. Rinse ducks inside and out. Place onion in each duck cavity. Cook ducks in water to cover in large kettle until very tender. Keep ducks warm in a small amount of broth; reserve remaining broth. Layer spaghetti, tomatoes, cheese, catsup and salt and pepper to taste alternately in large baking pan until all ingredients are used, ending with cheese. Pour reserved duck broth over layers. Bake at 375 degrees for 1 hour or until brown. Arrange ducks on top; place bacon over ducks. Bake for 10 to 15 minutes longer. When the Old Crow is gone, dinner will be ready. You can safely bet the old shotgun that if someone doesn't like this homely dish he doesn't know the thrill of whistling wings silhouetted against a glowing sunrise, as viewed from a duck blind on opening day. Yield: 4 servings.

Nutritional information for this recipe is not available.

Donna Pittenger
Lake Zurich, Illinois

WILD DUCK À LA BEER

4 ducks
2 12-ounce cans beer
1 6-ounce jar peach jam
1/4 cup soy sauce
1 tablespoon lemon juice
2 teaspoons dry mustard

Rinse ducks inside and out; pat dry. Sprinkle with salt and pepper to taste. Place in small roasting pan. Pour 1 can beer over ducks. Bake, covered, at 350 degrees for 2½ hours. Discard drippings. Skin, bone and slice ducks. Combine 1 can beer, peach jam, soy sauce, lemon juice and dry mustard in roaster; mix well. Place duck in sauce. Bake, covered, for 1 hour, basting frequently with sauce. Yield: 4 servings.

Approx Per Serving: Cal 880; Prot 60.4 g; T Fat 51.7 g; Chol 272 mg; Carbo 34.9 g; Sod 1235 mg; Potas 942 mg.

Tudy Nycklemoe
Fergus Falls, Minnesota

WILD DUCK

1 duck
1¹/2 tablespoons butter
3 to 4 tablespoons orange duck sauce

Rinse duck inside and out; pat dry. Place on large piece heavy-duty foil. Place butter and 1 to 2 tablespoons duck sauce in duck cavity. Spoon remaining sauce over duck. Seal foil around duck. Wrap in additional layer heavy-duty foil. Bake at 350 degrees for 1 hour. Reduce temperature to 275 degrees. Bake for 30 minutes. Reduce temperature to 200 degrees. Bake for 30 minutes. Duck will be very tender including legs, wings and skin. Serve with wild rice casserole, baked sweet potato, fresh spinach salad, corn bread and, if anyone is still hungry, orange-apple pie. Yield: 2 servings.

Approx Per Serving: Cal 473; Prot 29.8 g; T Fat 34.5 g; Chol 159 mg; Carbo 9.1 g; Sod 266 mg; Potas 434 mg.

J.B.VanderMale
Loxahatchee, Florida

WILD DUCK IN PEACH MARINADE

2 3-pound mallards
1 16-ounce can sliced peaches
1/2 cup soy sauce
1 1-inch piece fresh ginger, peeled, sliced
1 tablespoon butter
3 ounces fresh mushrooms, cut into quarters

Rinse ducks inside and out; pat dry. Place in large bowl. Drain peaches, reserving juice. Mix half the peach slices, soy sauce, ginger and reserved juice in bowl. Pour over ducks. Marinate overnight. Remove ducks from marinade; wipe off excess marinade. Brown ducks in butter in heavy skillet over medium heat. Place in shallow baking dish. Pour marinade over ducks. Add mushrooms. Bake, covered, at 350 degrees for 2 hours or until tender, adding a small amount of water if necessary to prevent scorching. Yield: 4 servings.

Approx Per Serving: Cal 673; Prot 47.3 g; T Fat 41.8 g; Chol 212 mg; Carbo 26.7 g; Sod 2234 mg; Potas 885 mg.

IGFCA World Championship Game Cookoff
Sioux City, Nebraska

ALASKAN DUCK BREASTS

6 to 8 duck breasts
1 package shrimp and crab boil
Peanut oil
1 package chicken Rice-A-Roni
1 6-ounce can water chestnuts, drained
1 4-ounce package slivered almonds
1 4-ounce can mushrooms, drained
Garlic and rosemary to taste
5 slices thick-sliced bacon

Rinse duck breasts; pat dry. Slice into 1/4-inch wide strips. Parboil with shrimp and crab boil for about 10 minutes; drain and pat dry. Heat about 2 inches peanut oil very hot in skillet. Add duck strips. Cook for 5 to 8 minutes or just until tender; drain. Drain oil from skillet; do not clean skillet. Prepare Rice-A-Roni in skillet according to package directions. Add duck, water chestnuts, almonds, mushrooms and seasonings. Cook according to package directions. Cook bacon until very crisp; drain well on paper towels. Crumble over Rice-A-Roni mixture. Yield: 3 servings.

Approx Per Serving: Cal 717; Prot 59.2 g; T Fat 36.3 g; Chol 173 mg; Carbo 39.3 g; Sod 853 mg; Potas 1050 mg. Nutritional information does not include peanut oil.

Jeffrey S. Behnken
Anchorage, Alaska

BLACKENED BREAST OF DUCK

Boned breast of 1 black duck or mallard
1/2 cup olive oil
1/2 cup Old Bay Seasoning

Place duck breast on cutting board. Place hand lightly on breast; slice into halves with sharp knife. Pound between waxed paper. Preheat seasoned cast iron skillet. Dip duck filets into olive oil; coat with seasoning. Place in skillet. Cook for 2 minutes on each side or until brown. Serve with baked sweet potatoes, steamed broccoli and crusty Italian or French bread. Yield: 2 servings.

Approx Per Serving: Cal 661; Prot 23.9 g; T Fat 59.9 g; Chol 82 mg; Carbo 9.7 g; Sod 68.2 mg; Potas 403 mg.

John and Jane Lugo
Palermo, New Jersey

DUCK BREASTS WITH RAISIN SAUCE

Duck breasts
Orange juice
Apple juice
1/4 cup butter
1/4 cup all-purpose flour
1 cup milk
1/2 cup orange juice
1 1/2 teaspoons paprika
1 teaspoon salt
1/4 teaspoon pepper
2/3 cup raisins

Rinse duck breasts; pat dry. Place in baking pan. Bake, uncovered, at 350 degrees for 1 1/2 hours, basting frequently with mixture of orange juice and apple juice. Melt butter in saucepan. Blend in flour. Stir in milk and 1/2 cup orange juice gradually. Cook until thickened, stirring constantly. Add paprika, salt, pepper and raisins; mix well. Heat to serving temperature. Serve duck breasts with raisin sauce over hot cooked brown or wild rice.

Nutritional information for this recipe is not available.

Doug Alexander
Bozeman, Montana

FRENCH BROAD RIVER WOODIES

4 wood duck breasts
1 cup red wine
1 cup water
1/4 cup olive oil
1 bay leaf
12 peppercorns
1/2 teaspoon thyme
1/2 cup all-purpose flour
1/2 cup butter
1/2 cup sour cream
1/4 cup sliced mushrooms
1/4 cup chicken broth

Rinse duck breasts; pat dry. Marinate in mixture of wine, water, olive oil and seasonings for 24 hours. Drain and pat dry. Coat with flour. Cook in butter in cast iron skillet until brown. Pour mixture of sour cream, mushrooms and broth over duck. Bake, covered, at 350 degrees for 40 minutes or until tender. Yield: 2 servings.

Approx Per Serving: Cal 1172; Prot 39.7 g; T Fat 92.7 g; Chol 273 mg; Carbo 27 g; Sod 707 mg; Potas 746 mg. Nutritional information includes all of marinade.

David McMahan
Kodak, Tennessee

TRASH'S FRIED DUCK BREAST STRIPS

4 duck breast filets
2 eggs, beaten
Milk
1/4 cup Tony's creole seasoning
Garlic powder to taste
Flour
Salt and pepper
Oil for deep frying

Rinse duck breasts; pat dry. Cut lengthwise into 1/4 inch strips. Beat eggs with enough milk to cover duck strips in large bowl. Add creole seasoning and garlic powder. Marinate duck strips in milk mixture in refrigerator for 12 to 24 hours. Mix flour, salt and pepper in large plastic bag. Drain strips; shake in flour mixture until coated. Fry in 1½-inches 350-degree oil until strips are brown and floating. Drain on paper towels. Serve with wild rice and green beans. Yield: 4 servings.

Nutritional information for this recipe is not available.

Mike Kimbriel (Trash)
Jackson, Mississippi

NINNESCAH DUCK DELIGHT

4 large duck breast filets
8   1-ounce slices Cheddar cheese
1 can cream of chicken soup
1   4-ounce can sliced mushrooms
1/2 cup cooking wine
1 cup herb-seasoned stuffing mix
6 tablespoons melted margarine

Rinse filets; pat dry. Cut lengthwise into 8 pieces. Arrange in 9x13-inch baking dish; top each with cheese slice. Mix soup, mushrooms and wine in bowl; spoon over cheese. Sprinkle stuffing mix over top. Drizzle with melted margarine. Bake, uncovered, at 350 degrees for 50 to 55 minutes or until brown and duck is tender. Yield: 8 servings.

Approx Per Serving: Cal 413; Prot 23.3 g; T Fat 23.5 g; Chol 73.8 mg; Carbo 24.4 g; Sod 1089 mg; Potas 270 mg.

Jane Queal
Pratt, Kansas

PINTAILS IN RED WINE ROUX

4 pintail breast filets
2 cups dry vermouth
1/2 cup bacon drippings
1/2 cup peanut oil
1/2 cup all-purpose flour
1/2 cup chopped green onions
1/2 cup chopped celery
1 cup chopped mushrooms
1/2 cup duck or chicken stock
1/2 cup red wine
1/2 teaspoon cayenne pepper
1/4 teaspoon white pepper
1/4 teaspoon black pepper
1/4 teaspoon sweet basil
1/4 teaspoon thyme
1/8 teaspoon oregano
1 teaspoon garlic

Rinse filets; pat dry. Marinate filets in vermouth for 2 to 4 hours. Drain and cut into cubes. Brown in bacon drippings in skillet. Drain and set aside. Heat oil in Dutch oven over high heat until very hot. Add flour gradually, stirring constantly. Cook until flour is rust-colored, stirring constantly; reduce heat. Add green onions, celery and mushrooms. Cook until vegetables are brown, stirring constantly. Add stock, wine, spices and duck. Simmer, covered, for 45 to 60 minutes, stirring occasionally and adding liquid as necessary. Serve over rice or with corn bread or dumplings. Yield: 4 servings.

Approx Per Serving: Cal 830; Prot 19.8 g; T Fat 59 g; Chol 230 mg; Carbo 21.4 g; Sod 715 mg; Potas 450 mg.

Paul Swacina
Corpus Christi, Texas

ROASTED DUCK BREASTS

4 duck breast filets
8 slices bacon
1 1/2 sticks butter, sliced
1 bay leaf, crushed
1 tablespoon poultry seasoning
1 teaspoon parsley flakes
1 teaspoon salt
Dash each of black pepper, red pepper and cinnamon

Rinse filets; pat dry. Wrap filets in bacon; arrange in baking dish lined with large piece foil. Add butter slices; sprinkle with seasonings. Seal foil tightly. Bake at 350 degrees for 1 hour and 15 minutes. Yield: 4 servings.

Approx Per Serving: Cal 519; Prot 26.9 g; T Fat 45.6 g; Chol 186 mg; Carbo 1 g; Sod 1090 mg; Potas 384 mg.

Greg McDonald
New Bern, North Carolina

MICROWAVE STUFFED DUCK BREASTS

6 duck breasts
1 package rice stuffing mix
Garlic powder to taste

Rinse duck breasts; pat dry. Cut pockets in breasts. Prepare stuffing mix using package directions. Sprinkle pockets with garlic powder and salt and pepper to taste. Spoon stuffing into pockets; secure with toothpicks. Arrange in greased glass baking dish. Microwave, covered, on Medium for 7 minutes. Spoon remaining stuffing mixture around breasts. Microwave on Medium for 10 minutes longer. Yield: 6 servings.

Approx Per Serving: Cal 172; Prot 23.3 g; T Fat 6.4 g; Chol 85.8 mg; Carbo 4.2 g; Sod 161 mg; Potas 308 mg.

Mrs. John D. Allan
Annada, Missouri

DUCK BREAST TERIYAKI

2 large duck breasts with skin
Garlic powder
Pepper
1 cup teriyaki sauce

Rinse duck breasts; pat dry. Sprinkle with garlic powder and pepper. Marinate in enough teriyaki sauce to cover breasts for 6 hours; drain. Place on grill over low coals. Cook for 4 minutes per side. Do not allow fire to flare up; duck breasts should be rare. Slice diagonally 1/4-inch thick; arrange slices in semi-circle on plate. Garnish with parsley sprigs. Serve with red wine sauce if desired. Duck legs prepared this way make great hors d'oeuvres. Yield: 2 servings.

Approx Per Serving: Cal 367; Prot 28.7 g; T Fat 17.7 g; Chol 90.7 mg; Carbo 24.7 g; Sod 5585 mg; Potas 639 mg. Nutritional information includes all of teriyaki sauce.

Steve Rucker
Reno, Nevada

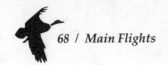

BIG AL'S GRILLED DUCK TERIYAKI

Duck breasts (1 per serving)
White onion
Bacon (2 slices per serving)
1 bottle of teriyaki sauce

Rinse duck breasts; pat dry. Pound to 1/8-inch thickness with meat mallet. Cut 3/4 inch wide strip of onion for each breast; place in center of each. Roll up to enclose onion; wrap 2 strips bacon around each and secure with toothpicks. Marinate in teriyaki sauce for 1 hour or longer. Drain, reserving teriyaki sauce. Grill over hot charcoal until bacon is crisp, basting frequently with reserved teriyaki sauce. May use only tenderloin strip of duck breast prepared as above to serve as appetizer or as a sampler for those who "hate duck." Great fun to watch their minds change right before your eyes!

Nutritional information for this recipe is not available.

Al Seyler
Cary, North Carolina

CHERRY BRANDY DUCK BREASTS

3 whole duck breasts
2 tablespoons shortening
2   21-ounce cans cherry pie
filling
1 tablespoon finely chopped
crystallized ginger
2 tablespoons shredded
orange rind
1/4 cup orange juice
1/2 cup Brandy
1/4 cup cherry Brandy
1 to 2 tablespoons cornstarch

Rinse duck breasts; pat dry. Cut breasts into quarters. Cook in a small amount of shortening in skillet until brown. Place in Crock•Pot. Combine pie filling, ginger, orange rind, orange juice and Brandies in saucepan. Bring to a boil, stirring constantly. Dissolve cornstarch in a small amount of water. Stir into cherry mixture. Cook until thickened, stirring constantly. Pour into Crock•Pot. Cook on Low for 5 to 6 hours. May bake in baking dish at 350 degrees for 45 to 60 minutes or until duck breasts are tender. Yield: 3 servings.

Approx Per Serving: Cal 790; Prot 24.5 g; T Fat 13.6 g; Chol 82 mg; Carbo 135 g; Sod 186 mg; Potas 810 mg.

Dianne Robison
Pocatello, Idaho

CREAMED DUCKS

8 duck breasts
1/4 teaspoon garlic salt
Pepper to taste
Meat tenderizer
2 cans cream of mushroom soup
1 can beef consommé
1 consommé can water
1 teaspoon Worcestershire sauce
1 teaspoon onion flakes

Rinse duck breasts; pat dry and cut into pieces. Sprinkle with garlic salt, pepper and tenderizer. Brown in a small amount of oil in skillet; drain on paper towels. Place in Crock•Pot. Add soup, consommé, 1 consommé can water, Worcestershire sauce and onion flakes. Cook on High for 2 to 4 hours or on Low all day. Serve over rice, noodles or toast. Yield: 8 servings.

Approx Per Serving: Cal 215; Prot 24.1 g; T Fat 10.3 g; Chol 82.9 mg; Carbo 5.5 g; Sod 826 mg; Potas 377 mg.

Virginia Aaron
Fort Greely, Alaska

CROCKED-BROILED DUCK

4 duck breasts
2 cups milk
1   12-ounce can beer
1/2 small onion, chopped
1/2 to 1 cup sliced mushrooms
1 teaspoon garlic salt
1 teaspoon minced garlic
1 teaspoon pepper
Dash each of thyme and basil
2 tablespoons Worcestershire sauce
6 drops of Tabasco sauce
1/2 cup melted margarine
2 tablespoons honey
4 slices bacon

Rinse duck breasts; pat dry. Marinate in mixture of milk and beer in refrigerator for 2 to 3 days. Drain and pat dry. Combine onion, mushrooms, seasonings, Worcestershire sauce and Tabasco sauce in Crock•Pot. Place duck breasts on onion mixture. Drizzle margarine over top. Cook on Low for 4 to 6 hours. Remove duck breasts from Crock•Pot. Blend 1/4 to 1/2 cup drippings with honey in small bowl. Brush over duck breasts; wrap each breast with bacon. Place on rack in broiler pan or on grill over hot coals. Broil for 2 to 3 minutes or until bacon is crisp. Place on serving plate. Spoon onion mixture from Crock•Pot over breasts. Yield: 2 servings.

Approx Per Serving: Cal 676; Prot 58.6 g; T Fat 25.8 g; Chol 208 mg; Carbo 40.9 g; Sod 1679 mg; Potas 1301 mg.

Sandy Lipson
Grand Junction, Colorado

BUFFALO CITY BEANS WITH TWICE SMOKED DUCK

1 pound dried navy beans
1 pound boned smoked duck
   (about 6 ducks)
1 large onion, sliced
1/2 cup packed brown sugar
5 tablespoons blackstrap
   molasses
1/2 cup catsup
1 teaspoon salt
1/2 teaspoon dry mustard
1/4 teaspoon peppercorns

Place beans in large saucepan; add water to cover. Bring to boil. Boil for 2 minutes; remove from heat. Let stand, covered, for 1 hour. Add water to cover. Bring to a simmer. Simmer, uncovered, for 50 minutes; do not boil. Drain beans, reserving liquid. Lay duck, beans and onion in greased 2-quart casserole or bean pot. Combine brown sugar, molasses, catsup and seasonings in bowl. Add 1 cup reserved bean liquid; mix well. Pour over bean mixture. Add enough reserved bean liquid or water to almost cover beans. Bake, covered, at 300 degrees for 3 to 3 1/2 hours. Bake, uncovered, for 30 minutes longer. Stir casserole if beans appear dry during baking. Yield: 8 servings.

Approx Per Serving: Cal 409; Prot 22.2 g; T Fat 9.4 g; Chol 45.4 mg; Carbo 60.3 g; Sod 501 mg; Potas 1502 mg.

Carol Kube
Arcadia, Wisconsin

HEARTY DUCK AND BEAN CASSEROLE

1 pound dried Northern beans
2 quarts water
4 duck breasts
1/4 teaspoon ground cloves
2 bay leaves
1 pound mild or hot pork
   sausage
1 large onion, chopped
1 cup apple juice
1 8-ounce can tomato sauce
1 teaspoon thyme
1 tablespoon parsley

Soak beans in water to cover overnight. Drain. Combine with 2 quarts water in saucepan. Rinse duck breasts. Add duck breasts, cloves and bay leaves to beans. Bring to a boil; skim foam. Simmer for 1 hour. Remove and slice duck breasts. Cook beans for 15 minutes longer. Remove bay leaves. Drain, reserving liquid. Cook sausage and onion in skillet until brown and crumbly; drain. Add apple juice, tomato sauce, thyme, duck, parsley and 2 cups reserved bean liquid; mix well. Heat for 3 minutes. Layer bean mixture and sausage mixture alternately in large casserole. Bake at 375 degrees for 1 hour. Serve with hot biscuits or corn bread and salad. Yield: 8 servings.

Approx Per Serving: Cal 524; Prot 30.4 g; T Fat 26.1 g; Chol 79.8 mg; Carbo 42.4 g; Sod 590 mg; Potas 1300 mg.

Pat Malloy
Ft. Thomas, Kentucky

DUCK CASSEROLE

3 ducks
2 small onions
1 medium potato
1 medium apple
3 bay leaves
1 stalk celery
5 cups water
1 8-ounce package herb-
seasoned stuffing mix
1½ cups milk
½ cup chopped celery
1 cup chopped onion
2 eggs, beaten
½ cup mayonnaise
10⅔ tablespoons melted butter
1 can cream of mushroom soup
¾ cup shredded Cheddar
cheese

Rinse ducks inside and out. Combine with onions, potato, apple, bay leaves, celery and water in large saucepan. Cook, covered, for 2 hours or until tender. Drain, reserving 1½ cups broth. Bone ducks. Pour reserved broth over stuffing mix in large bowl. Let stand for several minutes. Add milk, celery, chopped onion, eggs, mayonnaise and butter; mix well. Spoon into greased baking dish. Refrigerate overnight. Spread soup over top. Bake at 350 degrees for 1 hour or until set and brown. Sprinkle cheese over top. Bake until cheese melts.
Yield: 8 servings.

Approx Per Serving: Cal 779; Prot 33.2 g; T Fat 56.1 g; Chol 238 mg; Carbo 35.5 g; Sod 1169 mg; Potas 612 mg.

John Mason
Cairo, Georgia

WILD DUCK CASSEROLE

2 wild ducks
1 1-pound loaf white
bread, dried
1 teaspoon salt
1 teaspoon pepper
1½ teaspoons sage
¼ cup minced onion
¼ cup celery flakes
½ cup mayonnaise-type
salad dressing
1 egg
1 can cream of celery soup
2 cups shredded sharp
Cheddar cheese

Rinse ducks. Place in water to cover in large saucepan. Cook until tender. Drain, reserving 2 cups broth. Remove duck meat from bones; set aside. Cut bread into cubes. Combine bread cubes, salt, pepper, sage, onion and celery flakes in large stainless steel bowl; toss to mix. Add reserved 2 cups broth, salad dressing, egg and soup; toss until moistened. Chop boned duck; add to bread mixture. Spoon into well-greased large casserole. Bake at 350 degrees for 45 minutes. Sprinkle with cheese. Bake for 15 minutes longer. Let stand for 10 minutes before serving. Serve with tossed salad.
Yield: 8 servings.

Approx Per Serving: Cal 529; Prot 27.2 g; T Fat 31 g; Chol 105 mg; Carbo 34.3 g; Sod 1153 mg; Potas 358 mg.

Mrs. Kenneth E. Hardy
Bath, Illinois

DUCK McNUGGETS

2 or 3 ducks
1/2 cup all-purpose flour
Paprika to taste
1/2 cup oil

Rinse ducks inside and out; pat dry. Cut meat from bone; cut into 1-inch cubes. Sprinkle with salt and pepper to taste. Coat with mixture of flour and paprika. Heat oil in large heavy skillet over medium heat. Add duck. Cook until brown on all sides. Reduce heat to low. Cook, covered, for 30 to 60 minutes or until tender. Cook, uncovered, over medium heat for several minutes to crisp nuggets if desired. Serve with sweet and sour sauce, ranch dressing or other favorite dipping sauce. Yield: 4 servings.

Approx Per Serving: Cal 834; Prot 46 g; T Fat 66.2 g; Chol 204 mg; Carbo 11.1 g; Sod 144 mg; Potas 655 mg.

JoAnn Woodgerd
Stevensville, Montana

RUTHIE MAE'S DUCK PIE

3 ducks
2 cups chopped onion
2 stalks celery
1 tablespoon salt
2 tablespoons all-purpose flour
Worcestershire sauce to taste
1   2-crust recipe pie pastry

Rinse ducks inside and out. Place in large saucepan. Add onion, celery, 1 tablespoon salt and water to just cover. Cook over medium-low heat for 2 1/2 hours or until almost dry and duck is very tender. Bone ducks; place duck meat in loaf pan or casserole. Broil until brown and skin is crisp. Dissolve flour in a small amount of water. Discard celery stalks from saucepan. Stir flour mixture into broth. Cook until thickened, stirring constantly. Add salt, pepper and Worcestershire sauce to taste. Stir in enough water to make of gravy consistency. Place duck in pastry-lined deep-dish pie plate. Add gravy. Top with remaining pastry, sealing edge and cutting vents. Bake at 425 degrees until brown. Yield: 6 servings.

Approx Per Serving: Cal 723; Prot 33.9 g; T Fat 43.8 g; Chol 136 mg; Carbo 29.9 g; Sod 1550 mg; Potas 588 mg.

Ruthie Mae Jerger
Lake Iamonia, Leon County, Florida

BASHFUL BENJAMIN'S DOWN-EAST POTPIE

2 Idas
1 6-ounce package dried
apricots
Grated rind and segments of 1
large orange
Grated rind and segments of 1
small lemon
1¹/₂ cups Grand Marnier
¹/₂ cup all-purpose flour
¹/₂ cup sugar
6 large potatoes
¹/₄ cup butter
¹/₂ cup cream
1 16-ounce jar boiled
onions, drained
1 16-ounce can whole kernel
corn, drained
¹/₂ cup melted butter

Rinse ducks inside and out; pat dry. Rub with salt and pepper to taste; place on rack in deep baking dish. Sprinkle cavities with salt and pepper to taste; add 4 or 5 apricots, 2 or 3 orange segments, 1 teaspoon of each rind and 1 tablespoon of the Grand Marnier. Butter both sides of 2 paper bags (do not use bags made of recycled paper); place over ducks as for tent. Bake at 375 degrees until golden brown and tender. Remove bags. Bake for 15 minutes longer. Combine remaining Grand Marnier, remaining rinds, orange and lemon sections and remaining apricots in saucepan. Bring to a simmer. Dissolve flour in a small amount of water. Stir into hot mixture. Cook until thickened, stirring constantly. Add sugar; stir with wire whisk until very thick. Set aside. Boil unpeeled potatoes in water to cover in saucepan until tender; drain and peel. Place in large bowl. Add ¹/₄ cup butter and salt and pepper to taste. Add cream gradually, beating constantly until light and fluffy. Cool. Bone ducks; discard fruit from cavities. Place duck in glass pie plate. Add sauce, onions and corn. Spread potatoes over top; draw into random peaks and shape volcano-like depression in center. Drizzle melted butter over peaks and depression. Place on baking sheet. Bake at 375 degrees for 45 minutes. The smell alone would make Bashful Benjamin blush. Yield: 6 servings.

Approx Per Serving: Cal 1044; Prot 23.7 g; T Fat 39.9 g; Chol 138 mg; Carbo 121 g; Sod 277 mg; Potas 1466 mg.

Lisa Laurence
Sullivan Harbor, Massachusetts

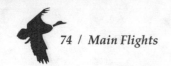
BEST I'VE EVER HAD WILD DUCK GUMBO

3 ducks (preferably mallards)
2 pounds unpeeled shrimp
1/2 cup butter
1/2 cup bacon drippings
1/2 cup (or more) all-purpose
flour
3 cloves of garlic, chopped
3 large green bell peppers,
chopped
2 cups chopped celery
2 large yellow onions, chopped
2 large bunches green onions,
chopped
2 6-ounce cans tomato paste
1 16-ounce can tomatoes
1 teaspoon thyme
1 teaspoon basil
1 teaspoon oregano
1/2 teaspoon (about) cayenne
pepper
2 teaspoons MSG
1 tablespoon seasoned salt
1 tablespoon pepper
1 tablespoon parsley flakes
1 tablespoon filé

Rinse ducks inside and out. Cook in water to cover in large saucepan until tender. Drain; strain and reserve broth. Cool ducks; skin and cut into bite-sized pieces. Peel shrimp; reserve heads and shells. Boil heads and shells in 2 quarts water in saucepan for 30 minutes. Strain and reserve broth. Cook butter, bacon drippings and flour in skillet until color of an old penny, stirring constantly. Add garlic, green pepper, celery and yellow and green onions. Cook until vegetables are light brown, stirring constantly. Add tomato paste and undrained tomatoes; mix well, breaking tomatoes with spoon. Add seasonings. Add enough duck and shrimp broth in equal amounts to make of desired consistency. Simmer, covered, for 1 hour or longer. Add duck 45 minutes before serving time. Add shrimp 30 minutes before serving. Add additional stock as necessary to make of desired consistency. Bring to a boil over high heat. Add filé. Cook for 3 minutes. Serve over hot cooked rice. May add 2 cans crab meat and/or fresh oysters with liquor. Yield: 15 servings.

Approx Per Serving: Cal 313; Prot 14.4 g; T Fat 24.4 g; Chol 122 mg; Carbo 9.5 g; Sod 1240 mg; Potas 474 mg.

Hal C. Matthews
Sherwood, Arkansas

Chandler Cheek of Biloxi, Mississippi, has the following suggestions for how much duck to serve. If serving roast domestic or large wild duck, plan on 1/4 to 1/2 duck per guest. For roasted or braised medium-sized wild duck, you will need 1/2 to 1 duck per person. Small wild duck and teal are served whole and require 1 to 2 ducks per person.

DUCK GUMBO

2 ducks
1¹/₂ cups margarine
1 cup all-purpose flour
1 bunch celery, chopped
3 cloves of garlic, chopped
4 medium onions, chopped
1 large green bell pepper,
chopped
1 bunch green onions, chopped
1 15-ounce can tomato paste
2 teaspoons MSG
1 teaspoon oregano
2 tablespoons salt
2 20-ounce cans tomatoes
2 tablespoons parsley flakes
1 teaspoon thyme
1 tablespoon black pepper
¹/₄ teaspoon red pepper
4 cups cut okra

Rinse ducks inside and out. Cook in water to cover in large saucepan until tender. Drain, reserving 2 quarts broth. Bone ducks. Melt margarine in skillet. Add flour. Cook until dark brown, stirring constantly. Stir into reserved broth in large saucepan. Cook until thickened, stirring constantly. Add duck and remaining ingredients. Cook over low heat for 2 hours or less, stirring frequently. Serve over hot cooked rice. Yield: 10 servings.

Approx Per Serving: Cal 411; Prot 18.1 g; T Fat 25.2 g; Chol 54.4 mg; Carbo 31.6 g; Sod 2585 mg; Potas 1128 mg.

Russell B. King III
Leland, Mississippi

DUCK DE SAL

2 mallards
2 to 4 tablespoons oil
1 cup chopped celery
1 cup chopped onion
1 cup chopped peeled carrots
1 4-ounce can sliced black
olives, drained
1 4-ounce can mushrooms,
drained
1 can chicken broth
1 cup red cooking wine
1 to 2 tablespoons soy sauce
2 tablespoons (about)
cornstarch

Rinse ducks inside and out; pat dry. Pour enough oil into heavy roasting pan to cover bottom. Add chopped vegetables, olives, mushrooms and salt and pepper to taste; stir to coat with oil. Place ducks on vegetables. Pour broth and wine over ducks. Bake, covered, at 300 degrees for 3 to 4 hours or until ducks are fork-tender. Bone and chop. Strain broth; reserve vegetables. Skim broth. Combine with soy sauce in saucepan. Bring to a boil. Dissolve enough cornstarch to thicken to desired consistency in a small amount of cold water. Stir into broth. Cook until thickened, stirring constantly. Add vegetables and chopped duck. Heat to serving temperature. Serve over hot cooked rice. Yield: 4 servings.

Approx Per Serving: Cal 616; Prot 33.3 g; T Fat 43 g; Chol 136 mg; Carbo 17.2 g; Sod 1047 mg; Potas 923 mg.

Salli Jackson
Grenada, Mississippi

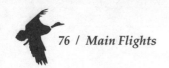

NANCY'S CROCK • POT DUCK STEW

5 small or 2 large ducks
3 tablespoons oil
3 tablespoons orange
marmalade
2 small yellow onions, sliced
3 cloves of garlic, chopped
5 or 6 carrots, peeled
3 large potatoes, peeled
1 cup 1-inch celery pieces
1   10-ounce can chicken broth

Rinse ducks inside and out; pat dry. Brown on all sides in hot oil in skillet over medium-high heat. Brush with marmalade; place breast side up in Crock•Pot. Sauté onions and garlic in drippings in skillet until brown; add to Crock•Pot. Cut carrots and potatoes into 1-inch pieces. Add vegetables, broth, garlic and salt and pepper to taste to Crock•Pot. Cook on High for 2¹/₂ hours. Serve with white or wild rice. Yield: 5 servings.

Approx Per Serving: Cal 519; Prot 27.6 g; T Fat 29.5 g; Chol 109 mg; Carbo 36.1 g; Sod 311 mg; Potas 1133 mg.

Nancy Malech
Coyote, California

WILD RICE AND DUCKY SHRIMP

2 wild ducks
2   6-ounce packages long grain
and wild rice mix
1 pound peeled shrimp
¹/₂ cup chopped green onions
2 cans cream of mushroom soup

Rinse ducks inside and out; pat dry. Sprinkle inside and out with salt and pepper to taste. Place in roasting pan. Bake, covered, at 325 degrees for 3 hours or until cooked through. Refrigerate ducks with drippings for 8 hours to overnight. Reserve drippings; bone and chop duck. Prepare rice mix using package directions, adding shrimp when rice comes to a boil. Sauté green onions in duck drippings in skillet; reduce heat. Add soup and enough water to make sauce of desired consistency. Stir in duck. Add salt to taste. Heat to serving temperature. Serve duck mixture over shrimp and rice mixture. May combine the two mixtures in casserole if desired. Yield: 8 servings.

Approx Per Serving: Cal 353; Prot 29.1 g; T Fat 19.4 g; Chol 155 mg; Carbo 14.2 g; Sod 707 mg; Potas 403 mg.

Gloria Pittman
Slidell, Louisiana

OTTERTAIL DUCK WITH MUSHROOMS

6 duck breasts
1 clove of garlic, chopped
3 tablespoons oil
1 small onion, chopped
1¹/₂ cups beef bouillon
1 pound fresh mushrooms,
sliced
3 tablespoons cornstarch
1 tablespoon soy sauce
4 cups cooked brown rice

Rinse duck breasts; pat dry. Slice ¹/₈ inch thick. Sauté garlic in oil in skillet; remove garlic. Add duck slices, onion and salt and pepper to taste. Cook until brown, stirring occasionally. Add bouillon and mushrooms. Cook, covered, over low heat for 30 minutes. Blend cornstarch with soy sauce and a enough water to make thin paste. Stir into duck mixture. Cook until thickened, stirring constantly. Serve over rice. Yield: 4 servings.

Approx Per Serving: Cal 594; Prot 42.5 g; T Fat 19.4 g; Chol 123 mg; Carbo 61.6 g; Sod 652 mg; Potas 1089 mg.

Janelle Scheidecker
Fergus Falls, Minnesota

SPICY MALAYSIAN DUCK

3 ducks
2 tablespoons cider vinegar
2 tablespoons fresh lime juice
1¹/₂ teaspoons chili powder
3 tablespoons oil
2¹/₂ cups thinly sliced onion
1   4-ounce can chopped mild
green chilies
1¹/₂ tablespoons minced fresh
ginger
1¹/₂ teaspoons salt
¹/₂ teaspoon turmeric
2 cloves of garlic, minced
1   28-ounce can tomatoes
³/₄ cup water
Chopped fresh cilantro

Rinse ducks inside and out; pat dry. Bone ducks; cut into 1-inch cubes. Marinate in mixture of vinegar, lime juice and chili powder for 15 minutes, turning frequently. Brown duck a small amount at a time in oil in heavy saucepan over medium-high heat. Remove duck with slotted spoon. Reduce heat to low. Add onion, green chilies, ginger, salt, turmeric and garlic. Cook for 5 to 10 minutes or until onion is wilted and clear. Drain and chop tomatoes, reserving juice. Add tomatoes, reserved juice, duck and water. Bring to a boil; reduce heat. Simmer, covered, for 1¹/₂ hours or until duck is tender and sauce is slightly thickened, stirring occasionally. Add salt and pepper to taste. Serve in soup bowls on bed of hot cooked rice. Garnish with cilantro. Yield: 6 servings.

Approx Per Serving: Cal 486; Prot 32.3 g; T Fat 33.4 g; Chol 136 mg; Carbo 14.6 g; Sod 854 mg; Potas 925 mg.

Jim Seltzer
Eagle, Idaho

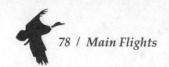

DUCK AND GARLIC SAUCE

2 ducks
3 tablespoons tapioca starch
1/2 cup oil
6 cloves of garlic, crushed
1 tablespoon sugar
2 tablespoons soy sauce
2 tablespoons tapioca starch
1/2 teaspoon ground ginger
1/8 teaspoon cayenne pepper
1 cup water
1 medium sweet onion
1 green bell pepper
1 stalk celery
2 tablespoons peanut oil
1 6-ounce can sliced bamboo shoots, drained
1 6-ounce can sliced water chestnuts, drained
1 14-ounce can baby corn ears, drained
1/4 cup unsalted Virginia peanuts
1 tablespoon oyster sauce

Rinse ducks inside and out; pat dry. Bone duck; cut into bite-sized pieces. Dust pieces with 3 tablespoons tapioca starch. Fry several pieces at a time in 1/2 cup hot oil in skillet. Set aside. Combine garlic, sugar, soy sauce, 2 tablespoons tapioca starch, ginger, cayenne pepper and water in saucepan; mix well. Cook until thickened, stirring constantly. Set aside. Cut onion and bell pepper into chunks. Slice celery into 1-inch pieces. Heat peanut oil in wok or heavy skillet. Add vegetables and peanuts. Stir-fry until tender-crisp. Add duck and oyster sauce; remove from heat. Stir in garlic sauce. Serve with hot cooked rice. For Szechuan style, increase cayenne pepper to the limit of your tolerance for pain. Yield: 4 servings.

Approx Per Serving: Cal 919; Prot 37.6 g; T Fat 65.9 g; Chol 136 mg; Carbo 47.8 g; Sod 646 mg; Potas 1145 mg.

Tom Borschel
Frankfort, New York

DUCK AND BROCCOLI STIR-FRY

6 to 8 duck breast filets
Garlic powder and tarragon to taste
6 slices bacon
2 medium onions, sliced
1 green bell pepper, sliced
1 small bunch broccoli, chopped
4 to 6 mushrooms, sliced
1/2 cup dry wine
1/2 cup orange marmalade

Rinse duck breasts; pat dry. Slice into 1/2-inch strips. Sprinkle with garlic powder and tarragon. Fry bacon in skillet until crisp; drain, reserving drippings. Brown duck in bacon drippings; remove from skillet. Add vegetables. Cook, covered, for several minutes or until broccoli is tender-crisp. Add duck and crumbled bacon. Add wine and marmalade. Simmer, covered, for 10 minutes or until heated through. Serve over hot cooked rice. Yield: 6 servings.

Approx Per Serving: Cal 318; Prot 33 g; T Fat 9.7 g; Chol 115 mg; Carbo 21.3 g; Sod 198 mg; Potas 746 mg.

Sandra L. Beitzel
Manitowoc, Wisconsin

KATH-AL DUCK ORIENTAL

4 duck breast filets
1/4 cup soy sauce
1/4 cup white wine
1/2 teaspoon ginger
1 teaspoon sugar
3/4 teaspoon garlic powder
2 egg whites
2 tablespoons cornstarch
1 cup oil
3 tablespoons oil
1/2 teaspoon ginger
1/4 teaspoon garlic powder
1 medium onion, sliced
1 green and 1 red bell pepper,
cut into strips
1 16-ounce can bean sprouts
1 6-ounce can water chestnuts
1 10-ounce package frozen
pea pods
2 tablespoons cornstarch

Rinse duck breasts; pat dry. Cut into 1/8-inch strips. Mix soy sauce, wine, 1/2 teaspoon ginger, sugar and 3/4 teaspoon garlic powder in bowl. Add duck. Marinate for 1 hour or longer. Drain, reserving marinade. Mix egg whites with 2 tablespoons cornstarch in small bowl. Dip duck into mixture to coat. Deep-fry in 1 cup hot oil until brown. Drain; set aside and keep warm. Heat 3 tablespoons oil with 1/2 teaspoon ginger and 1/4 teaspoon garlic powder in wok. Stir-fry vegetables one at a time for 1 to 2 minutes. Combine onion, peppers, drained bean sprouts, drained water chestnuts, pea pods, duck and reserved marinade in wok. Heat through. Dissolve 2 tablespoons cornstarch in a small amount of water. Stir into wok. Cook until thickened, stirring constantly. Yield: 4 servings.

Approx Per Serving: Cal 875; Prot 30.8 g; T Fat 72.8 g; Chol 82 mg; Carbo 25.7 g; Sod 1139 mg; Potas 764 mg.

Kathi and Al Seyler
Cary, North Carolina

ORIENTAL DUCK WITH SNOW PEAS

12 duck breast filets
1/2 cup soy sauce
1/2 cup oil
1/2 cup white wine
2 cloves of garlic, minced
1/2 teaspoon ground ginger
1 to 2 tablespoons oil
1 large onion, sliced
6 to 8 fresh mushrooms, sliced
1 10-ounce package frozen
pea pods

Rinse duck breast; pat dry. Slice thinly. Mix soy sauce, oil, wine, garlic and ginger in bowl. Add duck. Marinate in refrigerator for 4 hours or longer. Drain, reserving 1/4 cup marinade. Heat 1 to 2 tablespoons oil in wok. Add duck. Stir-fry until cooked through; remove from wok. Add onion and mushrooms. Stir-fry until tender-crisp. Add duck, pea pods and reserved marinade. Heat to serving temperature. May thicken sauce with a small amount of cornstarch dissolved in a small amount of water if desired. Serve with steamed rice. Yield: 8 servings.

Approx Per Serving: Cal 398; Prot 36.5 g; T Fat 23.7 g; Chol 123 mg; Carbo 6.6 g; Sod 1129 mg; Potas 652 mg. Nutritional information includes all of marinade.

Barbara Springer
Fairbanks, Alaska

DRUNKEN WILD GOOSE

1 large apple, cut into quarters
1 medium onion
Whole cloves
2 oranges, cut into quarters
4 half-stalks celery
2 cups gin
1 wild goose
8 ounces salt pork
2 tablespoons butter
2 tablespoons all-purpose flour
1 cup chicken broth

Combine apple, onion studded with whole cloves, oranges, celery and gin in large plastic container. Cover tightly and shake vigorously until fruit and vegetables are bruised. Marinate in refrigerator overnight. Rinse goose inside and out; pat dry. Drain fruit and vegetables, reserving marinade. Stuff goose cavity with marinated fruit and vegetables. Place goose in roasting pan. Cover legs and breast with salt pork. Drizzle 1 to 2 tablespoons reserved marinade over goose. Cover goose with foil; vent with small air hole. Bake at 325 degrees for 4 to 5 hours, basting occasionally with mixture of pan drippings and reserved marinade. Cook butter and flour in small saucepan until brown, stirring constantly. Stir in broth gradually. Cook until thickened, stirring constantly. Pour over goose before serving. Yield: 4 servings.

Approx Per Serving: Cal 675; Prot 40.8 g; T Fat 20.1 g; Chol 212 mg; Carbo 21.2 g; Sod 933 mg; Potas 492 mg. Nutritional information includes all of marinade.

Judy Nugent
Waupun, Wisconsin

MOIST AND TENDER GOOSE

1 goose
Onion
Carrot
Celery
2 envelopes dry onion
soup mix
4 cups water

Rinse goose inside and out; pat dry. Stuff cavity with onion, carrot and celery. Place in large oven cooking bag. Add soup mix and water; seal bag. Shake filled bag vigorously; place in roasting pan. Cut vents in bag using manufacturer's instructions. Bake at 275 degrees for 4 1/2 hours. Yield: 4 servings.

Nutritional information for this recipe is not available.

Greg Seitzer
St. Peter, Minnesota

ROAST GOOSE

1 goose
2 tablespoons pickling spice
4 small onions, cut into
quarters
2 oranges, peeled, sectioned
1 16-ounce can sauerkraut
1 cup dry wine
1 cup apple juice
1 bay leaf
1/2 teaspoon marjoram
1/2 teaspoon thyme

Rinse goose inside and out; drain. Combine goose, pickling spice, 2 onions and water to cover in large pan. Parboil for 30 minutes; drain. Stuff with remaining onions and oranges. Place half the sauerkraut, wine, apple juice and bay leaf in roasting pan. Place goose breast side down in prepared pan. Cover with remaining sauerkraut; sprinkle with marjoram and thyme. Bake, covered, at 300 degrees for 5 hours. Remove bay leaf. Discard stuffing. Yield: 4 servings.

Approx Per Serving: Cal 282; Prot 28.4 g; T Fat 4.6 g; Chol 161 mg; Carbo 26 g; Sod 756 mg; Potas 544 mg.

David Atkins
Kremmling, Colorado

ROASTED WILD GOOSE

1 wild goose, skinned
Buttermilk
Apples, quartered
Bacon

Soak goose in salted water for 45 minutes; drain. Place goose in plastic bag in large pan. Add buttermilk to cover. Soak for 4 hours to overnight. Drain; rinse inside and out with cold water and pat dry. Stuff cavity with unpeeled apples. Place in roasting pan. Cover breast with bacon; secure with toothpicks. Bake, covered, at 500 degrees for 30 minutes. Reduce temperature to 350 degrees. Bake for 20 minutes per pound total cooking time. Yield: 1 goose.

Nutritional information for this recipe is not available.

Cecil R. Allbright
Eaton, Ohio

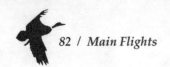

SMOKED WILD GOOSE

3 large wild geese
1 cup red wine
1 tablespoon rosemary
1/2 cup Worcestershire sauce
6 bay leaves
1 tablespoon thyme
1 large onion, chopped
6 cloves of garlic, crushed

Rinse geese inside and out; pat dry. Marinate in mixture of remaining ingredients overnight, turning several times. Drain. Place on grill in covered grill or smoker over low coals. Smoke until thermometer registers medium-rare. Cut meat from bones. May reserve bones to prepare stock for other recipes. Yield: 3 smoked geese.

Nutritional information for this recipe is not available.

Harold J. Heno
Metairie, Louisiana

DR. MILLER'S ORIENTAL WATERFOWL

Fileted breast of 1 goose
3 medium onions, chopped
2 8-ounce cans sliced
mushrooms, drained
1 2 1/2-ounce package slivered
almonds
2 packages Oriental
Rice-A-Roni
3 large stalks celery, cut into
1 1/2-inch pieces
2 green or red bell peppers, cut
into strips

Rinse goose breast; pat dry. Cut into 1 inch thick slices. Parboil for 20 minutes. Drain, reserving broth. Cool and cut into 1-inch cubes. Sauté goose, onions, mushrooms and almonds in butter in skillet for 15 minutes. Add salt, pepper and seasoned salt to taste. Prepare Rice-A-Roni according to package directions using reserved broth and adding celery and bell peppers halfway through cooking time. Combine duck mixture and rice mixture. Simmer for 15 minutes. Yield: 6 servings.

Approx Per Serving: Cal 253; Prot 21 g; T Fat 13.9 g; Chol 54.6 mg; Carbo 12.5 g; Sod 433 mg; Potas 535 mg.

Dr. John L. Miller
Greenville, Pennsylvania

Pat Mowbray of Florida places chunks of fresh papaya in the cavities of geese and ducks and in the roasting pan as well. It serves to tenderize the birds, imparts a delicious flavor and is a good addition to the meal.

GOOSE ESCALLOPS

4 Canada goose breasts
1/4 cup oil
2 tablespoons butter
3 tablespoons minced
green onions
1/2 cup red wine
1/4 cup beef bouillon
Juice of 1 lemon

Rinse goose breasts; pat dry. Slice diagonally 3/8 inch thick; discard any skin, fat and filaments. Flatten to 1/4-inch thickness. Rinse and pat dry. Cook 5 or 6 pieces at a time in oil in skillet over high heat for 5 to 6 minutes on each side; remove to plate. Pour oil from skillet. Add any drained juices from cooked escallops and butter to skillet. Add green onions. Sauté for 1 minute, stirring constantly with wooden spoon. Add wine, bouillon and lemon juice. Deglaze skillet. Boil until reduced to about 6 tablespoons. Arrange escallops on hot serving plate; pour juices over top. Surround with hot cooked rice. Garnish with parsley. Yield: 6 servings.

Approx Per Serving: Cal 403; Prot 33.1 g; T Fat 27.4 g; Chol 120 mg; Carbo 1.4 g; Sod 154 mg; Potas 486 mg.

Blackwell C. Dunnam
Troy, Ohio

GOOSE IN A SACK

Fileted breast of 1 goose
1/2 cup oil
1/2 cup soy sauce
1 large onion, sliced
8 ounces mushrooms, sliced
1/4 cup Parmesan cheese
1 clove of garlic, mashed
1/2 teaspoon pepper
1/2 cup beer or wine
Pita bread rounds
Shredded Cheddar cheese
Shredded lettuce
Tomato quarters
Mayonnaise or mustard

Cut breast in 1/4 x 3-inch strips. Rinse and pat dry. Marinate in mixture of oil, soy sauce, onion, mushrooms, Parmesan cheese, garlic, pepper and beer in closed container in refrigerator for overnight to 7 days. Drain, reserving 1/4 cup liquid, onion and mushrooms. Place goose, onion and mushrooms in broiler pan. Sprinkle with reserved liquid. Broil for 7 minutes. Turn over with spatula. Broil for 7 minutes longer; goose strips should be slightly pink inside. Cut pita bread rounds into halves; open to form pockets. Fill pockets with broiled mixture, Cheddar cheese, lettuce, tomato and add choice of mayonnaise or mustard.

Nutritional information for this recipe is not available.

Paula W. Yeatman
Oak Ridge, Tennessee

GRILLED MARINATED GOOSE

Fileted breast of 1 goose
2 tablespoons Dijon mustard
3/4 cup oil
1/4 cup wine vinegar
1/2 teaspoon salt
1/4 teaspoon pepper

Rinse goose breast; pat dry. Cut lengthwise into 2 portions. Marinate in mixture of mustard, oil, vinegar, salt and pepper. Drain, reserving marinade. Grill over hot coals to desired degree of doneness, basting frequently with reserved marinade. May marinate in mixture of 2 table-spoons brown sugar, 1 clove of garlic, 1/2 cup soy sauce, 2 tablespoons Worcestershire sauce and 1 tablespoon lemon juice or in Italian salad dressing instead of mustard mixture.
Yield: 2 servings.

Approx Per Serving: Cal 1143; Prot 50 g; T Fat 104 g; Chol 164 mg; Carbo 3 g; Sod 858 mg; Potas 715 mg. Nutritional information includes all of marinade.

Cindy Delaney
Washington, Indiana

GOOSE BREAST IN PORT WINE

2 goose breast filets
6 tablespoons butter
8 juniper berries, crushed
1/2 medium onion, finely chopped
10 sprigs parsley, finely chopped
4 cloves of garlic, minced
Marjoram to taste
Freshly ground pepper to taste
1 1/3 cups red Port
3/4 cup chicken broth
2 tablespoons tomato paste
1/2 cup heavy cream

Rinse goose; pat dry. Set aside. Melt butter in large skillet. Add juniper berries, onion, parsley, garlic, marjoram and pepper. Sauté until soft. Add Port and broth. Cook until well mixed. Add goose. Coddle for 3 minutes. Remove goose. Cook until liquid is reduced by half. Add tomato paste and cream. Simmer until thickened, stirring constantly. Place goose in sauce. Simmer for 4 minutes or until tender. Slice goose diagonally 1/4-inch thick. Ladle a small amount of sauce onto serving plate; arrange goose slices in semi-circle. Ladle remaining sauce on top. Garnish with parsley sprigs and pickled apples. This recipe was developed by 3 hobby cooks, Kosta Arger, Keith Vowels and me.
Yield: 4 servings.

Approx Per Serving: Cal 544; Prot 26.7 g; T Fat 39.4 g; Chol 169 mg; Carbo 8.6 g; Sod 512 mg; Potas 629 mg.

Steve Rucker
Reno, Nevada

FRYE'S GOURMET GOOSE

1 Canada goose
16 ounces fresh mushrooms,
chopped
1 3-inch onion, chopped
4 large stalks celery, chopped
4 Hungarian hot peppers,
chopped
1 tablespoon salt
1 teaspoon pepper
1 can cream of mushroom soup
1/2 soup can milk
1/3 cup all-purpose flour

Skin goose; filet breast and remove legs and thighs. Rinse well; pat dry. Cut breast into 3 portions. Place breast, legs and thighs in Crock•Pot. Add chopped vegetables, salt, pepper, soup and milk. Cook on Low for 8 to 10 hours or until very tender. Mix flour with a small amount of water. Stir into Crock•Pot. Cook for 20 to 30 minutes longer. Serve over rice, wild rice, noodles or mashed potatoes. Yield: 4 servings.

Approx Per Serving: Cal 292; Prot 26.1 g; T Fat 10.4 g; Chol 126 mg; Carbo 26.5 g; Sod 1167 mg; Potas 773 mg.

Richard E. Frye
Cleo, Michigan

HUNTER'S GOOSE STEW

2 pounds boned goose
6 slices bacon, chopped
1/2 cup (about) all-purpose flour
2 cloves of garlic, minced
3 beef bouillon cubes
3 cups water
2 cups red or white wine
1 8-ounce can tomato sauce
2 teaspoons lemon juice
2 teaspoons steak sauce
1 teaspoon thyme
2 bay leaves
1 large onion, cut into quarters
6 small onions
6 carrots
6 potatoes, peeled
1 cup chopped celery
2 tablespoons all-purpose flour
1/2 cup water

Rinse goose; pat dry. Cut into bite-sized pieces. Cook bacon in large heavy pan until brown. Coat goose pieces with mixture of 1/2 cup flour and salt and pepper to taste. Add to pan. Cook until brown on all sides. Add garlic. Cook for 1 minute. Add bouillon cubes, 3 cups water, wine, tomato sauce, lemon juice, steak sauce, thyme and bay leaves. Simmer, covered, for 2 hours or until tender. Cut vegetables into bite-sized pieces. Add to stew with salt and pepper to taste. Simmer for 1 hour. Mix 2 tablespoons flour with 1/2 cup water. Stir into stew. Cook until thickened, stirring constantly. Remove bay leaves. Yield: 6 servings.

Approx Per Serving: Cal 457; Prot 42.1 g; T Fat 9.2 g; Chol 220 mg; Carbo 52.5 g; Sod 449 mg; Potas 1016 mg.

Deanna V. Klint
Deering, New Hampshire

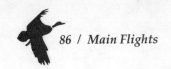

WILD GOOSE STEW

3 geese, boned, cubed
1/2 cup (about) all-purpose flour
1/2 cup oil
2 envelopes dry onion soup mix
5 carrots, cut into quarters
4 stalks celery, chopped
8 small onions
2 cups frozen green beans
8 ounces fresh mushrooms, sliced
1 teaspoon sweet basil
1 teaspoon tarragon
2 cloves of garlic, crushed
2 bay leaves
2 tablespoons Cavendars Greek Seasoning
6 potatoes, peeled, cut into halves

Rinse goose meat; pat dry. Coat with mixture of flour and salt and pepper to taste. Brown in oil in skillet. Place in large roaster. Add soup mix, carrots, celery, onions, green beans, mushrooms, seasonings and water to cover. Bake at 325 degrees for 2 hours. Reduce temperature to 275 degrees. Add potatoes. Bake for 1 hour longer. Thicken if desired. Bake until goose is tender. Remove bay leaves. Yield: 10 servings.

Approx Per Serving: Cal 487; Prot 33.8 g; T Fat 24.4 g; Chol 98.3 mg; Carbo 33.2 g; Sod 239 mg; Potas 1055 mg.

James C. Tennant

GOOSE PÂTÉ

Boned breast of 1 goose
Goose livers (optional)
1 pound ground veal
1 cup shelled pistachios
2 ounces green peppercorns
1 tablespoon sage
1 teaspoon salt
Several bay leaves
Bacon
2 boneless chicken breasts

Rinse goose; pat dry. Grind goose breast and livers in food processor container. Combine with ground veal, pistachios, peppercorns, sage and salt in bowl; mix well. Arrange bay leaves in decorative pattern in bottoms of two 5x9-inch loaf pans. Line pans with bacon strips. Fill each about half full with goose mixture. Make indentation down center of each. Place chicken breast in indentation. Add goose mixture to fill pans; press firmly. Cover with bacon strips. Place pans in large roaster. Add 1-inch water. Bake in covered roaster at 350 degrees for 1 1/2 hours. Remove pans; place heavy weight on each. Let stand at room temperature until completely cooled. Refrigerate overnight before slicing. Serve with chutney or cranberry relish.

Nutritional information for this recipe is not available.

Will Fox
Chestertown, Maryland

Open Season

Game and Game Birds

White Tail Buck

Ken Carlson *(courtesy of Russell A. Fink Gallery, Lorton, Virginia)*

VENISON CURRY

1 large onion, chopped
1 tart green apple, peeled,
chopped
2 tablespoons butter
2 tablespoons all-purpose
flour
1 tablespoon curry
powder
1 cup warm beef stock
1/2 cup pale dry Sherry
1 tablespoon lemon juice
1/4 teaspoon nutmeg
Salt and pepper to taste
2 cups cubed, cooked
venison

Sauté onion and apple in butter in skillet for 5 minutes or until onion is transparent. Remove onion and apple; set aside. Stir in flour and curry powder. Cook over low heat for 4 to 5 minutes; do not brown. Add stock and Sherry, stirring constantly. Add lemon juice, nutmeg and salt and pepper. Cook over low heat until sauce thickens, stirring constantly. Stir in sautéed onion, apple and venison. Simmer for 3 to 4 minutes. Serve hot over rice with chutney and condiments such as raisins or dried currants, fresh pineapple and roasted peanuts.
Yield: 4 servings.

Mary Lea Carlson

ASHLEY HALL PLANTATION VENISON

1 venison roast
Vinegar
Red wine
Bacon slices
1 package dry onion soup mix

Marinate venison in equal parts water and vinegar to cover in bowl in refrigerator for 24 hours. Drain. Add enough red wine to cover. Marinate in refrigerator for 24 hours. Drain; pat dry. Cut slits in roast. Fill each slit with small piece bacon. Place in baking pan. Add enough red wine to partially fill. Sprinkle dry onion soup mix over venison. Cover with foil. Roast at 350 degrees for 2 to 4 hours or until tender. Yield: 1 roast.

Nutritional information for this recipe is not available.

Mr. and Mrs. Harold Seignious
Charleston, South Carolina

BACON WRAPS

Tenderloin of deer
Dales steak sauce
Bacon slices

Cut tenderloin into 3 or 4-inch strips. Tenderize with meat mallet. Coat each strip with steak sauce. Wrap each slice with slice of bacon; secure with toothpick. Cook in smoker for 1 1/2 to 2 hours or to desired degree of doneness.

Nutritional information for this recipe is not available.

Mary Ann Beckwith
West Point, Mississippi

Shirley Horner of Friendship, Wisconsin, has a popular recipe for Stir-Fry Venison. Partially freeze the venison so that it can be sliced very thin. Cut slices into 1 to 2-inch wide strips. Stir-fry for 1 minute on each side in skillet or on griddle. Serve with onion slices sautéed in butter.

PARTY DEER BALLS

1 pound ground venison
³/4 cup cracker crumbs
2 eggs
1/2 cup finely chopped onion
1¹/2 tablespoons
Worcestershire sauce
1/2 teaspoon pepper
1/2 teaspoon paprika
Barbecue sauce

Combine venison, cracker crumbs, eggs, onion, Worcestershire sauce, pepper and paprika in large bowl; mix well. Shape into balls. Brown in skillet. Place in slow cooker. Add barbecue sauce to cover. Cook on low until heated through. Yield: 4 servings.

Nutritional information for this recipe is not available.

Randy Ricketts
Evansville, Indiana

VENISON BOURGUIGNON

2 pounds venison, cubed
2 tablespoons shortening
4 cups boiling water
1 tablespoon lemon juice
1 teaspoon Worcestershire
sauce
1 clove of garlic
1 medium onion, sliced
1 to 2 bay leaves
1 tablespoon salt
1 tablespoon sugar
1/2 teaspoon pepper
1/2 teaspoon paprika
Dash of cloves or allspice
6 carrots, cut into quarters
6 small new potatoes
8 ounces fresh mushrooms
1/2 cup Sherry

Brown venison in shortening in large saucepan. Add water, lemon juice, Worcestershire sauce, garlic, onion and seasonings. Simmer for 2 hours or longer, stirring occasionally. Remove bay leaves and garlic. Add carrots, potatoes, mushrooms and Sherry. Cook for 30 minutes or until vegetables are tender. Thicken cooking liquid for gravy if desired. Yield: 8 servings.

Approx Per Serving: Cal 340; Prot 36.5 g; T Fat 6.1 g; Chol 73.7 mg; Carbo 30 g; Sod 927 mg; Potas 1030 mg.

Sandra L. Beitzel
Manitowoc, Wisconsin

VENISON BUNS

1 pound ground venison
1 onion
1 egg, beaten
1 tablespoon mustard
1/2 cup catsup
1 teaspoon salt
1 teaspoon pepper
8 hamburger buns, split
2 tablespoons butter, softened

Combine venison, onion, egg, mustard, catsup, salt and pepper in bowl; mix well. Spread buns with butter. Spread venison mixture on each bun half. Place on baking sheet. Broil at 350 degrees for 5 minutes or until venison is cooked through. Garnish with shredded cheese if desired. Serve with French fries. Yield: 16 servings.

Approx Per Serving: Cal 137; Prot 10.9 g; T Fat 3.7 g; Chol 39.4 mg; Carbo 14.2 g; Sod 406 mg; Potas 179 mg.

Robbie Kuehlem
Plano, Illinois

VENISON WITH CAPERS AND CREAM

6³/4-inch thick venison
loin chops
2 tablespoons butter
2 tablespoons olive oil
Freshly ground pepper to taste
2 tablespoons minced shallots
1/2 cup beef broth
1/4 cup dry vermouth
1 tablespoon fresh lemon juice
1/2 cup heavy cream
2 tablespoons capers,
rinsed, drained
2 tablespoons minced
fresh parsley

Pat venison dry with paper towels. Brown on one side in mixture of butter and olive oil in large heavy skillet over medium heat. Turn chops over. Sprinkle with salt and pepper to taste. Cook for about 7 minutes or just until springy to touch and pink in center. Transfer to heated platter. Cover and keep warm. Sauté shallots in 2 tablespoons pan drippings for 2 minutes. Add broth, vermouth and lemon juice. Cook until mixture is reduce by half, stirring frequently to deglaze skillet. Stir in cream and capers. Simmer for 5 minutes or until thickened. Adjust seasoning. Pour over warm chops. Sprinkle with parsley. Yield: 6 servings.

Approx Per Serving: Cal 322; Prot 34.2 g; T Fat 18.2 g; Chol 111 mg; Carbo 1.5 g; Sod 186 mg; Potas 420 mg.

IGFCA World Championship Wild Game Cookoff
Sioux City, Nebraska

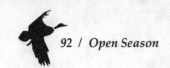

BREADED VENISON CUTLETS

8 2-ounce boned venison
loin cutlets
2 tablespoons all-purpose flour
3 tablespoons Parmesan cheese
1 egg, beaten
1 teaspoon minced parsley
1/2 teaspoon salt
1/4 teaspoon pepper
1/4 teaspoon nutmeg
1/2 cup milk
6 tablespoons butter
Juice of 3/4 lemon

Pound venison with meat mallet until very thin. Coat each cutlet with flour. Combine cheese, egg, parsley, seasonings and milk in bowl; mix well. Dip cutlets into batter. Brown in 4 tablespoons butter in skillet over low heat. Remove to heated platter; keep warm. Add remaining 2 tablespoons butter to skillet. Cook until butter browns. Add lemon juice ; stir to deglaze skillet. Pour over cutlets. Yield: 4 servings.

Approx Per Serving: Cal 390; Prot 38.2 g; T Fat 23.4 g; Chol 196 mg; Carbo 5.3 g; Sod 592 mg; Potas 464 mg.

Jeri L. Nelson
Springfield, South Dakota

DECOY CARVER'S ELK CHILI

2 pounds elk or deer burger
1 large white onion, chopped
1 medium green bell
pepper, chopped
1 28-ounce can peeled
tomatoes, chopped
1 15-ounce can tomato sauce
1 15-ounce can dark red
kidney beans
1 15-ounce can chili beans
10 to 15 drops of Tabasco sauce
2 small chili peppers, chopped
2/3 cup hamburger dill pickle
chips, chopped
2 tablespoons dill pickle juice
1/3 cup pimento-stuffed
olives, sliced

Brown elk burger with half the onion and half the green pepper in skillet, stirring until crumbly; drain. Add remaining onion, green pepper, tomatoes, tomato sauce, beans, Tabasco sauce, chili peppers, pickles, pickle juice and olives. Sprinkle with seasoning salt, black pepper, chili powder and cayenne pepper to taste. Simmer for 3 to 4 hours or to desired consistency. Garnish each serving with shredded Cheddar cheese.
Yield: Enough chili for 4 hungry decoy carvers.

Approx Per Serving: Cal 616; Prot 82.7 g; T Fat 9.2 g; Chol 147 mg; Carbo 53 g; Sod 2806 mg; Potas 2359 mg.

Gordon Alcorn
Bozeman, Montana

NORMAN'S ZESTY CHAMPIONSHIP CHILI

1 pound venison back strap
1 pound venison loin
1 pound lean beef stew meat
1 pound venison sausage
1½ pounds twice-ground chuck
3 cups chopped onions
1 cup finely chopped green
bell peppers
1 cup finely chopped celery
2 tablespoons oil
3 tablespoons comino
¼ cup chili powder
2 tablespoons freshly
ground pepper
½ teaspoon cayenne pepper
2 10-ounce cans Ro-Tel
tomatoes
1 4-ounce can chopped
green chilies
1 8-ounce can tomato sauce
1 16-ounce bottle of Bloody
Mary mix
1 cup dry Sherry

Cut venison and beef stew meat into ½-inch cubes. Brown venison, beef, sausage and ground chuck 1 pound at a time in skillet, stirring ground meat until crumbly. Remove each as cooked to large saucepan. Sauté onions, green peppers and celery in oil in skillet. Add to meats. Add seasonings, Ro-Tel, green chilies, tomato sauce, Bloody Mary mix and Sherry; cover. Bring to a boil. Reduce heat. Simmer for 2 hours, stirring occasionally. Remove from heat. Let stand for 45 minutes to blend flavors. Simmer for 1 hour longer. Garnish each serving with chopped onion and shredded sharp cheese. Yield: 12 servings.

Nutritional information for this recipe is not available.

Norman Smith
Memphis, Tennessee

SPICY CROCK • POT VENISON

1 3-pound venison roast
¼ cup sugar
½ teaspoon cinnamon
½ teaspoon cloves
1 6-ounce package mixed
dried fruit
½ cup Sherry

Place roast in Crock•Pot. Sprinkle with mixture of sugar, cinnamon and cloves. Arrange dried fruit over roast. Pour Sherry over all. Cook on High for 1 hour. Cook on Low for 3 or 4 hours or until roast is tender. Yield: 6 servings.

Approx Per Serving: Cal 461; Prot 67.7 g; T Fat 5.1 g; Chol 147 mg; Carbo 28.3 g; Sod 166 mg; Potas 1007 mg.

John Hudson
Cedarville, Illinois

VENISON FAJITAS

2 pounds venison, cut
into strips
1 teaspoon garlic powder
1 teaspoon cumin
1 teaspoon black pepper
³/₄ cup soy sauce
3 ounces Tequila
³/₄ cup lime juice
6 tablespoons pineapple juice
¹/₄ cup packed brown sugar
¹/₂ cup dried jalapeño peppers
1 teaspoon ginger
2 tablespoons Tabasco sauce

Sprinkle venison with mixture of garlic powder, cumin and black pepper. Place in bowl. Chill for 2 hours. Combine soy sauce, Tequila, lime juice, pineapple juice, brown sugar, peppers, ginger and Tabasco sauce in large bowl; mix well. Add venison; mix well. Marinate in refrigerator for 8 to 10 hours. Drain. Grill over hot coals with green bell peppers and onions if desired until cooked through. Serve with flour tortillas, guacamole, sour cream and picante sauce. Yield: 8 servings.

Approx Per Serving: Cal 251; Prot 35.4 g; T Fat 2.8 g; Chol 73.7 mg; Carbo 18.5 g; Sod 1771 mg; Potas 573 mg. Nutritional information includes all of marinade.

Michelle Marquardt
Kremmling, Colorado

STUFFED DEER LOAF

¹/₂ cup chopped onion
2 tablespoons butter
¹/₂ cup shredded carrot
¹/₂ cup shredded potato
2 pounds ground venison
1 large tomato, peeled, chopped
2 eggs
1 cup bread crumbs
Pepper to taste
¹/₂ teaspoon nutmeg
¹/₂ teaspoon garlic powder

Sauté onion in butter in skillet. Add carrot and potato. Cook, covered, for 5 minutes. Combine with venison, tomato, eggs, bread crumbs, salt to taste and seasonings in bowl; mix well. Shape into loaf in greased shallow baking pan. Bake at 350 degrees for 1 hour. Yield: 8 servings.

Approx Per Serving: Cal 285; Prot 37.3 g; T Fat 7.5 g; Chol 151 mg; Carbo 14.9 g; Sod 218 mg; Potas 545 mg.

Janice Schaefer
Evansville, Indiana

GRILLED VENISON LOINS

1¹/₂ cups oil
³/₄ cups soy sauce
¹/₄ cup Worcestershire sauce
2 tablespoons dry mustard
2¹/₄ teaspoons salt
1 tablespoon freshly
ground pepper
¹/₂ cup wine vinegar
1¹/₂ teaspoons dried
parsley flakes
2 cloves of garlic, crushed
¹/₂ cup fresh lemon juice
2   2¹/₂-pound venison
loins, trimmed

Combine oil, soy sauce, Worcestershire sauce, dry mustard, salt, pepper, wine vinegar, parsley flakes, garlic and lemon juice in glass dish; mix well. Add venison loins. Marinate at room temperature for 2 to 3 hours, turning venison several times. Grill over hot coals for 7 to 9 minutes on each side for medium-rare. Marinade is good on other types of meat. Yield: 8 servings.

Approx Per Serving: Cal 801; Prot 85.3 g; T Fat 47.2 g; Chol 184 mg; Carbo 5.8 g; Sod 2152 mg; Potas 1096 mg. Nutritional information includes all of marinade.

Judy Nugent
Waupun, Wisconsin

MATTY'S DADDY'S HUNTER'S SURPRISE

3 pounds venison
¹/₄ cup apple cider vinegar
¹/₂ cup soy sauce
¹/₄ handful black pepper
¹/₄ handful ground ginger
Minced garlic to taste
1 cup sugar
2 cups oil

Combine venison, vinegar, soy sauce, seasonings, ¹/₂ cup sugar and 1¹/₂ cups oil in bowl. Marinate for several hours, turning venison occasionally. Heat remaining ¹/₂ cup oil in large skillet. Add venison and marinade. Cook over high heat until brown on both sides. Reduce heat. Cook until tender, sprinkling with remaining ¹/₂ cup sugar during cooking. This tastes great with rice and corn and is extremely tender. Use London broil if the deer got away. Yield: 6 servings.

Approx Per Serving: Cal 1115; Prot 68.1 g; T Fat 77.7 g; Chol 147 mg; Carbo 35.8 g; Sod 1532 mg; Potas 817 mg.

Lisa Laurence
Sullivan Harbor, Massachusetts

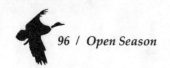

MOOSE FOR COMPANY

2 pounds moose round steak
1 tablespoon bacon drippings
1½ cups red wine
½ cup beef broth
1 teaspoon salt
½ teaspoon thyme
2 cloves of garlic, chopped
1 onion, chopped
½ orange
2 tablespoons cornstarch
2 tablespoons water
8 ounces fresh mushrooms,
sliced
1 16-ounce can small
onions, drained
½ cup pitted black olives
1 10-ounce package
frozen peas

Brown moose steak in bacon drippings in skillet. Add wine, broth, salt, thyme, garlic, onion and orange. Simmer, covered, for 1½ hours or until tender. Add mixture of cornstarch and water. Cook until thickened, stirring constantly. Add mushrooms, onions, olives and peas. Cook until heated through. Remove orange half before serving. Yield: 6 servings.

Approx Per Serving: Cal 501; Prot 39.1 g; T Fat 7.7 g; Chol 124 mg; Carbo 23.5 g; Sod 607 mg; Potas 645 mg.

Nancy Murkowski
Fairbanks, Alaska

VENISON ROAST

1 3-pound venison roast
8 2-inch pieces bacon
8 cloves of garlic
2 tablespoons margarine,
softened
Pepper to taste
½ cup Catalina salad dressing
½ cup creamy French
salad dressing
½ cup Italian salad dressing

Cut 4 slits on each side of roast. Insert 1 piece bacon and 1 clove of garlic in each slit. Spread margarine over roast. Season with salt and pepper to taste. Brown in skillet over high heat. Add salad dressings. Cook, covered, over low heat for 2½ to 4 hours or until tender. Yield: 8 servings.

Approx Per Serving: Cal 541; Prot 52.8 g; T Fat 35.2 g; Chol 126 mg; Carbo 5.2 g; Sod 647 mg; Potas 644 mg.

Carol Allen
Wabasha, Minnesota

RAGOÛT OF VENISON

2 pounds boneless venison loin
2 large onions, finely chopped
2 tablespoons oil
2 tablespoons tomato paste
2 bay leaves
1 teaspoon thyme
Pepper to taste
1 cup beef broth
1 pound mushrooms (wild if possible), sliced
Juice and grated rind of 1 orange
1 cup dry white wine
1 cup whipping cream
1 tablespoon all-purpose flour
1 bunch parsley, finely chopped
Several drops of fresh lemon juice

Trim venison; cut into cubes. Wash in cold water; drain in colander. Sauté onions in oil in skillet until pale yellow. Add tomato paste. Cook over high heat for 3 minutes, stirring constantly. Add venison. Brown over high heat for 5 minutes, stirring occasionally. Add bay leaves, thyme, salt and pepper to taste. Cook, covered, over medium heat until venison is tender, adding broth as necessary. Add mushrooms, orange juice and rind; mix gently. Add wine. Cook over low heat for several minutes. Add mixture of whipping cream, flour, parsley and lemon juice. Bring to a boil; reduce heat. Simmer for 2 to 3 minutes. Adjust seasonings. Remove bay leaves. Serve with wild rice or mashed potatoes.
Yield: 6 servings.

Approx Per Serving: Cal 478; Prot 48.6 g; T Fat 23.1 g; Chol 153 mg; Carbo 12.2 g; Sod 264 mg; Potas 1058 mg.

Laszlo Varju
Greenup, Illinois

SAVORY VENISON

2 pounds venison
3/4 cup beef bouillon
1/4 cup packed brown sugar
2 tablespoons soy sauce
1/2 teaspoon garlic powder
1/4 teaspoon ginger
Pepper to taste

Cut venison into finger-width strips. Combine bouillon, brown sugar, soy sauce, garlic powder, ginger and salt and pepper to taste in bowl. Add venison. Let stand for 1 hour to overnight, turning venison several times. Place in shallow baking pan. Roast at 350 degrees for 1½ hours, turning venison and basting with pan juices several times. Yield: 4 servings.

Approx Per Serving: Cal 391; Prot 68 g; T Fat 5.1 g; Chol 148 mg; Carbo 14.4 g; Sod 826 mg; Potas 855 mg.

Sandra Polkinghorn
Britton, South Dakota

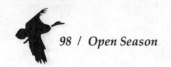

JUDY'S VENISON SCALLOPINI

*2 pounds venison filets, cut
into 1/4-inch slices
1 egg
3 tablespoons milk
11/4 cups dried bread crumbs
1/4 cup Parmesan cheese
1 teaspoon salt
1 teaspoon pepper
2 tablespoons butter
2 cloves of garlic
6 tablespoons butter
1 beef bouillon cube
3/4 cup water
2 teaspoons all-purpose flour
1/4 cup butter
1/2 to 1 cup Marsala wine
1/4 cup minced parsley*

Trim venison filets. Mix egg and milk in pie plate. Combine bread crumbs, cheese, salt and pepper in shallow dish. Dip filets into egg mixture; coat with crumb mixture. Melt 2 tablespoons butter in skillet. Add garlic and 1/4 of the filets. Cook until light brown. Remove to heated platter; keep warm. Repeat with remaining filets, using 6 additional tablespoons butter. Dissolve bouillon cube in water. Add flour; mix well. Melt remaining 1/4 cup butter in skillet. Add bouillon mixture, wine and parsley. Cook until thickened, stirring constantly. Add filets. Simmer over low heat for about 20 minutes or until filets are tender. Yield: 8 servings.

Approx Per Serving: Cal 517; Prot 40.4 g; T Fat 23.2 g; Chol 159 mg; Carbo 29.3 g; Sod 933 mg; Potas 498 mg.

*Judy Barton
Cumberland, Maryland*

VENISON SCALLOPINI

*11/2 pounds 3/8-inch thick
venison steak
Pepper to taste
2 tablespoons all-purpose flour
1 egg
1/3 cup half and half
1 cup fine bread crumbs
1 cup Parmesan cheese
1/4 cup minced parsley
1/4 cup butter
1 clove of garlic
1/2 cup Sherry
1/2 cup beef broth*

Cut venison into serving-sized pieces. Pound with meat mallet. Season with salt and pepper to taste. Coat with flour. Combine egg and cream in bowl; mix well. Combine cracker crumbs, cheese and parsley in bowl; mix well. Dip venison into egg mixture; coat with crumb mixture. Heat butter and garlic in Dutch oven. Add venison. Cook until brown on both sides. Add wine and broth. Bake, covered, at 350 degrees for 1 hour or until tender. Yield: 4 servings.

Approx Per Serving: Cal 638; Prot 65 g; T Fat 26.4 g; Chol 235 mg; Carbo 23.7 g; Sod 904 mg; Potas 742 mg.

*Mrs. Eugene Harris
Durham, California*

VENISON STEAKS IN PEPPER SAUCE

4   *8-ounce venison steaks*
1/4 cup olive oil
1/2 cup dry red wine
2 teaspoons chopped garlic
1 tablespoon tomato paste
1/4 teaspoon crushed dried
red peppers

Brown steaks in olive oil in skillet until of desired degree of doneness. Remove to heated platter; keep warm. Reserve 2 tablespoons drippings. Add wine to reserved drippings, stirring to deglaze skillet. Add garlic, tomato paste and dried peppers. Cook until of sauce consistency. Add steaks; coat with sauce.
Yield: 4 servings.

Approx Per Serving: Cal 480; Prot 67.4 g; T Fat 18.5 g; Chol 147 mg; Carbo 2.3 g; Sod 163 mg; Potas 849 mg.

John P. Merickel
Willmar, Minnesota

HUNTER'S VENISON STEW

1 1/2 pounds venison, cubed
3 tablespoons all-purpose flour
1 teaspoon salt
1/8 teaspoon pepper
1 onion, chopped
1 clove of garlic, minced
2 tablespoons oil
2 cups water
3/4 cup dry red wine
1 beef bouillon cube,
6 carrots, cut into 2-inch strips
2 stalks celery, cut into
2-inch strips
1 cup cranberries
1 teaspoon sugar
1 tablespoon steak sauce
2 teaspoons Hungarian paprika
4 juniper berries
2 whole cloves
1 bay leaf

Coat venison with flour seasoned with salt and pepper. Brown venison with onion and garlic in oil in skillet. Add water, wine and bouillon cube. Bring to a boil. Simmer, covered, for 1 hour and 15 minutes. Add carrots, celery, cranberries, sugar, steak sauce, paprika, juniper berries, cloves and bay leaf. Simmer, covered, for 45 minutes longer. Remove cloves and bay leaf. Thicken with enough cornstarch mixed with a small amount of water to make of desired consistency if desired. Yield: 6 servings.

Approx Per Serving: Cal 253; Prot 35.1 g; T Fat 2.8 g; Chol 73.7 mg; Carbo 15.7 g; Sod 541 mg; Potas 727 mg.

Lynn M. Carr
Pensacola, Florida

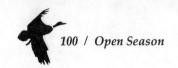

WILD GAME STEW

4 pounds venison, elk or
antelope, cut into
1¹/2-inch cubes
³/4 cup all-purpose flour
¹/4 teaspoon salt
¹/8 teaspoon pepper
¹/4 cup bacon drippings
2 cups water
2 cups Burgundy
1 medium onion, sliced
2 large cloves of garlic, chopped
2 bay leaves
1 tablespoon fines herbs
4 medium potatoes, cut
into quarters
5 carrots, cut into 2-inch pieces
3 stalks celery, cut into
2-inch pieces

Coat venison with mixture of flour, salt and pepper. Brown in bacon drippings in large skillet. Add water, Burgundy, onion, garlic, bay leaves and herbs. Simmer, covered, for 1 hour. Add potatoes, carrots and celery. Simmer for 2 to 3 hours longer or until vegetables are tender. Remove bay leaves. Serve with tossed salad, Billy Joe Cross's beer biscuits and a hearty red wine. Yield: 8 servings.

Approx Per Serving: Cal 558; Prot 70 g; T Fat 12.3 g; Chol 189 mg; Carbo 28.3 g; Sod 332 mg; Potas 1252 mg.

Judy Nugent
Waupun, Wisconsin

VENISON STROGANOFF

1¹/2 pounds venison round steak
¹/3 cup all-purpose flour
¹/2 cup butter
1 cup chopped onion
1 6-ounce can sliced
mushrooms, drained
1 teaspoon salt
1 teaspoon Worcestershire
sauce
1 12-ounce can beef bouillon
1 cup sour cream
6 cups hot cooked noodles

Cut venison into very thin slices diagonally. Coat with flour. Brown in butter in skillet. Remove from skillet. Add onion and mushrooms. Cook until onion is tender, stirring frequently. Add salt, Worcestershire sauce and bouillon. Simmer, covered, for 45 to 60 minutes or until venison is tender. Stir in sour cream. Cook just until heated through. Serve over noodles. Yield: 6 servings.

Nutritional information for this recipe is not available.

Maxine White Allan
Annada, Missouri

PAT'S VENISON STROGANOFF

3 pounds venison steak
2 large sweet onions, minced
4 cloves of garlic, minced
1/4 cup butter
Pepper to taste
2 10-ounce cans beef
consommé
2 teaspoons Worcestershire
sauce
12 ounces fresh mushrooms,
sliced
2 tablespoons butter
2 cups sour cream

Trim venison; cut into bite-sized cubes. Brown venison, onions and garlic in 1/4 cup butter in skillet. Season with salt and pepper to taste. Add consommé and Worcestershire sauce. Cook until venison is very tender, adding small amounts of water as necessary. Sauté mushrooms in 2 tablespoons butter in skillet. Add to venison. Stir in sour cream gradually just before serving. Venison mixture should not be boiling when sour cream is added. Serve over hot rice or noodles. Yield: 10 servings.

Approx Per Serving: Cal 377; Prot 43 g; T Fat 19.8 g; Chol 128 mg; Carbo 5.3 g; Sod 282 mg; Potas 705 mg.

Pat Rossman
McFarland, Wisconsin

ELK TENDERLOIN WITH BRANDY MUSTARD SAUCE

2 10-ounce elk tenderloins
1 clove of garlic, peeled,
cut in half
Thyme and freshly ground
black pepper to taste
2 slices bacon
1/2 cup sliced mushrooms
1/4 cup finely chopped onion
1/4 cup finely chopped green
bell pepper
1/4 cup Brandy
1/2 cup brown gravy
1 tablespoon Dijon-style
mustard

Remove silverskin from elk tenderloins. Rub with garlic. Sprinkle with thyme and pepper. Wrap 1 slice bacon around each tenderloin; secure with toothpicks. Sauté in hot skillet until bacon is crisp and tenderloin is medium-rare. Remove to heated platter; keep warm. Add mushrooms, onion and green pepper. Sauté until tender. Add Brandy; flambé. Let flame subside. Add gravy and mustard; mix well. Pour over tenderloin. Serve with wild rice or pilaf and green vegetables. Yield: 2 servings.

Approx Per Serving: Cal 557; Prot 87.2 g; T Fat 10.2 g; Chol 190 mg; Carbo 17.6 g; Sod 622 mg; Potas 1129 mg.

IGFCA World Championship Game Cookoff
Sioux City, Nebraska

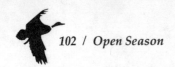

SWEET AND SOUR VENISON TENDERLOIN

4 pounds venison tenderloin
1 medium onion, thinly sliced
1 clove of garlic, minced
1/4 cup butter
3 tablespoons lemon juice
1 tablespoon brown sugar
1 tablespoon Worcestershire
sauce
2 teaspoons salt
8 medium mushrooms

Cut venison into cubes if desired. Sauté onion and garlic in butter in skillet just until onion is translucent. Add lemon juice, brown sugar, Worcestershire sauce, salt and mushrooms; mix well. Spoon over venison. Bake in preheated 400-degree oven for 45 minutes for roast or in 350-degree oven for 30 minutes if venison is cubed, basting occasionally. Serve hot with sauce. Yield: 10 servings.

Approx Per Serving: Cal 318; Prot 54 g; T Fat 8.7 g; Chol 130 mg; Carbo 2.9 g; Sod 609 mg; Potas 692 mg.

Greg McDonald
New Bern, North Carolina

TENNESSEE TENDERLOIN

2 2-pound venison tenderloins
1/4 cup Jack Daniels sour
mash whiskey
1/4 olive oil
1/4 teaspoon pepper
1/4 cup Worcestershire sauce
1/4 teaspoon thyme
2 cloves of garlic, chopped
2 green bell peppers, cut
into quarters
2 medium onions, cut
into quarters
8 mushrooms

Marinate venison in mixture of whiskey, olive oil, pepper, Worcestershire sauce, thyme and garlic in bowl in refrigerator for 4 to 8 hours. Drain, reserving marinade. Cut venison into cubes. Thread onto skewers alternately with green peppers, onions and mushrooms. Cook over low to medium coals until medium-rare, basting frequently with reserved marinade. Serve over rice. Yield: 4 servings.

Approx Per Serving: Cal 856; Prot 136 g; T Fat 23.9 g; Chol 295 mg; Carbo 9.1 g; Sod 468 mg; Potas 1896 mg.

David McMahan
Kodak, Tennessee

Ben Moise of Charleston, South Carolina, makes an easy venison marinade of 1 cup of soy sauce, 1 cup of Worcestershire sauce, 1/2 cup of waffle syrup, 1 teaspoon of garlic powder and 1/2 teaspoon pepper. Marinade cubes of venison for 2 hours or longer and deep-fry in hot oil.

VENISON THAT ANYONE WILL EAT

5 pounds venison loin
1 cup minced onion
1/3 cup margarine
3 tablespoons brown sugar
1/3 cup water
1 tablespoon pepper
Crushed dried red peppers
to taste
1 32-ounce bottle of catsup
1 cup apple cider vinegar

Trim venison. Cook in a small amount of water in covered saucepan or in pressure cooker using manufacturer's instructions until venison is very tender. Drain. Cool to room temperature. Chop to desired consistency. Place in large baking pan. Sauté onion in margarine in skillet until tender. Add brown sugar, water, pepper and red peppers. Cook over high heat for 1 to 2 minutes, stirring constantly. Reduce heat to low. Add catsup; mix well. Remove from heat. Stir in vinegar. Add sauce to venison. Bake at 300 degrees until heated through. Serve on seeded sandwich buns with dill pickles and coleslaw. This dish was concocted when I was more efficient at harvesting deer than at making money to buy groceries and works equally well with bear, beaver, woodchuck and other red meats. Yield: 20 servings.

Approx Per Serving: Cal 230; Prot 34.4 g; T Fat 3.1 g; Chol 73.7 mg; Carbo 15 g; Sod 559 mg; Potas 581 mg.

Gary Doster
Athens, Georgia

WEST TEXAS FRIED VENISON

2 pounds venison
1/4 cup all-purpose flour
1 teaspoon salt
Pepper to taste
3 tablespoons bacon drippings
2 stalks celery, chopped
1 large onion, chopped
1 teaspoon Worcestershire
sauce
2 24-ounce cans tomatoes
1 8-ounce can mushrooms,
drained
8 ounces noodles, cooked

Soak venison in salted water to cover in bowl overnight. Drain. Cut venison into serving pieces. Coat with mixture of flour, salt and pepper. Brown on both sides in bacon drippings in skillet. Add celery and onion. Cook until brown. Add Worcestershire sauce, tomatoes and mushrooms. Cook, covered, for 1 to 2 hours or until venison is tender. Serve over noodles. Yield: 6 servings.

Approx Per Serving: Cal 503; Prot 53 g; T Fat 11.5 g; Chol 140 mg; Carbo 45.6 g; Sod 1082 mg; Potas 1210 mg.

Diane and Lisa Blazevich

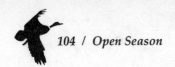

VENISON WELLINGTON

1   2-pound boneless venison
loin roast
1 recipe 2-crust pie pastry
1 tablespoon Dijon-
style mustard
8 ounces mushrooms, sliced
1/8 teaspoon salt
1/8 teaspoon pepper
2 tablespoons prepared
horseradish
1 cup sour cream
2 tablespoons white wine
1/8 teaspoon pepper
1/4 teaspoon salt

Trim roast. Roll pie pastry large enough to completely cover roast. Spread mustard along 1 side to within 1 inch of edge and covering an area about as wide as roast. Arrange mushrooms on mustard. Place roast on top of mushrooms. Sprinkle with 1/8 teaspoon salt and 1/8 teaspoon pepper. Bring edges of pastry up to enclose roast; seal edge and pinch ends. Place on lightly greased baking sheet. Bake at 400 degrees for 20 minutes for rare or to desired degree of doneness. Cover pastry with foil if necessary to prevent over browning. Cut into thin slices. Combine horseradish, sour cream, wine, 1/8 teaspoon pepper and 1/4 teaspoon salt in bowl. Let stand until serving time. Serve with venison. Yield: 4 servings.

Approx Per Serving: Cal 1312; Prot 142. g; T Fat 49.2 g; Chol 320 mg; Carbo 41.4 g; Sod 1157 mg; Potas 1903 mg.

Tom Borschel
Frankfort, New York

VENISON AND WILD RICE CASSEROLE

2 1/2 pounds ground venison
1 medium onion, chopped,
1 medium green bell
pepper, chopped
3 stalks celery, chopped
1 to 2 cups sliced mushrooms
1   10-ounce can cream
of mushroom soup
1   10-ounce can cream of
celery soup
1   10-ounce can cream of
chicken soup
3/4 cup water
3 tablespoons soy sauce
3 cups cooked wild rice
1 cup cooked brown rice
1 1/2 cups biscuit mix
1/3 cup milk

Brown venison in skillet; drain. Add onion, green pepper, celery and mushrooms. Sauté until tender. Combine soups, water and soy sauce. Add wild rice and brown rice to venison mixture; mix well. Stir in soup mixture. Spoon into greased 3 1/2-quart casserole. Bake at 350 degrees for 45 minutes. Increase temperature to 400 degrees. Combine biscuit mix and milk in bowl; mix well. Drop by spoonfuls on top of casserole. Bake for 15 to 20 minutes or until biscuits are brown. Yield: 10 servings.

Approx Per Serving: Cal 474; Prot 40.9 g; T Fat 13.5 g; Chol 80.6 mg; Carbo 44.9 g; Sod 1547 mg; Potas 639 mg.

Janet L. Franke
Decatur, Illinois

Game Birds

Canyon Crossing

David Maass *(courtesy of Wild Wings, Inc., Lake City, Minnesota)*

MUSHROOM WOODCOCK

4 woodcock breasts
1/2 teaspoon salt
1/2 teaspoon pepper
4 slices bacon
4 toothpicks
1 small can sliced button
mushrooms, drained
3/4 cup butter, melted

Sprinkle woodcock breasts with salt and pepper. Wrap slices of bacon around each breast; secure with toothpick. Place in broiler pan. Add mushrooms. Broil for 18 to 20 minutes or until breasts are tender, basting frequently with melted butter.
Yield: 4 servings.

Ann Maass

BARBECUED DOVE

12 dove breasts
1 bay leaf
1 cup Worcestershire sauce
1/2 cup catsup
2 teaspoons sugar
2 tablespoons melted butter
1 teaspoon garlic salt

Wash dove breasts and pat dry. Cook in water to cover with 1 bay leaf for 45 minutes or until tender; drain. Arrange in baking dish. Combine Worcestershire sauce, catsup, sugar, butter and garlic salt in bowl; mix well. Pour over dove breasts. Bake, covered, at 350 degrees for 20 minutes. Yield: 12 servings.

Approx Per Serving: Cal 90; Prot 7.3 g; T Fat 2.5 g; Chol 32.4 mg; Carbo 7.2 g; Sod 508 mg; Potas 202 mg.

Donna Pittenger
Lake Zurich, Illinois

NORMAN'S DOVE À L'ORANGE

12 dove breasts
1/2 cup all-purpose flour
1/2 cup oil
1 1/2 cups orange juice
1 1/2 cups Burgundy

Wash dove breasts and pat dry. Combine flour with salt and pepper to taste. Roll dove breasts in flour mixture, coating well. Brown in oil in 10-inch skillet. Remove to baking dish. Pour mixture of orange juice and wine over top. Bake at 350 degrees for 1 hour, adding additional orange juice and wine if necessary to cover dove. Remove dove to platter. Serve with pan juices and long grain and wild rice. Yield: 6 servings.

Approx Per Serving: Cal 435; Prot 16.1 g; T Fat 19.5 g; Chol 54.4 mg; Carbo 35.4 g; Sod 5.3 mg; Potas 554 mg.

Norman Smith
Memphis, Tennessee

Dean Ettinger of Sierra Vista, Arizona, grills dove breasts. He makes 2 parallel slits next to the fin bone on the breasts; sprinkles smoked garlic salt, ground ginger or curry powder into the slits; and wraps each dove breast with thickly sliced bacon. Grill for 5 minutes on each side over coals mixed with hickory or mesquite chips.

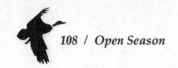

BRAISED DOVE

Cleaned dove
Melted butter
All-purpose flour
2 tablespoons butter
1/2 to 1 onion, chopped
2 to 4 carrots, chopped
1/2 to 1 green bell pepper,
chopped
1 can beef bouillon
1/4 to 1/2 cup Sherry or Port
5 whole cloves
Sliced mushrooms

Wash dove and pat dry. Dip in melted butter. Roll in flour, coating well. Sauté in 2 tablespoons butter in skillet until light brown. Place in baking dish. Add onion, carrots and green pepper to skillet. Sauté over medium heat for 3 to 5 minutes. Add beef bouillon, Sherry and cloves; mix well. Pour over dove. Cook, covered, at 350 degrees for 1 hour. Add mushrooms. Bake for 30 minutes longer; do not allow dove to cook dry. Serve over rice.

Nutritional information for this recipe is not available.

Gil Russell
Tucson, Arizona

DOVE MONTERREY STYLE

10 dove breasts
2 12-ounce bottles of
ginger ale
1/2 teaspoon rosemary
1/2 teaspoon parsley flakes
1/2 teaspoon sage
1/2 teaspoon thyme
1 teaspoon seasoned salt
1 teaspoon pepper
1/4 cup margarine
11/2 cups corn syrup
2 fresh limes
2 large fresh oranges

Wash dove and pat dry. Marinate in ginger ale in bowl in refrigerator overnight; drain. Place in baking dish. Sprinkle with mixture of rosemary, parsley flakes, sage, thyme, salt and pepper. Melt margarine in double boiler. Stir in corn syrup and juice of limes and oranges. Grate lime rind and cut orange rind into fine strips. Add to double boiler. Cook until heated through. Pour over dove breasts. Bake at 350 degrees for 40 minutes. Yield: 5 servings.

Approx Per Serving: Cal 517; Prot 14.1 g; T Fat 10.3 g; Chol 54.4 mg; Carbo 94.8 g; Sod 603 mg; Potas 146 mg. Nutritional information includes all of ginger ale marinade.

Dr. Eric. W. Gustafson
Monterrey, Nuevo León, Mexico

HUNTER'S DOVE STEW

8 dove breasts
1 onion, chopped
2 green bell peppers, chopped
1 can cream of mushroom soup
1 soup can water
¹/4 cup Sherry
Dash of Worcestershire sauce
¹/4 cup toasted sesame seed
¹/2 teaspoon celery salt
2 tablespoons cornstarch

Wash dove breasts and pat dry. Sprinkle with salt and pepper to taste. Brown on both sides in large oiled skillet. Add onion and green peppers. Cook, covered, over low heat for several minutes. Combine soup, water, Sherry, Worcestershire sauce, sesame seed and celery salt in saucepan. Bring to a simmer. Add dove breast mixture. Simmer for 30 minutes or longer. Dissolve cornstarch in a small amount of water. Stir into stew. Cook until thickened. Serve with buttermilk biscuits. May substitute spaghetti sauce or chili for soup if preferred. Yield: 4 servings.

Approx Per Serving: Cal 257; Prot 17.4 g; T Fat 11.7 g; Chol 55.2 mg; Carbo 12.7 g; Sod 850 mg; Potas 179 mg.

S. J. Rosinski
Priest River, Idaho

POTTED DOVE

12 dove
1 cup catsup
1 onion, sliced
3 tablespoons Worcestershire sauce
1 tablespoon melted butter
6 slices bacon

Wash dove and pat dry. Steam in a small amount of water in a saucepan for 20 minutes. Drain, reserving water. Combine catsup, onion, Worcestershire sauce, butter and salt and pepper to taste in bowl; mix well. Spread in 8x12-inch baking dish. Arrange dove in sauce. Lay bacon slices over dove. Bake, covered, at 275 degrees for 1 hour, adding reserved water if necessary to keep dove from drying out. Yield: 6 servings.

Approx Per Serving: Cal 292; Prot 24.4 g; T Fat 9.4 g; Chol 97.3 mg; Carbo 20.4 g; Sod 997 mg; Potas 407 mg.

Betty Ann Smith
Merritt Island, Florida

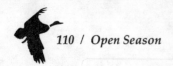

SMOTHERED DOVE BREASTS

24 *dove breasts*
1 *cup all-purpose flour*
Garlic powder to taste
1/2 *cup safflower oil*
2 *large white onions, sliced*
1 *pound fresh mushrooms,*
sliced
2 *teaspoons all-purpose flour*
1 *cup water*
2 *cups rice, cooked*

Wash dove breasts and pat dry. Combine 1 cup flour with garlic powder and salt and pepper to taste. Coat 6 dove breasts at a time in flour mixture. Brown dove on both sides in oil in skillet over medium heat. Remove dove to heavy 5-quart saucepan. Sauté onions and mushrooms in pan drippings in skillet over low heat. Blend 2 teaspoons flour with 1 cup water. Stir into skillet. Cook until thickened, stirring constantly. Pour over dove. Simmer for 45 minutes, stirring occasionally. Serve over rice. Yield: 8 servings.

Approx Per Serving: Cal 376; Prot 23.9 g; T Fat 15.7 g; Chol 81.6 mg; Carbo 27.6 g; Sod 3.8 mg; Potas 263 mg.

David Weintraub
Stone Mountain, Georgia

CREAMED PHEASANT

1 *pheasant, cut up*
1/2 *cup all-purpose flour*
Garlic powder and paprika
to taste
Oil for frying
1 *can cream of chicken soup*
1 *can cream of mushroom soup*
1 *tablespoon Worcestershire*
sauce
1/3 *cup chopped onion*
1/4 *to* 1/2 *cup milk*

Wash pheasant and pat dry. Combine flour with garlic powder, paprika and salt and pepper to taste. Roll pheasant pieces in flour mixture, coating well. Brown in oil in skillet. Remove to baking dish. Combine soups, Worcestershire sauce, onion and enough milk to make of desired consistency in bowl; mix well. Pour over pheasant. Sprinkle with additional paprika. Bake, covered, at 325 to 350 degrees for 1 1/2 to 2 hours. Yield: 4 servings.

Approx Per Serving: Cal 415; Prot 30.1 g; T Fat 20.6 g; Chol 90.4 mg; Carbo 25.7 g; Sod 1224 mg; Potas 464 mg. Nutritional information does not include oil for frying.

Sandra Polkinghorn
Britton, South Dakota

CREAMY WILD RICE WITH PHEASANT

1¹/2 *cups wild rice*
2 stalks celery, chopped
1 medium onion, chopped
4 ounces fresh mushrooms,
sliced
¹/2 *cup butter*
1 can cream of mushroom soup
8 ounces sour cream
1 teaspoon salt
¹/4 *teaspoon pepper*
¹/4 *cup melted butter*
2 tablespoons lemon juice
1 teaspoon Worcestershire
sauce
³/4 *cup evaporated milk*
1 teaspoon salt
¹/4 *teaspoon pepper*
6 pheasant breasts

Cook wild rice according to package directions. Sauté celery, onion and mushrooms in ¹/2 cup butter in skillet just until onions are transparent. Mix soup and sour cream in bowl. Add soup and rice to onion mixture. Season with 1 teaspoon salt and ¹/4 teaspoon pepper. Spoon into 3¹/2-quart baking dish. Combine ¹/4 cup melted butter, lemon juice, Worcestershire sauce, evaporated milk, 1 teaspoon salt and ¹/4 teaspoon pepper in bowl. Wash pheasant breasts and pat dry. Dip in evaporated milk mixture. Arrange over rice mixture; press into rice. Bake at 350 degrees for 1 hour and 15 minutes or until pheasant is tender. Yield: 6 servings.

Approx Per Serving: Cal 713; Prot 45.1 g; T Fat 42 g; Chol 170 mg; Carbo 39.1 g; Sod 1412 mg; Potas 744 mg.

William G. Quarles
Gastonia, North Carolina

FAISAN À LA CRÈME

1 pheasant
2 onions, chopped
2 ounces butter, softened
1 tablespoon all-purpose flour
¹/2 *cup cream*

Wash pheasant and pat dry inside and out. Place pheasant and onions in buttered baking dish. Bake at 325 degrees for 1 hour. Carve pheasant. Place in shallow serving dish. Purée pan juices and onions in blender container. Pour into saucepan. Stir in flour and cream. Season with salt and pepper to taste. Cook until thickened, stirring constantly. Pour over pheasant. Yield: 4 servings.

Approx Per Serving: Cal 424; Prot 25.8 g; T Fat 32.6 g; Chol 152 mg; Carbo 6.7 g; Sod 152 mg; Potas 379 mg.

Jill Probert
England

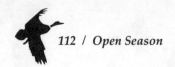
GOLDEN PHEASANT CASSEROLE

1 pheasant, cut up
All-purpose flour
Salt and pepper to taste
Butter
Bacon drippings
Potatoes, thickly sliced
Onion, sliced
Carrots, sliced
1 can cream of mushroom soup
1 cup sour cream
1 tablespoon Worcestershire
    sauce
1½ cups water
1 recipe baking powder biscuits

Wash pheasant and pat dry. Coat well with mixture of flour, salt and pepper. Brown in equal parts butter and bacon drippings in heavy skillet. Remove to deep baking dish. Layer potatoes, onion and carrots over pheasant. Combine soup, sour cream, Worcestershire sauce and water in bowl; mix well. Pour over pheasant. Bake, covered, at 325 degrees for 1½ hours or until tender. Top with biscuits. Bake, uncovered, until biscuits are brown. Yield: 4 servings.

Nutritional information for this recipe is not available.

Jeri L. Nelson
Springfield, South Dakota

FAISAN IN ROTWEIN

1   3½-pound pheasant
4 tablespoons butter
½ cup finely chopped onion
1 cup dry red wine
½ cup chicken stock
½ small bay leaf
½ teaspoon salt
2 slices lean bacon
1 cup thinly sliced fresh
    mushrooms
2 tablespoons butter
1 tablespoon all-purpose flour
⅓ cup heavy cream

Wash pheasant and pat dry inside and out. Rub cavity with 1 tablespoon softened butter. Sprinkle with salt and pepper to taste. Truss pheasant. Brown in 3 tablespoons butter in heavy saucepan. Remove to platter. Add onion. Sauté until tender. Add wine, stirring to deglaze saucepan. Add stock, bay leaf, ½ teaspoon salt and pepper to taste. Add pheasant and juices. Arrange bacon across breast. Simmer, covered, for 45 minutes or until juices run clear. Remove to warm platter, reserving stock. Let stand, covered with foil, for several minutes. Sauté mushrooms in 2 tablespoons butter in skillet for 3 minutes. Stir in flour. Cook for 1 minute, stirring constantly. Scrape into saucepan in which pheasant was cooked; remove bay leaf. Stir in cream. Simmer until slightly thickened, stirring constantly. Carve pheasant. Serve with sauce and wild rice. Yield: 5 servings.

Approx Per Serving: Cal 422; Prot 21.8 g; T Fat 29 g; Chol 125 mg; Carbo 5.4 g; Sod 493 mg; Potas 378 mg.

Betty Hrdlicka
Dorchester, Nebraska

FAVORITE PHEASANT

1 pheasant, cut up
1/2 cup all-purpose flour
1/4 cup margarine
1/2 cup chopped onion
1 clove of garlic, minced
1 can cream of chicken soup
1/2 cup dry white wine or water

Filet pheasant breast; remove tendons from legs with pliers. Combine flour with salt and pepper to taste. Roll pheasant in flour, coating well. Brown in margarine in Dutch oven over medium-high heat. Remove to plate. Add onion and garlic to Dutch oven. Cook over medium heat until transparent. Return pheasant to Dutch oven. Stir in mixture of soup and wine. Bake, covered, at 325 degrees for 1 1/4 to 1 1/2 hours. Yield: 4 servings.

Approx Per Serving: Cal 439; Prot 28 g; T Fat 25.7 g; Chol 85.4 mg; Carbo 18.1 g; Sod 755 mg; Potas 378 mg.

Gwendolyn Tyler
Winfield, Kansas

LEE'S BRB

2 pheasant, partridge,
or sharptail
1 onion, sliced
Marjoram and thyme to taste
1 can cream of mushroom soup
1 can cream of chicken soup
1   16-ounce package
frozen broccoli
1/2 cup uncooked instant rice
1 can cream of celery soup
1   16-ounce jar of Cheez Whiz
1 can cream of celery soup
1 cup cheese-flavored croutons

Combine game birds with water to cover, onion, marjoram and thyme in large saucepan. Cook, covered, for 2 hours; drain. Bone and cut into bite-sized pieces. Place in greased baking pan. Layer mushroom soup, chicken soup, broccoli, rice, Cheez Whiz, celery soup and croutons over pheasant. Bake, covered, at 350 degrees for 1 hour. Yield: 10 servings.

Approx Per Serving: Cal 441; Prot 32.4 g; T Fat 25.6 g; Chol 101 mg; Carbo 20.2 g; Sod 1505 mg; Potas 526 mg.

Lee Silha
Bowman, North Dakota

Paul Craig of Halifax, Pennsylvania, browns pheasant pieces in butter and adds 1/2 cup of chopped onion, 1 cup of sliced mushrooms, 1 cup of dry white wine, 1/2 teaspoon of basil and salt and pepper to taste. Bake, covered, at 325 degrees for 2 hours. Add 1 cup of sour cream and cook for 5 minutes.

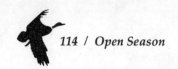

PAPRIKA PHEASANT

2 pheasant, split
1/2 cup apple cider
1/2 cup chopped onion
1 clove of garlic, pressed
1 tablespoon Worcestershire
sauce
Paprika to taste
1 can cream of mushroom soup
1   4-ounce can button
mushrooms, drained

Wash pheasant and pat dry. Place in baking dish. Mix remaining ingredients in sauce pan. Simmer for 10 minutes. Pour over pheasant. Bake at 350 degrees for 1½ hours, basting with sauce and sprinkling with additional paprika every 15 minutes. Yield: 4 servings.

Approx Per Serving: Cal 489; Prot 50.4 g; T Fat 25.3 g; Chol 160 mg; Carbo 12.6 g; Sod 819 mg; Potas 705 mg.

Ellen Henson
Trinidad, Washington

PARMESAN PHEASANT

1 pheasant, cut up
1/4 cup all-purpose flour
2 tablespoons Parmesan cheese
1 teaspoon MSG
1/2 teaspoon paprika
3/4 teaspoon salt
1/8 teaspoon pepper
1/4 cup butter
1/2 cup chicken stock

Wash pheasant and pat dry. Combine flour, cheese, MSG, paprika, salt and pepper. Roll pheasant in flour, coating well. Let stand on rack for 30 minutes. Brown in butter in skillet heated to 340 to 360 degrees for 15 minutes on each side. Add stock. Simmer, covered, for 20 minutes or until tender. Cook, uncovered, for 10 minutes longer. Yield: 4 servings.

Approx Per Serving: Cal 336; Prot 26.5 g; T Fat 22.3 g; Chol 113 mg; Carbo 6.1 g; Sod 1756 mg; Potas 288 mg.

Jeri L. Nelson
Springfield, South Dakota

PHAVORITE PHEASANT

2 pheasant, cut into quarters
1/4 cup butter
1/4 cup all-purpose flour
1/4 teaspoon pepper
1/8 teaspoon garlic powder
Thyme and ginger to taste
2 bay leaves
1 cup chicken broth
1 cup white May wine
4 cups cooked wild rice

Wash pheasant and pat dry. Brown in butter in skillet. Sift mixture of flour, pepper, garlic powder, thyme and ginger over pheasant. Add bay leaves, broth and wine. Simmer, covered, for 1 hour or until tender. Remove bay leaves. Serve over hot rice. Yield: 6 servings.

Approx Per Serving: Cal 431; Prot 39.7 g; T Fat 13.4 g; Chol 120 mg; Carbo 29.6 g; Sod 251 mg; Potas 514 mg.

Janelle Scheidecker
Fergus Falls, Minnesota

PHANTASTIC PHEASANT

1/2 cup finely chopped onion
6 green onions, finely chopped
1 clove of garlic, chopped
2 tablespoons oil
2 tablespoons chopped parsley
1/4 cup all-purpose flour
1 pheasant, cut up
8 fresh mushrooms,
thinly sliced
1/2 cup dry red wine

Sauté onion, green onions and garlic in oil in large heavy skillet. Add parsley. Cook for 2 minutes longer. Remove with slotted spoon. Combine flour with salt and pepper to taste. Wash pheasant and pat dry. Roll in flour, coating well. Add to skillet. Cook until lightly browned. Add sautéed vegetables, mushrooms and wine. Simmer for 45 minutes. Place pheasant in serving dish. Pour sauce over top. Yield: 4 servings.

Approx Per Serving: Cal 321; Prot 26.2 g; T Fat 17 g; Chol 79.7 mg; Carbo 10.2 g; Sod 47.7 mg; Potas 508 mg.

Bill and Serena Hendryx
Dallas, Texas

PHEASANT BREAST IN BRANDY HORSERADISH CREAM

1/2 cup butter
1/2 cup all-purpose flour
8 pheasant breasts
1/4 cup butter
2 tablespoons bacon drippings
1/2 cup Brandy
1 1/2 cups chicken stock
1 cup horseradish
1/2 teaspoon salt
Pepper to taste
3 cups heavy cream
1 pound bacon, crisp-fried

Melt 1/2 cup butter in skillet. Stir in flour. Cook until medium brown; set aside. Wash pheasant breasts and pat dry. Brown in 1/4 cup butter and bacon drippings in saucepan. Remove pheasant to baking dish. Stir Brandy into saucepan. Bring to a boil; reduce heat. Simmer for several minutes. Add stock, horseradish, 1/2 teaspoon salt and pepper. Stir in cream. Bring just to a simmer. Add browned flour. Cook until thickened, stirring constantly. Pour over pheasant. Bake, covered, at 350 degrees for 30 minutes or until tender. Sprinkle with crumbled bacon. Yield: 8 servings.

Approx Per Serving: Cal 1088; Prot 56.2 g; T Fat 86.7 g; Chol 320 mg; Carbo 17 g; Sod 1472 mg; Potas 825 mg.

Mary Jane Waltemate
Steeleville, Illinois

This recipe for Nevada Chicken or sage grouse comes from Janell Ahlvers of Ely, Nevada. Partially freeze sage hen (the bigger the better) and cut meat off bones in very thin slices. Sprinkle with lemon pepper, coat with flour and cook in butter in skillet until rare to medium-rare.

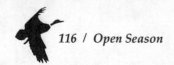

PHEASANT BREASTS WITH CINNAMON MARMALADE

4 pheasant breast filets
2 tablespoons butter
4 teaspoons all-purpose flour
1/4 teaspoon cinnamon
1/2 cup orange juice
2 tablespoons orange
marmalade
3/4 teaspoon instant
chicken bouillon
1 tablespoon orange liqueur
1/2 cup green seedless grapes
1 orange, peeled, cut
into sections
1/4 cup toasted sliced almonds

Line 8x8-inch baking pan with heavy aluminum foil, leaving 1½-inch foil collar. Wash pheasant breasts and pat dry. Arrange in prepared pan. Melt butter in saucepan over medium heat. Stir in flour and cinnamon. Cook until smooth. Stir in orange juice, marmalade and bouillon. Cook until thickened, stirring constantly. Stir in liqueur. Spoon over pheasant. Seal foil tightly. Bake at 325 degrees until pheasant is tender. Spoon grapes and orange sections over pheasant. Bake, uncovered, for 5 minutes longer. Sprinkle with almonds. Serve with hot cooked rice. Yield: 4 servings.

Approx Per Serving: Cal 370; Prot 36.9 g; T Fat 13.7 g; Chol 97.3 mg; Carbo 22.7 g; Sod 102 mg; Potas 607 mg.

IGFCA World Championship Wild Game Cookoff
Sioux City, Nebraska

PHEASANT AND DUMPLINGS

2 pheasant, cut up
1/2 teaspoon parsley flakes
1 bay leaf
1/2 cup white wine
1/2 teaspoon salt
1/2 teaspoon pepper
1 can cream of chicken soup
1/4 cup butter
1½ cups buttermilk baking mix
1/2 cup milk
Curry powder to taste

Wash pheasant and pat dry. Combine with parsley flakes, bay leaf, wine, salt, pepper and water to cover in large saucepan. Cook for 1½ hours or until tender. Bone pheasant and return meat to saucepan. Stir in soup and butter. Remove bay leaf. Combine baking mix, milk and curry powder in bowl; mix well. Roll on floured surface. Cut into strips. Drop into simmering broth. Cook, uncovered, for 10 minutes. Cook, covered, for 10 minutes longer. Yield: 6 servings.

Approx Per Serving: Cal 428; Prot 34.8 g; T Fat 25.4 g; Chol 134 mg; Carbo 10 g; Sod 779 mg; Potas 433 mg.

Jeri L. Nelson
Springfield, South Dakota

PHEASANT MULLIGAN WITH DUMPLINGS

2 young pheasant, cut up
2 cups chopped carrots
1 cup chopped onion
1 cup finely shredded cabbage
2 cups chopped potatoes
2 tablespoons shortening
2 cups sifted all-purpose flour
1 tablespoon baking powder
1/2 teaspoon salt
1 egg
3/4 cup milk

Wash pheasant and pat dry. Combine with carrots, onion, cabbage and water to cover in saucepan. Simmer until nearly tender. Add potatoes, shortening and salt and pepper to taste. Cook until tender. Sift flour, baking powder and 1/2 teaspoon salt into bowl. Add mixture of beaten egg and milk; mix well, adding additional milk if needed for desired consistency. Drop by tablespoonfuls into stew. Simmer, covered, for 15 minutes; do not lift cover. Yield: 8 servings.

Approx Per Serving: Cal 421; Prot 30.3 g; T Fat 15 g; Chol 117 mg; Carbo 39.5 g; Sod 333 mg; Potas 654 mg.

Marlene Robertson
Amaranth, Manitoba, Canada

SPECIAL PHEASANT

1 pheasant, cut up
1 cup all-purpose flour
1 teaspoon salt
1/2 teaspoon pepper
1/2 cup butter-flavored
shortening
1 cup white wine
2 1/2 cups chicken broth
1/4 cup chopped onion
1 teaspoon tarragon
2 cups spinach noodles
1 cup heavy cream

Wash pheasant and pat dry. Shake in mixture of flour, salt and pepper in bag, coating well. Brown in shortening in skillet. Stir in wine, broth, onion and tarragon. Simmer for 30 to 40 minutes or until tender. Cook noodles according to package directions; drain. Layer noodles and pheasant in serving dish; keep warm. Stir cream into pan juices. Simmer for 3 minutes. Pour over pheasant. Yield: 4 servings.

Approx Per Serving: Cal 1236; Prot 47.8 g; T Fat 63 g; Chol 162 mg; Carbo 108 g; Sod 1126 mg; Potas 1038 mg.

James E. Vanauken
Columbus Junction, Iowa

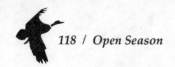
PHEASANT WITH CRANBERRY CREAM SAUCE

6 cups apple cider
2 cups dry white wine
1/2 cup chopped onion
1/4 cup chopped carrots
1/4 cup chopped celery
1/4 cup chopped parsley stems
6 juniper berries
3 bay leaves
1 1/2 teaspoons thyme
1 1/2 teaspoons whole
peppercorns
4 pheasant
1 tablespoon peanut oil
2 cups chicken stock
2 tablespoons butter
2 tablespoons all-purpose flour
1/2 cup whipping cream
2 tablespoons jellied
cranberry sauce
1/4 cup clarified butter

Combine cider, wine, onion, carrots and celery in large shallow dish. Tie parsley stems, juniper berries, bay leaves, thyme and peppercorns in cheesecloth bag. Add to cider mixture. Wash pheasant and pat dry inside and out. Place in marinade. Marinate, covered, in refrigerator for 4 days, turning occasionally. Drain marinade through strainer, reserving 2 cups clear liquid, bag of seasonings and vegetables. Place pheasant in roasting pan. Roast at 425 degrees for 20 minutes or until rare. Cool. Carve breast meat and bone legs. Set meat aside. Chop pheasant bones and carcasses. Brown in peanut oil in saucepan. Add reserved vegetables. Sauté until light brown. Add 2 cups reserved marinade, bag of seasonings and stock. Simmer for 2 hours. Strain mixture. Return to saucepan. Cook until reduced to 2 cups liquid. Blend 2 tablespoons butter and flour in small bowl. Whisk into sauce. Season with salt and freshly ground pepper to taste. Simmer until thickened, stirring constantly. Degrease and adjust seasonings. Add cream and cranberry sauce. Cook until thickened to desired consistency. Cover and keep warm. Sauté pheasant leg meat in clarified butter in heavy skillet. Add breast meat, turning to coat well. Heat in oven for 2 to 3 minutes or until heated through. Serve immediately with warm sauce. This recipe was created by Chef Kevin Grenzig of Alfredo's in the Westin Hotel in Vail, Colorado. Yield: 12 servings.

Approx Per Serving: Cal 761; Prot 35.6 g; T Fat 57.1 g; Chol 258 mg; Carbo 20.1 g; Sod 287 mg; Potas 671 mg.

Frances Szczesniak
Rosemount, Minnesota

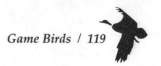

GROUSE AUX CHOUX

4 grouse breast filets
3 slices bacon
1 medium onion, sliced
1 carrot, sliced
1 large head of cabbage,
chopped
2 cups apple juice or
white wine

Wash grouse and pat dry. Fry bacon in Dutch oven until crisp. Remove bacon. Brown grouse in bacon drippings, turning frequently. Remove to plate. Add onion and carrot. Cook until light brown. Add cabbage and apple juice. Place grouse in cabbage, covering well. Simmer for 1 hour or until tender or bake at 350 degrees for 1½ hours. Place grouse on serving platter. Arrange vegetables around grouse. Crumble bacon over top. Yield: 2 servings.

Approx Per Serving: Cal 445; Prot 41 g; T Fat 6.5 g; Chol 160 mg; Carbo 44.9 g; Sod 220 mg; Potas 1052 mg.

Tom Clark
Atikokan, Ontario, Canada

STIR-FRIED GROUSE

2 grouse
1 teaspoon soy sauce
Pepper to taste
2 tablespoons peanut oil
1 clove of garlic, crushed
2 scallions, cut into
1-inch lengths
1 carrot, diagonally sliced
1 red bell pepper, coarsely
chopped
1 10-ounce package frozen
snow peas
1 7-ounce can sliced water
chestnuts, drained
1 tablespoon tapioca starch
½ cup water

Wash grouse and pat dry. Bone and cut into bite-sized pieces. Sprinkle with soy sauce and pepper. Let stand for several minutes. Heat oil in wok or heavy skillet. Add garlic. Stir-fry for 1 minute. Add grouse. Stir-fry until tender. Add vegetables. Cook, covered, for several minutes or until tender-crisp. Blend tapioca starch and water in small bowl. Stir into grouse and vegetable mixture. Cook until thickened, stirring constantly. Serve with rice. Yield: 4 servings.

Approx Per Serving: Cal 297; Prot 28.8 g; T Fat 7.9 g; Chol 106 mg; Carbo 19.1 g; Sod 177 mg; Potas 270 mg.

Tom Borschel
Frankfort, New York

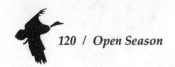

GROUSE AND WILD RICE

2/3 cup wild rice *2 cups chicken broth* *1/4 cup butter* *Grouse breast filets* *Eggs, beaten* *All-purpose flour* *Garlic salt, oregano, basil and* *pepper to taste* *Butter* *Chicken broth* *Mozzarella cheese, sliced*	Combine wild rice with 2 cups broth and 1/4 cup butter in saucepan. Cook, covered, until tender; keep warm. Wash grouse filets and pat dry. Pound filets between waxed paper with meat mallet until tender. Combine with eggs in bowl. Let stand for 1 hour. Combine flour, garlic salt, oregano, basil and pepper in bowl. Roll filets in flour mixture, coating well. Brown on both sides in butter in skillet. Add enough broth to cover bottom of skillet. Simmer, covered, for 10 minutes. Place 1 slice cheese on each filet. Cook just until cheese is melted. Serve with rice.

Nutritional information for this recipe is not available.

Marge Olson
Webster, Wisconsin

PARTRIDGE CORDON BLEU

1 egg *1/2 cup milk* *1 cup cornflake crumbs* *1 teaspoon parsley flakes* *1/2 teaspoon paprika* *1/2 teaspoon salt* *1/2 teaspoon pepper* *8 ruffed grouse breast filets* *4 slices ham* *4 slices Swiss cheese* *Oil for frying*	Beat egg and milk in small bowl. Combine cornflake crumbs, parsley flakes, paprika, salt and pepper in bowl. Wash grouse filets and pat dry. Pound thin with meat mallet. Place ham slices and cheese slices on 4 filets. Top with remaining filets, pressing edges to seal. Dip in egg mixture. Coat well with crumb mixture. Place on plate. Chill in refrigerator for 1 hour or longer. Fry in 1/2 inch oil in skillet over medium heat for 2 minutes on each side. Serve with baked potato and favorite vegetable. Yield: 4 servings.

Nutritional information for this recipe is not available.

Vernon Herbert
Atikokan, Ontario, Canada

Mark Looney of Texarkana, Texas makes a favorite cooking sauce for quail. Mix 1/2 cup of apple jelly, 1/2 cup of white wine, 1/4 cup of butter, 1 minced clove of garlic, 1/4 teaspoon of coarsely ground pepper and a dash of cinnamon. Pour over browned quail in skillet and simmer, covered, for 1 hour.

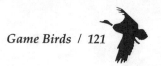

BAKED QUAIL WITH SHERRY

6 quail
1/4 cup margarine
1 small onion, chopped
1/2 cup chopped celery
1 1/2 tablespoons all-purpose flour
1 cup chicken broth
1/2 cup Sherry

Wash quail and pat dry. Brown in margarine in skillet. Place in baking dish. Sprinkle with salt and pepper to taste. Sauté onion and celery until tender. Stir in flour. Cook until bubbly. Add broth. Cook until thickened, stirring constantly. Stir in Sherry. Pour over quail. Bake, covered, at 325 degrees for 1 hour. Yield: 4 servings.

Approx Per Serving: Cal 654; Prot 52 g; T Fat 42.5 g; Chol 0.3 mg; Carbo 4.1 g; Sod 499 mg; Potas 691 mg.

Dolores Rhoades
Ashepoo Plantation

QUAIL WITH WHITE GRAPES

4 quail
1 tablespoon lemon juice
1/2 teaspoon seasoned salt
White pepper to taste
1/2 cup all-purpose flour
1/3 cup butter
1/3 cup dry white wine
1/3 cup chicken broth
1 tablespoon lemon juice
1/4 cup seedless white grapes
2 tablespoons sliced toasted almonds

Wash quail and pat dry inside and out. Drizzle with 1 tablespoon lemon juice. Sprinkle with seasonings. Let stand for 1 hour. Coat with flour. Sauté in butter in sauce-pan until golden. Add wine, broth and 1 table-spoon lemon juice. Simmer, covered, for 20 minutes. Add grapes and almonds. Cook for 5 minutes or until quail are tender. Yield: 2 servings.

Approx Per Serving: Cal 1120; Prot 72.4 g; T Fat 75.1 g; Chol 82.2 mg; Carbo 30 g; Sod 1106 mg; Potas 948 mg.

William G. Quarles
Gastonia, North Carolina

SIMPLICITY QUAIL

6 quail, skinned
1 can cream of mushroom soup
1 cup white wine
1 tablespoon teriyaki sauce
1 envelope dry onion soup mix

Wash quail and pat dry inside and out. Place quail in baking pan. Pour mixture of soup, wine and sauce over quail. Sprinkle with soup mix. Seal foil loosely. Bake at 350 degrees for 1 hour. Yield: 6 servings.

Approx Per Serving: Cal 408; Prot 34.5 g; T Fat 24.1 g; Chol 0.6 mg; Carbo 4.9 g; Sod 694 mg; Potas 437 mg.

William G. Quarles
Gastonia, North Carolina

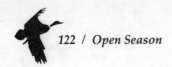

QUAIL WITH LEMON SAUCE

4 ounces smoked bacon
3 carrots, sliced
1 parsnip, sliced
2 large onions, sliced
3/4 teaspoon sugar
7 peppercorns
Breasts and drumsticks of
15 quail
1 cup (or more) chicken broth
2 tablespoons butter
1 tablespoon all-purpose flour
Juice and grated rind of
1 lemon
3 tablespoons sour cream

Combine first 6 ingredients in skillet. Cook for 10 minutes. Wash quail and pat dry. Add to skillet. Simmer, covered, until tender, stirring occasionally. Add a small amount of broth if necessary. Remove quail to platter; keep warm. Remove peppercorns. Purée vegetables in blender container. Blend butter and flour in skillet. Add 1 cup broth. Cook until thickened, stirring constantly. Add lemon juice and rind. Simmer for 10 minutes. Stir in puréed vegetables and sour cream. Bring to a boil. Add salt to taste. Pour over quail. Serve with wild rice.
Yield: 8 servings.

Approx Per Serving: Cal 540; Prot 78.1 g; T Fat 20.8 g; Chol 22.2 mg; Carbo 6 g; Sod 536 mg; Potas 1056 mg.

Laszlo Varju
Greenup, Illinois

SAUTÉED QUAIL MEDALLIONS IN CURRANT SAUCE

12 quail
2 tablespoons oil
1 stalk celery with leaves,
finely chopped
1 carrot, finely chopped
1 small onion, finely chopped
1/4 cup butter
1/2 cup Sherry
1/2 cup red wine
4 cups chicken stock
1 bay leaf
Thyme to taste
1/4 cup butter
6 tablespoons butter
6 tablespoons all-purpose flour
1/2 cup currants
1/2 cup currant jelly

Bone quail breasts. Chop bones and carcasses. Brown bones in oil in skillet; set aside. Sauté celery, carrot and onion in 1/4 cup butter in saucepan. Add Sherry, red wine, stock, bay leaf, thyme and browned quail bones. Simmer for 1 hour. Strain, reserving liquid. Season filets with thyme and salt and pepper to taste. Sauté in 1/4 cup butter in skillet. Place in baking dish. Blend 6 tablespoons butter and flour in saucepan. Cook until medium brown, stirring constantly. Stir in reserved liquid. Cook until thickened, stirring constantly. Stir in currants and jelly. Brush on filets. Bake at 400 degrees for 10 minutes. Broil until light brown. Ladle sauce over filets or serve in small bowl. Yield: 6 servings.

Approx Per Serving: Cal 1121; Prot 72.0 g; T Fat 73.4 g; Chol 73.1 mg; Carbo 35.1 g; Sod 943 mg; Potas 1111 mg.

Mary Jane Waltemate
Steeleville, Illinois

Off Season

Meats, Poultry and Seafood

Releasing A Spawner

John P. Cowan

TROUT AMANDINE

*1/2 cup thinly sliced
almonds
4 to 6 fillets of trout
3 cups milk
1 teaspoon dry mustard
1 cup all-purpose flour
Salt and pepper to taste
1 cup margarine*

Brown almonds in a small amount of margarine in saucepan. Marinate trout in mixture of milk and mustard in bowl for 10 minutes. Remove from marinade. Drain. Coat with mixture of flour and salt and pepper. Brown in 1 cup margarine in skillet, turning once. Drain on paper towel. Spoon almonds and margarine over trout. Serve hot. Yield: 4 to 6 servings.

GRILLED TENDERLOIN

1 *2-pound beef tenderloin*
1 *12-ounce bottle of Italian Salad Dressing*

Combine tenderloin with dressing in large plastic bag; seal well. Refrigerate overnight, turning several times. Remove from refrigerator 2 hours before cooking; drain well. Grill over hot coals for 40 minutes for medium-rare or 50 minutes for medium. Yield: 8 servings.

Approx Per Serving: Cal 415; Prot 32.8 g; T Fat 34 g; Chol 92.1 mg; Carbo 4.3 g; Sod 281 mg; Potas 444 mg. Nutritional information includes all of salad dressing.

Mrs. Fred King
Clarksville, Tennessee

BEEF TENDERLOIN IN PUFF PASTRY

8 ounces mushrooms, finely chopped
1 large onion, finely chopped
3 tablespoons clarified butter
1 *3-pound beef tenderloin*
1/4 cup Grand Marnier
10 thin slices cooked ham
3 tablespoons clarified butter, softened
1 sheet frozen puff pastry, thawed
1 egg yolk

Sauté mushrooms and onion in 3 tablespoons butter in skillet until tender. Add salt and freshly ground pepper to taste. Trim tenderloin, removing ends. Brush with Grand Marnier. Cut into 12 slices, cutting almost to but not through bottom. Place 1 slice of ham between each slice, trimming to fit tenderloin. Spread small amount of mushroom mixture between slices; reserve remaining mushroom mixture. Press slices together; secure with skewers. Place in roasting pan. Roast at 375 degrees for 15 to 20 minutes or until partially cooked. Cool slightly; remove skewers. Spread with softened butter. Season with salt and pepper to taste. Spread with reserved mushroom mixture. Roll pastry into thin sheet on lightly floured surface. Place tenderloin on pastry; wrap pastry to enclose tenderloin. Place on baking sheet. Brush with cold water. Bake at 450 degrees for 12 minutes. Brush with egg yolk. Bake until light brown. Serve with Bearnaise sauce seasoned with curry powder. Yield: 12 servings.

Nutritional information for this recipe is not available.

Herbert E. Barthels
Santa Barbara, California

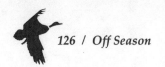

MEXICAN KABOBS

1 tablespoon vinegar
1 tablespoon water
1 envelope Italian salad
dressing mix
1 teaspoon chili powder
1 tablespoon oil
1/3 cup orange juice
1 pound round steak
1 large green bell pepper
1 large onion
12 large cherry tomatoes

Combine vinegar, water, salad dressing mix and chili powder in jar with tight-fitting lid; shake well. Add oil and orange juice; shake well. Cut steak into cubes. Combine with marinade in glass dish. Marinate in refrigerator overnight. Drain, reserving marinade. Cut green pepper into chunks. Cut onion into 12 wedges. Alternate steak and vegetables on 4 skewers. Broil or grill over hot coals for 4 to 5 minutes on each side, brushing frequently with marinade. May use elk, venison or antelope round steak if available. Yield: 4 servings.

Approx Per Serving: Cal 468; Prot 39.7 g; T Fat 28.1 g; Chol 108 mg; Carbo 21.4 g; Sod 200 mg; Potas 1199 mg.

Frances Szczesniak
Rosemount, Minnesota

ITALIAN BEEF

1 4-pound chuck roast
Garlic powder and oregano
to taste
1 16-ounce jar mild
pepper rings
2 onions, sliced
1 12-ounce can beef broth
1 12-ounce can beer

Sprinkle roast on both sides with garlic powder and oregano to taste. Add salt and pepper to taste. Place in roasting pan. Drain peppers, reserving liquid. Layer peppers and onions over roast. Pour broth, beer and reserved pepper liquid over top. Bake, covered, at 300 degrees for 4 hours. Remove roast to plate. Shred with 2 forks. Serve on long Italian rolls with onion if desired. Yield: 12 servings.

Approx Per Serving: Cal 436; Prot 47.8 g; T Fat 23.4 g; Chol 160 mg; Carbo 3.7 g; Sod 754 mg; Potas 486 mg.

Teresa Shank
Brighton, Illinois

Sharron Wasser of Fairbanks, Alaska, makes an easy blender basting sauce of 1/2 cup of soy sauce, 1/2 cup catsup, 1/4 cup of dry Sherry, 3/4 cup of brown sugar, 2 cloves of minced garlic and 1 teaspoon of salt.

CONTINENTAL STEW

1/2 cup all-purpose flour
1 pound stew beef
4 medium onions, sliced
3 potatoes, peeled, coarsley chopped
4 carrots, sliced
1 can beef consommé
1 can tomato soup
1 soup can water

Mix flour with salt and pepper to taste. Roll stew beef in flour mixture, coating well. Layer onions, potatoes, carrots and beef in large baking pan. Combine consommé, soup and water in bowl; mix well. Pour over layers. Bake, covered, at 325 degrees for 3 hours. Yield: 6 servings.

Approx Per Serving: Cal 370; Prot 28 g; T Fat 12.8 g; Chol 80.2 mg; Carbo 35.5 g; Sod 557 mg; Potas 772 mg.

Mrs. John Henry Smith
Forsyth, Montana

SCALOPPINE AL CARCIOFI

1/2 cup all-purpose flour
1/2 teaspoon sugar
1/8 teaspoon salt
Cayenne pepper, nutmeg, dry mustard, MSG, sage to taste
11/2 pounds thinly sliced veal steaks
2 tablespoons olive oil
2 tablespoons butter
2 tablespoons Cognac
5 mushrooms, sliced
1 10-ounce package frozen artichokes, thawed, drained
1/2 cup beef stock
1/2 teaspoon BV meat extract
1/2 teaspoon tomato paste
11/2 teaspoons potato starch
1/2 cup dry Marsala
1 tablespoon currant jelly
1/4 teaspoon salt
1/2 teaspoon pepper
1/2 cup Parmesan cheese
1/2 teaspoon oregano

Combine flour, sugar, 1/8 teaspoon salt, cayenne pepper, nutmeg, dry mustard, MSG and sage in bowl; mix well. Cut veal into serving-sized pieces. Pound to 1/8-inch thickness between waxed paper with meat mallet. Coat well with flour mixture. Brown veal quickly on both sides in olive oil and butter in large skillet. Add Cognac, stirring to deglaze skillet. Ignite Cognac. Remove veal to baking dish when flames sub-side. Add mushrooms and artichokes to skillet. Sauté until light brown. Stir in beef stock, BV and tomato paste gently. Dissolve potato starch in wine. Add to skillet. Cook until thickened, stirring constantly. Stir in jelly, 1/4 teaspoon salt and 1/2 teaspoon pepper. Spoon mixture over veal. Sprinkle with cheese and oregano. Bake at 375 degrees for 15 minutes. Serve with rice cooked in chicken broth with a pinch of saffron. Yield: 6 servings.

Approx Per Serving: Cal 400; Prot 43 g; T Fat 15.7 g; Chol 171 mg; Carbo 16.6 g; Sod 487 mg; Potas 733 mg. Nutritional information does not include rice.

Jean Auchterionie
Birmingham, Michigan

HAMBURGER PIE

1 pound ground beef
1 small onion, chopped
1/2 cup chopped green
bell pepper
1 16-ounce can green beans
1 can tomato soup
1 tablespoon sugar
1 teaspoon chili powder
1 4-ounce package instant
mashed potatoes
1/2 cup Parmesan cheese

Brown ground beef with onion and green pepper in skillet, stirring until ground beef is crumbly; drain. Add undrained green beans, soup, sugar and chili powder; mix well. Spoon into deep 3-quart baking dish. Prepare mashed potatoes according to package directions. Season with salt and pepper to taste. Spoon in a circle around top of casserole. Sprinkle with Parmesan cheese. Bake at 375 degrees for 30 minutes. Yield: 4 servings.

Approx Per Serving: Cal 475; Prot 35.5 g; T Fat 27.4 g; Chol 107 mg; Carbo 24 g; Sod 1154 mg; Potas 743 mg.

Joann Goodell
Cedar Rapids, Iowa

LAZY LASAGNA

1 pound ground beef
1 16-ounce package
lasagna noodles
1 32-ounce jar spaghetti sauce
1 cup cottage cheese
2 cups shredded mozzarella
cheese
1/2 cup Parmesan cheese

Brown ground beef in skillet, stirring until ground beef is crumbly; drain. Cook noodles according to package directions. Reserve 1 cup spaghetti sauce. Combine remaining spaghetti sauce, ground beef, noodles, cottage cheese and mozzarella cheese in bowl; mix well. Spoon into 2-quart baking dish. Spread reserved spaghetti sauce over top. Sprinkle with Parmesan cheese. Bake at 350 degrees for 30 minutes. Serve with garlic bread. May substitute ground venison for ground beef. Yield: 6 servings.

Approx Per Serving: Cal 928; Prot 52.7 g; T Fat 41.2 g; Chol 135 mg; Carbo 83.8 g; Sod 1359 mg; Potas 1062 mg.

Brenda E. Stauffer
Ephrata, Pennsylvania

CREOLE CABBAGE

1 *pound ground chuck*
1 *pound smoked sausage, sliced*
1 *large onion, chopped*
3 *heads cabbage, chopped*
1/4 *teaspoon crushed red pepper*
2 *teaspoons Creole seasoning*

Brown ground chuck and sausage with onion in heavy skillet, stirring until ground chuck is crumbly; drain. Steam cabbage just until tender. Add ground beef mixture; mix well. Stir in seasonings. Cook until heated through.
Yield: 12 servings.

Approx Per Serving: Cal 271; Prot 20.6 g; T Fat 17.8 g; Chol 70.8 mg; Carbo 7 g; Sod 535 mg; Potas 525 mg.

Dovard Mitchell
Greenville, Mississippi

BUTTERFLIED LEG OF LAMB

1   *5-pound leg of lamb,*
trimmed, boned,
butterflied
4 *teaspoons soy sauce*
1 *tablespoon finely chopped*
fresh tarragon
or rosemary
1/2 *cup (about) olive oil*
2 *cloves of garlic*
3 *tablespoons lemon juice*
1 *clove of garlic, crushed*
1 *tablespoon lemon juice*
1 *cup molasses*
3/4 *teaspoon chopped fresh*
thyme or 1/2 teaspoon
dried
1 *tablespoon finely chopped*
parsley

Rub lamb with mixture of soy sauce, 2 teaspoons tarragon and 1 tablespoon olive oil. Cut 2 cloves of garlic into 12 slices each. Make 24 slits in boned side of lamb and insert 1 sliver of garlic in each slit. Rub with mixture of remaining olive oil and tarragon. Drizzle with 3 tablespoons lemon juice. Place lamb boned side down on rack in broiler pan. Roast at 400 degrees for 20 minutes or to 120 degrees on meat thermometer. Set oven to Broil. Broil 5 inches from heat source for 2 to 3 minutes or until lamb begins to brown. Place lamb on carving board. Let stand for 10 minutes; keep warm. Add 1 clove of garlic, 1 tablespoon lemon juice, molasses and thyme to pan juices; mix well. Carve lamb; place slices on serving plate. Stir parsley into sauce just before serving. Pour into serving bowl. Serve with lamb.
Yield: 12 servings.

Approx Per Serving: Cal 354; Prot 30.7 g; T Fat 18.2 g; Chol 99.3 mg; Carbo 15.7 g; Sod 217 mg; Potas 1183 mg.

Herbert E. Barthels
Santa Barbara, California

SAUSAGE CASSEROLE

1 pound bulk sausage
1 16-ounce can whole kernel
corn, drained
1/2 8-ounce package croutons
2 cans cream of chicken soup
1 1/2 soup cans milk

Brown sausage in skillet, stirring until crumbly; drain. Add corn and croutons; mix well. Place in greased baking dish. Combine soup with milk in bowl; mix well. Pour over casserole. Bake at 350 degrees for 1 hour. Yield: 6 servings.

Approx Per Serving: Cal 578; Prot 18.2 g; T Fat 39.9 g; Chol 68.8 mg; Carbo 38.7 g; Sod 1703 mg; Potas 463 mg.

Wylma Colehour
Mt. Carroll, Illinois

BARBECUED BABY BACK RIBS

6 pounds baby back pork ribs
1 cup water
2 medium onions, thinly sliced
2 lemons, thinly sliced
2 cups Barbecue Sauce

Cut ribs into serving-sized pieces. Sprinkle with salt and pepper to taste. Grill over medium high coals for 5 minutes on each side. Place in aluminum baking pan. Pour water over top; cover well. Place on grill; close cover. Grill over low coals for 1 hour. Sprinkle onion and lemon slices over ribs. Pour Barbecue Sauce over top. Grill for 1 hour longer, basting and rearranging after 30 minutes. Yield: 6 servings.

Approx Per Serving: Cal 782; Prot 51.3 g; T Fat 51.9 g; Chol 206 mg; Carbo 25.8 g; Sod 1553 mg; Potas 972 mg.

Barbecue Sauce

1/2 cup Worcestershire sauce
1 cup catsup
1/2 cup water
3 tablespoons brown sugar
1 teaspoon Tabasco sauce
2 teaspoons salt
2 teaspoons chili powder
1 teaspoon garlic powder

Combine Worcestershire sauce, catsup, water, brown sugar, Tabasco sauce and seasonings in bowl; mix well. Microwave on High for 3 to 4 minutes or until boiling. Omit water if ribs are to be cooked in oven. Yield: 2 cups.

Nutritional information for Barbecue Sauce is included in Barbecued Baby Back Ribs recipe.

Nelson Lyles
Columbia, Tennessee

STUFFED PORK TENDERLOIN

1 1½-pound pork tenderloin
½ cup chopped onion
¼ cup butter
1 cup fresh bread crumbs
1¼ cups packed brown sugar
¼ cup minced parsley
¼ teaspoon sage
¼ teaspoon rosemary
1 egg, slightly beaten
4 slices thick-sliced bacon

Cut tenderloin almost through lengthwise, leaving 1 side attached. Open out and pound with meat mallet to flatten. Sauté onion in butter in skillet until translucent. Add bread crumbs. Cook until crumbs are almost crisp, stirring constantly. Add brown sugar, parsley, herbs and salt and pepper to taste. Cool. Add enough egg to just moisten; mix well. Spread on half the tenderloin, leaving ¼-inch edge. Fold over remaining half of tenderloin. Top with bacon; secure with string. Place on rack in roasting pan. Roast at 350 degrees for 1 hour. Do not overbake.
Yield: 6 servings.

Approx Per Serving: Cal 611; Prot 40.5 g; T Fat 27.6 g; Chol 190 mg; Carbo 49.2 g; Sod 288 mg; Potas 709 mg.

Herbert E. Barthels
Santa Barbara, California

NANCY'S COMPANY QUICHE

2 cups shredded mild
Cheddar cheese
2 cups shredded Swiss cheese
1 medium yellow onion,
chopped
2 green onions, chopped
8 ounces fresh mushrooms,
sliced
1 pound cooked ham, cut into
1-inch cubes
6 slices bacon, crisp-fried,
crumbled
12 eggs
2 cups milk
2 cups buttermilk baking mix
1 teaspoon parsley flakes
1 teaspoon salt
1 teaspoon pepper

Layer Cheddar cheese, Swiss cheese, onion, green onions, mushrooms, ham and bacon in 2 greased 10-inch pie plates. Combine eggs, milk, baking mix, parsley, salt and pepper in bowl. Beat with fork until well mixed. Pour over layers. Bake at 350 degrees for 50 to 60 minutes or until knife inserted in center comes out clean. Let stand for 10 minutes before serving.
Yield: 12 servings.

Approx Per Serving: Cal 393; Prot 27.3 g; T Fat 22.6 g; Chol 331 mg; Carbo 19 g; Sod 1223 mg; Potas 410 mg.

Nancy Malech
Coyote, California

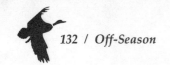

CHICKEN AND WILD RICE HOT DISH

1 6-ounce can mushrooms,
drained
1/4 cup chopped onion
2 tablespoons chopped green
bell pepper
2 tablespoons chopped pimento
2 tablespoons butter
2 cups cooked rice
2 cups cooked wild rice
2 cans cream of mushroom soup
2 7-ounce cans chunky chicken
1 can cream of mushroom soup
1/4 cup butter
1 6-ounce can mushrooms,
drained

Sauté 1 can mushrooms, onion, green pepper and pimento in 2 tablespoons butter in skillet. Combine rice, wild rice, 2 cans soup and chicken in bowl. Add sautéed vegetables; mix well. Spoon into medium baking dish. Bake at 350 degrees for 40 minutes. Combine 1 can soup, 1/4 cup butter and 1 can mushrooms in small saucepan. Heat until bubbly. Serve over casserole. Yield: 6 servings.

Approx Per Serving: Cal 514; Prot 27.8 g; T Fat 25.6 g; Chol 88.5 mg; Carbo 43.4 g; Sod 1538 mg; Potas 405 mg.

Darla Glawe
Vergas, Minnesota

CHICKEN HOT DISH

1/2 cup chopped onion
1/2 cup chopped green
bell pepper
1 cup chopped celery
1/4 cup butter
Garlic powder to taste
2 cups chopped cooked chicken
3 cups cooked rice
1 can cream of mushroom soup
1 can cream of chicken soup
1 cup chicken broth
1 4-ounce can mushroom
pieces, drained
1 2-ounce jar chopped pimento

Saute onion, green pepper and celery in butter in saucepan. Stir in garlic powder, salt and pepper to taste. Add chicken, rice, soups, broth, mushrooms and pimento; mix well. Spoon into 11x13-inch baking dish. Bake at 350 degrees for 1 hour. Yield: 8 servings.

Approx Per Serving: Cal 294; Prot 14.5 g; T Fat 14.6 g; Chol 50.2 mg; Carbo 26.4 g; Sod 985 mg; Potas 275 mg.

Colleen Seifert
Pelican Rapids, Minnesota

CHICKEN AND BROCCOLI CASSEROLE

2   10-ounce packages
frozen broccoli
2 cups sliced cooked chicken
2 cans cream of chicken soup
1 cup mayonnaise
2 cups cooked wild rice
1 teaspoon lemon juice
1/2 teaspoon curry powder
1/2 cup shredded Cheddar
cheese
1/4 cup fine bread crumbs

Cook broccoli according to package directions. Place in greased 9x13-inch baking dish. Sprinkle chicken over broccoli. Combine soup, mayonnaise, wild rice, lemon juice and curry powder in bowl; mix well. Spoon over chicken. Top with cheese and bread crumbs. Bake at 350 degrees for 25 to 30 minutes. Yield: 8 servings.

Nutritional information for this recipe is not available.

Robyn Bayless
Billings, Montana

CHICHARRONES DE POLLO

1 pound chicken breast filets
1/4 cup lemon juice
1 tablespoon soy sauce
1/2 teaspoon salt
1 cup all-purpose flour
1/2 teaspoon paprika
1/2 teaspoon salt
1 teaspoon pepper
1 1/2 cups oil for deep frying

Wash chicken and pat dry. Cut into bite-sized pieces. Combine with mixture of lemon juice, soy sauce and 1/2 teaspoon salt in bowl; mix well. Marinate for 2 hours; drain. Combine flour, paprika, 1/2 teaspoon salt and pepper in bowl. Add chicken; toss to coat well. Deep-fry in 365-degree oil until crisp. Serve with lemon slices. Yield: 4 servings.

Approx Per Serving: Cal 308; Prot 38.5 g; T Fat 5.5 g; Chol 95.6 mg; Carbo 23.8 g; Sod 882 mg; Potas 344 mg. Nutritional information does not include oil for deep-frying. It does include all of marinade.

Susan Algard
Helena, Montana

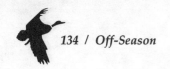

CHICKEN ELEGANT

4 chicken breasts
1/2 cup margarine
1 package dry Italian salad dressing mix
3 ounces cream cheese, softened
1/3 cup white wine
1 can mushroom soup
1 cup mushrooms
1 tablespoon chopped chives
2 cups cooked rice

Remove skin from chicken. Wash chicken and pat dry. Melt margarine in skillet. Sprinkle salad dressing mix over margarine. Add chicken. Sauté until chicken is brown on both sides; drain. Place chicken in greased 3-quart baking dish. Blend cream cheese, wine and soup in bowl. Add mushrooms and chives. Pour over chicken. Bake at 350 degrees for 1 hour, basting every 15 minutes. Serve over rice.
Yield: 4 servings.

Approx Per Serving: Cal 774; Prot 40.6 g; T Fat 53.7 g; Chol 120 mg; Carbo 33.9 g; Sod 1135 mg; Potas 473 mg.

Joann Goodell
Cedar Rapids, Iowa

CHICKEN ITALIANO

1 cup Parmesan cheese
2 tablespoons chopped parsley
1 tablespoon oregano
2 teaspoons paprika
1 teaspoon salt
1 teaspoon garlic salt
1/2 teaspoon pepper
1   3-pound chicken, cut up
1/2 cup melted margarine

Combine cheese, parsley, oregano, paprika, salt, garlic salt and pepper in bowl; mix well. Wash chicken and pat dry. Dip chicken in melted margarine in bowl. Roll in cheese mixture, coating well. Place in foil-lined 9x13-inch baking dish. Drizzle with remaining margarine. Bake at 350 degrees for 1 hour and 15 minutes.
Yield: 4 servings.

Approx Per Serving: Cal 942; Prot 107 g; T Fat 54.2 g; Chol 319 mg; Carbo 1 g; Sod 2041 mg; Potas 869 mg.

Joan Peabody
Alexandria, Minnesota

COMPANY'S COMING

8 chicken breast filets
1 3-ounce package dried beef
8 1-inch cubes mozzarella
cheese
1 can cream of mushroom soup
1/4 cup Sherry
1/2 cup shredded mild
Cheddar cheese
8 ounces sour cream
1/2 cup shredded Cheddar cheese
1/2 cup seasoned bread crumbs
4 slices bacon, crisp-fried,
crumbled

Wash chicken and pat dry. Pound with meat mallet to flatten. Place dried beef slices on chicken. Top with cube of mozzarella cheese. Roll chicken to enclose filling. Combine soup, wine, 1/2 cup Cheddar cheese and sour cream in bowl; mix well. Spoon a small amount into 9x12-inch baking dish. Arrange chicken rolls in prepared dish. Pour remaining sauce over top. Sprinkle with 1/2 cup Cheddar cheese, bread crumbs and bacon. Bake, covered, at 350 degrees for 1 hour. Bake, uncovered, for 15 minutes longer. May substitute game bird breasts for chicken if desired. Yield: 8 servings.

Approx Per Serving: Cal 482; Prot 49.8 g; T Fat 26.3 g; Chol 165 mg; Carbo 6.3 g; Sod 1017 mg; Potas 448 mg.

Sandi Thomas
Sackets Harbor, New York

HOT CHICKEN SALAD

2 cups chopped cooked chicken
2 cups finely chopped celery
1/4 cup chopped green
bell pepper
1/2 can cream of chicken soup
2 tablespoons chopped pimento
2 tablespoons lemon juice
2 tablespoons Worcestershire
sauce
2 tablespoons grated onion
1/2 cup mayonnaise
1/2 teaspoon salt
3/4 cup shredded Cheddar cheese
1/2 cup slivered almonds
3 cups crushed potato chips

Combine chicken, celery, green pepper, soup, pimento, lemon juice, Worcestershire sauce, onion, mayonnaise and salt in bowl; mix well. Spoon into baking dish. Sprinkle cheese, almonds and crushed potato chips over top. Bake at 350 degrees for 45 minutes to 1 hour. Yield: 8 servings.

Approx Per Serving: Cal 722; Prot 20.9 g; T Fat 51.8 g; Chol 50.2 mg; Carbo 50.2 g; Sod 906 mg; Potas 1409 mg.

Helen Shank
Clayton, Illinois

WAGAS SPECIAL

1   *3-pound chicken*
1/4 cup oil
1/2 cup honey
2 cups hot water
1   *10-ounce bottle of soy sauce*
1   *10-ounce bottle of teriyaki marinade*
1 *teaspoon garlic powder*

Wash chicken and pat dry. Cut into quarters. Place meaty side down in 8x8-inch dish. Combine oil, honey, hot water, soy sauce and marinade in bowl; mix well. Pour over chicken. Refrigerate, covered, for 24 hours. Drain well. Place on rack in baking pan. Sprinkle with garlic powder. Bake at 375 degrees for 40 minutes. This is a favorite at the duck hunting club, where it is usually made with duck halves in a Chinese oven. May cook on grill if preferred.
Yield: 4 servings.

Approx Per Serving: Cal 640; Prot 60.7 g; T Fat 21.6 g; Chol 143 mg; Carbo 52.7 g; Sod 6902 mg; Potas 736 mg. Nutritional information includes all of marinade.

Colleen Withro
Rosamond, California

CASEY'S POPPY SEED CHICKEN CASSEROLE

6 chicken breasts
1 can cream of chicken soup
8 ounces sour cream
35 butter crackers, crushed
6 tablespoons melted butter
2 tablespoons poppy seed

Wash chicken and pat dry. Cook in water to cover in saucepan until tender. Bone chicken. Place in baking dish. Combine soup and sour cream in bowl; mix well. Pour over chicken. Top with cracker crumbs. Drizzle with melted butter. Sprinkle with poppy seed. Bake at 325 degrees until bubbly. Yield: 6 servings.

Approx Per Serving: Cal 526; Prot 39.4 g; T Fat 34.2 g; Chol 147 mg; Carbo 18.2 g; Sod 752 mg; Potas 414 mg.

Joan Marsh
Humboldt, Tennessee

MEXICAN CHICKEN

1 3-pound chicken, cooked
¼ cup chopped onion
4 ounces Velveeta hot
cheese, sliced
1 8-ounce package
tortilla chips
1 can cream of mushroom soup
1 can cream of chicken soup
1 10-ounce can Ro-Tel
tomatoes

Bone and chop chicken. Place in baking dish. Sprinkle with onion. Top with cheese slices. Reserve ½ cup tortilla chips. Sprinkle remaining tortilla chips over casserole. Combine soups and Ro-Tel in bowl; mix well. Pour over layers. Top with reserved chips. Bake at 325 degrees for 1 hour. Yield: 6 servings.

Approx Per Serving: Cal 566; Prot 42 g; T Fat 29.5 g; Chol 118 mg; Carbo 33.2 g; Sod 1339 mg; Potas 547 mg.

Mrs. J. P. Stotts
DeWitt, Arkansas

WISCONSIN CHICKEN BOOYAH

1 pound dried beans
1 pound dried peas
35 pounds stewing chickens
3 pounds beef sirloin, cubed
1 pound onions, chopped
6 24-ounce cans tomatoes
4 cloves of garlic
2 bay leaves
2 tablespoons pickling spice
4 bunches celery, chopped
4 pounds carrots, chopped
6 pounds potatoes, chopped
1 16-ounce package frozen
wax beans
1 16-ounce package frozen
green beans
1 16-ounce package whole
kernel corn

Soak dried beans and peas in water to cover overnight. Cut up chicken. Combine chicken and beef with water to cover in 50-quart kettle. Cook over wood fire for 2 hours. Add drained beans and peas, onions and tomatoes. Add water to within 6 inches of top of kettle. Simmer for 2 hours or longer. Tie 2 cloves of garlic, 1 bay leaf and 1 tablespoon pickling spice in each of 2 cheesecloth bags. Chop celery, carrots and potatoes coarsely. Add spice bags, celery, carrots and potatoes to stew. Simmer for 2½ hours, stirring occasionally. Add frozen vegetables. Simmer for 30 minutes longer. Remove spice bags. Ladle into deep soup bowls. Serve with oyster crackers and beer. Yield: 40 servings.

Approx Per Serving: Cal 614; Prot 74.0 g; T Fat 18.6 g; Chol 203 mg; Carbo 36 g; Sod 396 mg; Potas 1459 mg.

Ellen Olson
DePere, Wisconsin

LIVERS FOR TWO

1¹/₄ pounds chicken livers
3 tablespoons margarine
2 tablespoons lemon juice
2 tablespoons Worcestershire
sauce
4 dashes Tabasco sauce
¹/₂ onion, chopped
¹/₂ green bell pepper, chopped
¹/₂ teaspoon hot and spicy
seasoning salt
1 cup rice
2 cups water
1 teaspoon salt
1 teaspoon margarine
3 drops butter flavoring

Wash livers and pat dry. Melt 3 tablespoons margarine in saucepan over low heat. Stir in lemon juice, Worcestershire sauce and Tabasco sauce. Add livers, onion and green pepper; mix gently. Spoon into baking dish. Sprinkle with seasoning salt. Bake at 375 degrees for 30 to 45 minutes or until brown. Combine rice, water, salt and 1 teaspoon margarine in saucepan. Bring to a boil; reduce heat. Stir in butter flavoring. Simmer, covered, until rice is tender and water is absorbed. Spoon rice onto plates. Top with liver mixture. Serve with garlic bread and a good rosé. Yield: 2 servings.

Approx Per Serving: Cal 1498; Prot 159 g; T Fat 53.1 g; Chol 3934 mg; Carbo 85.5 g; Sod 1790 mg; Potas 1147 mg.

Art Wilkirson
Findlay, Ohio

TURKEY BROCCOLI CASSEROLE

2   10-ounce packages
frozen broccoli
1 tablespoon lemon juice
2 tablespoons margarine
2 tablespoons all-purpose flour
2 cups milk
¹/₂ cup shredded Swiss cheese
2 cups chopped cooked turkey
³/₄ cup soft bread crumbs
¹/₄ cup Parmesan cheese
1 tablespoon melted margarine

Cook broccoli according to package directions; drain well. Place in 1¹/₂-quart baking dish. Sprinkle with lemon juice. Melt 2 tablespoons margarine in saucepan. Blend in flour. Add milk all at once. Cook until thickened, stirring constantly. Remove from heat. Stir in Swiss cheese until melted. Stir in turkey. Spoon over broccoli. Combine bread crumbs, Parmesan cheese and 1 tablespoon melted margarine. Sprinkle over casserole. Bake at 350 degrees for 20 to 25 minutes or until bubbly. Yield: 6 servings.

Approx Per Serving: Cal 311; Prot 27.1 g; T Fat 16.5 g; Chol 63.3 mg; Carbo 14.4 g; Sod 304 mg; Potas 459 mg.

Kathy Meyer
Medford, Oregon

DEEP FRIED TURKEY

1 12-ounce bottle of
Thousand Island
salad dressing
10 ounces Creole seasoning
4 ounces red pepper
2 ounces pepper
2 ounces garlic powder
2 ounces Worcestershire sauce
1 12-pound turkey
Peanut oil for deep frying

Combine salad dressing, Creole seasoning, red pepper, pepper, garlic powder and Worcestershire sauce in bowl; mix to form a paste. Rub on turkey, rubbing under skin as well. Deep-fry in peanut oil for 4 minutes per pound.
Yield: 8 servings.

Approx Per Serving: Cal 768; Prot 101 g; T Fat 32.1 g; Chol 271 mg; Carbo 12.9 g; Sod 609 mg; Potas 1199 mg. Nutritional information does not include peanut oil for deep frying.

Dovard Mitchell
Greenville, Mississippi

BAKED FISH FILLETS

1/2 cup mayonnaise
2 tablespoons chopped
green onions
Dillweed to taste
1/4 cup fine dry bread crumbs
1/4 cup Parmesan cheese
Pepper to taste
1 pound redfish fillets
Paprika to taste

Combine mayonnaise, green onions and dillweed in small bowl; mix well. Mix bread crumbs, cheese and pepper in bowl. Brush fish fillets with mayonnaise mixture. Roll in bread crumb mixture, coating well. Arrange in single layer in shallow baking dish. Sprinkle with paprika. Bake at 425 degrees for 20 minutes or until fish flakes easily. Yield: 4 servings.

Approx Per Serving: Cal 374; Prot 32.5 g; T Fat 25.5 g; Chol 73.5 mg; Carbo 2.5 g; Sod 330 mg; Potas 618 mg.

Sis Reilly
Lookout Mountain, Tennessee

Shirley Cartoscelli of Yuba City, California, dips bass or sturgeon fillets in Caesar salad dressing, sprinkles with shredded Cheddar cheese and crushed potato chips and bakes at 500 degrees for 10 to 15 minutes or until fish flakes easily.

MUSTARD BAKED FISH

1 *3-pound red snapper*
1 teaspoon Creole seasoning
1/4 cup Italian salad dressing
1/4 cup mayonnaise
1/4 cup butter
1 teaspoon Creole seasoning
2 tablespoons wine vinegar
1 1/2 tablespoons mustard
1/2 teaspoon Worcestershire
sauce
1 stalk celery, thinly sliced
1/2 medium onion, chopped
1/4 green bell pepper, chopped

Wash fish and pat dry. Sprinkle inside and out with 1 teaspoon Creole seasoning. Place in baking dish. Combine salad dressing, mayonnaise, butter, 1 teaspoon Creole seasoning, vinegar, mustard and Worcestershire sauce in saucepan. Bring to a boil; reduce heat. Simmer for 7 minutes. Add celery, onion and green pepper. Simmer for 10 to 12 minutes or until vegetables are tender-crisp. Pour over fish. Bake, covered with foil, at 350 degrees for 1 hour. Yield: 2 servings.

Approx Per Serving: Cal 995; Prot 91.2 g; T Fat 69 g; Chol 238 mg; Carbo 8 g; Sod 865 mg; Potas 1932 mg.

James D. Sandefur
Oakdale, Louisiana

BLACKENED BASS

1 teaspoon pepper
1 teaspoon white pepper
1 teaspoon red pepper
1 teaspoon thyme
1 teaspoon sage
1/2 teaspoon salt
8 *8-ounce bass fillets*
1/2 cup butter

Combine pepper, white pepper, red pepper, thyme, sage and salt in heavy plastic bag. Wash fillets and pat dry. Add 2 at a time to plastic bag; shake to coat well. Heat 2 tablespoons butter in skillet over medium-high heat. Add 2 fillets. Cook until fish is blackened and flakes easily. Remove to serving plate. Repeat process with remaining butter and fillets. Garnish with sliced green onions. Yield: 8 servings.

Approx Per Serving: Cal 388; Prot 54.7 g; T Fat 20.6 g; Chol 213 mg; Carbo 0.7 g; Sod 401 mg; Potas 887 mg.

Robert Platt
Lucedale, Mississippi

BUTTER-BATTERED NUTTY CATS

2 cups Grape Nuts cereal
8 vanilla wafers
1 cup cornmeal
2 teaspoons salt
1 teaspoon pepper
1/2 cup Cajun seasoning
2 eggs
1 1/2 cups buttermilk
4 3/4-pound catfish fillets
Peanut oil for frying
1/2 cup Parmesan cheese

Crush cereal and vanilla wafers to fine crumbs. Combine with cornmeal, salt, pepper and Cajun seasoning in paper bag; mix well. Beat eggs with buttermilk in bowl. Wash fish and pat dry. Dip in egg mixture. Shake in crumb mixture in bag, coating well. Fry in 360-degree peanut oil until brown. Sprinkle with cheese. Yield: 4 servings.

Approx Per Serving: Cal 1097; Prot 118 g; T Fat 32.2 g; Chol 466 mg; Carbo 80.3 g; Sod 2149 mg; Potas 2338 mg. Nutritional information does not include peanut oil for frying.

Norman Smith
Memphis, Tennessee

SMOKED CATFISH

1 10-ounce bottle of soy sauce
1 10-ounce bottle of Worcestershire sauce
10 drops of liquid smoke
3 pounds catfish fillets

Combine soy sauce, Worcestershire sauce and liquid smoke in bowl. Add catfish. Marinate for 2 hours. Heat coals and hickory chips in round smoker. Drain catfish. Place in smoker. Smoke for 2 hours or until fish flakes easily; do not overcook. Serve with butter-dill sauce and lemon wedges. Yield: 6 servings.

Approx Per Serving: Cal 325; Prot 44.7 g; T Fat 9.7 g; Chol 132 mg; Carbo 12.5 g; Sod 3307 mg; Potas 1254 mg. Nutritional information includes all of marinade.

Greg Robinson
Memphis, Tennessee

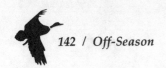

MARINATED CATFISH

1/2 cup soy sauce
Juice of 1 lemon
1 tablespoon Worcestershire
sauce
1/3 cup Burgundy
2 cloves of garlic, minced
1 pound catfish fillets
Cinnamon to taste

Combine soy sauce, lemon juice, Worcestershire sauce, wine and garlic in bowl; mix well. Add catfish. Marinate in refrigerator for 10 hours; drain. Place fillets in oiled wire broiler. Grill over medium coals for 10 minutes on each side. Sprinkle with cinnamon, salt and pepper to taste. Yield: 2 servings.

Approx Per Serving: Cal 335; Prot 45.3 g; T Fat 9.7 g; Chol 132 mg; Carbo 8.9 g; Sod 4286 mg; Potas 1004 mg. Nutritional information includes all of marinade.

Norman Smith
Memphis, Tennessee

ENGLISH FISH AND CHIPS SANDWICHES

1 cup all-purpose flour
1 tablespoon baking powder
1 tablespoon sugar
1 tablespoon vinegar
2 pounds fish fillets
4 potatoes, sliced
Oil for deep frying

Combine flour, baking powder, sugar and salt and pepper to taste in bowl. Add enough water to make a batter the consistency of thick cream; mix well. Place in freezer for 20 minutes. Remove batter from freezer. Add vinegar; mix well. Cut fish into 2-inch pieces. Place each piece of fish between 2 slices of potato. Dip into batter. Deep-fry in 5 inches hot oil until golden brown. Drain on paper towel. Yield: 4 servings.

Approx Per Serving: Cal 500; Prot 46.6 g; T Fat 10.1 g; Chol 132 mg; Carbo 53 g; Sod 397 mg; Potas 1269 mg. Nutritional information does not include oil for deep frying.

Jan McGuire
Bartlesville, Oklahoma

FISH FLORENTINE

1 pound fresh fish fillets
1 10-ounce package frozen
spinach soufflé, thawed
1/3 cup cracker crumbs
3 tablespoons Parmesan cheese

Grease bottom of 7x12-inch baking dish. Arrange fish in single layer in prepared dish. Spoon soufflé over top. Sprinkle with mixture of crumbs and cheese. Bake at 400 degrees for 20 minutes or until fish flakes easily.
Yield: 4 servings.

Nutritional information for this recipe is not available.

Sis Reilly
Lookout Mountain, Tennessee

HALIBUT HAWAIIAN

1 3-pound piece halibut
3 slices bacon
1 13-ounce can pineapple
tidbits
1 1/2 tablespoons cornstarch
3 tablespoons sugar
1/3 cup vinegar
1 1/2 tablespoons soy sauce
1/2 green bell pepper, cut
into strips

Place halibut in baking dish. Sprinkle with salt and pepper to taste. Place bacon over top of fish. Bake at 375 degrees for 45 minutes. Drain pineapple, reserving juice. Add enough water to reserved juice to measure 1 cup. Blend with cornstarch, sugar, vinegar and soy sauce in saucepan. Cook until thickened, stirring constantly. Add green pepper and pineapple. Cook until heated through. Place fish on serving plate. Spoon sauce over top. Yield: 6 servings.

Approx Per Serving: Cal 334; Prot 48.7 g; T Fat 7.1 g; Chol 75.2 mg; Carbo 17 g; Sod 431 mg; Potas 1135 mg.

Marilyn Tuttle
Homer, Alaska

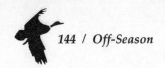

HOTSY TOTSY HALIBUT

1/2 cup melted butter
1 large clove of garlic, minced
1 1/2 teaspoons sweet
hot mustard
1/2 teaspoon Worcestershire
sauce
2 pounds halibut fillets
1 cup seasoned Italian
bread crumbs
Pepper to taste

Mix melted butter, garlic, mustard and Worcestershire sauce in bowl. Cut fish into small pieces. Dip in butter mixture. Roll in mixture of crumbs and pepper, coating well. Arrange in single layer in shallow baking dish. Drizzle with remaining butter mixture. Bake at 450 degrees for 20 to 25 minutes or until fish flakes easily. Yield: 4 servings.

Approx Per Serving: Cal 486; Prot 48.5 g; T Fat 28.7 g; Chol 135 mg; Carbo 6 g; Sod 404 mg; Potas 1051 mg.

Barbara Springer
Fairbanks, Alaska

HALIBUT WITH SHERRY SAUCE

2 pounds halibut steaks
1 tablespoon melted butter
1 teaspoon salt
Pepper to taste
1 tablespoon melted butter
1/4 cup finely chopped onion
1 clove of garlic, minced
1 tablespoon butter
1 tablespoon all-purpose flour
1/4 cup sour cream
1/2 cup chicken broth
1   2 1/2-ounce jar mushrooms,
drained
1 tablespoon Sherry

Cut fish into 6 portions. Brush with 1 tablespoon butter. Sprinkle with salt and pepper. Grill over medium coals for 5 to 8 minutes or until fish flakes easily. Brush with 1 tablespoon butter; keep warm. Sauté onion and garlic in 1 tablespoon butter in saucepan. Stir in flour, sour cream and chicken broth. Cook until bubbly, stirring constantly. Stir in mushrooms and Sherry. Cook until heated through. Place fish on serving plate. Spoon sauce over top. Yield: 6 servings.

Approx Per Serving: Cal 238; Prot 32.7 g; T Fat 9.5 g; Chol 63.1 mg; Carbo 2.8 g; Sod 590 mg; Potas 744 mg.

Betty Breeding
Anchorage, Alaska

HANUS BAY HALIBUT

2 pounds halibut
2 8-ounce jars marinated
artichoke hearts
2 8-ounce cans button
mushrooms
1/2 cup butter
1/2 cup all-purpose flour
3 cups milk
1/2 cup white wine
1 tablespoon Accent
1/2 teaspoon garlic salt
11/2 teaspoons Tabasco sauce
1 cup shredded Cheddar cheese

Cut fish into cubes. Place fish, artichoke hearts and mushrooms in 9x13-inch baking dish. Melt butter in saucepan. Stir in flour. Add milk, wine, Accent, garlic salt, Tabasco and cheese. Cook until sauce is thickened and cheese is melted. Pour over mixture in baking dish. Bake at 350 degrees for 50 minutes. Yield: 6 servings.

Approx Per Serving: Cal 597; Prot 44.7 g; T Fat 35.4 g; Chol 126 mg; Carbo 23.6 g; Sod 3425 mg; Potas 1182 mg.

Barbara Springer
Fairbanks, Alaska

POOR MAN'S LOBSTER

Halibut fillets
2 quarts water
2/3 cup sugar
1/4 cup salt

Cut halibut into 1-inch cubes. Bring water, sugar and salt to a boil in saucepan. Add fish in small amounts to water. Cook until fish floats to top of water. Remove with slotted spoon. Serve with garlic butter.

Nutritional information for this recipe is not available.

Pat McGrorty
Homer, Alaska

Janet Franke of Decatur, Illinois, makes an easy batter for deep frying fish fillets by mixing equal parts of flour and beer.

HEAVENLY FISH

2 pounds fish fillets
2 tablespoons lemon juice
1/4 cup butter, softened
3 tablespoons mayonnaise
3 tablespoons chopped
green onion
1/2 cup Parmesan cheese
Dash of hot pepper sauce
1/4 teaspoon salt

Place fish in single layer on greased rack in broiler pan. Brush with lemon juice. Let stand for 10 minutes. Combine butter, mayonnaise, green onion, cheese, pepper sauce and salt in bowl; mix well. Broil fish 4 inches from heat source for 6 to 8 minutes or until fish flakes easily. Spread with cheese sauce. Broil for 2 to 3 minutes longer or until light brown.
Yield: 6 servings.

Approx Per Serving: Cal 325; Prot 30.6 g; T Fat 21.6 g; Chol 118 mg; Carbo 1 g; Sod 415 mg; Potas 553 mg.

Miriam Burchell

REDFISH

2 pounds redfish
1/2 cup butter
Juice of 1 lemon
2 tablespoons dry white wine
1/4 cup Parmesan cheese
Paprika to taste

Sprinkle fish with salt and pepper to taste. Place butter in shallow baking dish. Heat in 450-degree oven until butter is melted and browned. Place fish in hot butter. Bake at 450 degrees for 15 minutes. Turn fish and baste with butter. Sprinkle with lemon juice, wine, cheese and paprika. Bake for 5 to 10 minutes longer or until fish flakes easily. Yield: 4 servings.

Approx Per Serving: Cal 522; Prot 62 g; T Fat 28.4 g; Chol 173 mg; Carbo 0.6 g; Sod 417 mg; Potas 1206 mg.

Sis Reilly
Lookout Mountain, Tennessee

SALMON PIE

1 unbaked 9-inch pie shell
1 10-ounce package frozen
broccoli spears
1 16-ounce can salmon
1 cup chopped celery
1 cup chopped green onions
3 hard-cooked eggs, chopped
1 cup mayonnaise
1 cup shredded Swiss cheese
Dillweed to taste

Place pie shell in glass pie plate. Bake according to package directions until light golden brown. Cook broccoli according to package directions; drain. Place in pie shell. Drain and flake salmon. Combine with celery, green onions, eggs, mayonnaise, cheese and dillweed in bowl; mix well. Pour over broccoli. Microwave on High for 6 to 8 minutes or until heated through.
Yield: 8 servings.

Approx Per Serving: Cal 440; Prot 16.5 g; T Fat 35.8 g; Chol 156 mg; Carbo 14.1 g; Sod 372 mg; Potas 437 mg.

Karma Pehrson
West Jordan, Utah

STUFFED BAKED FISH

2 cups bread crumbs
2 teaspoons chopped parsley
2 tablespoons chopped pickle
2 teaspoons chopped onion
2 tablespoons lemon juice
1/2 teaspoon salt
1/4 teaspoon pepper
1/2 cup melted butter
1 6-pound salmon
3 slices bacon
3/4 cup all-purpose flour

Combine bread crumbs, parsley, pickle, onion, lemon juice, salt, pepper and melted butter in bowl; mix well. Add a small amount of hot water if needed for desired consistency. Wash fish and pat dry inside and out. Stuff with bread crumb mixture; sew cavity closed. Season with salt and pepper to taste. Cut slits 2 inches apart in fish. Chop 1 piece of bacon. Place bacon pieces in slits. Wrap remaining bacon around fish. Coat well with flour. Place in baking dish. Bake at 350 degrees for 12 to 14 minutes per pound. Yield: 4 servings.

Approx Per Serving: Cal 1348; Prot 141 g; T Fat 69.6 g; Chol 440 mg; Carbo 30.8 g; Sod 1006 mg; Potas 3440 mg.

Frances Szczesniak
Rosemount, Minnesota

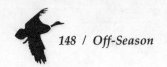

MONTANA FISH FRY

Fish fillets	Arrange fish skin side down on sheet of aluminum foil. Place on grill over hot coals. Brush with mixture of equal parts butter and lemon juice seasoned with garlic salt, salt and pepper. Grill, uncovered, just until fish begins to flake; do not overcook. Remove from foil with spatula; skin will stick to foil.
Butter	
Fresh lemon juice	
Garlic salt	
Salt	
Pepper	

Nutritional information for this recipe is not available.

Doug Alexander
Bozeman, Montana

BARBECUED TROUT

1 1½ to 2-pound rainbow trout	Clean trout, leaving fins, head and tail. Rinse and pat dry. Season with salt, pepper, garlic powder and ginger to taste. Fill cavity with onions. Sprinkle lemon juice over onions. Wrap with bacon. Double wrap in foil. Bake over medium coals in covered grill for 45 minutes. Yield: 3 servings.
Salt and pepper to taste	
Garlic powder and ginger to taste	
Chopped onions	
Lemon juice	
7 bacon slices	

Nutritional information for this recipe is not available.

Ruth and Larry Ruppenthal
Kitchener, Ontario

BEER BATTER TROUT

1 cup all-purpose flour	Combine flour, cornstarch, baking powder, sugar and red pepper in bowl. Add beer; mix well. Cut fish into 1-inch strips. Dip in batter. Fry in hot oil until golden brown. Yield: 6 servings.
1 cup cornstarch	
1 teaspoon baking powder	
1 teaspoon sugar	
1 teaspoon red pepper	
1 12-ounce bottle of beer	
2 pounds trout fillets	
Oil for frying	

Approx Per Serving: Cal 404; Prot 42.1 g; T Fat 6.9 g; Chol 110 mg; Carbo 36.4 g; Sod 110 mg; Potas 998 mg. Nutritional information does not include oil for frying.

Sandra L. Beitzel
Manitowoc, Wisconsin

HUDSON'S BEER BATTER FISH FILLETS

1 cup all-purpose flour
1 cup Hungry Jack pancake mix
2 eggs
1 12-ounce can beer
Fish fillets
Oil for deep frying

Combine flour, pancake mix, eggs and beer in large bowl; mix well. Add salt and pepper to taste. Dip fish fillets in batter. Deep-fry a few at a time in hot oil until golden brown.

Nutritional information for this recipe is not available.

John Hudson
Cedarville, Illinois

SHEP'S CLAM CASSEROLE

1¹/2 cups coarsely crushed butter crackers
1¹/2 cups drained chopped clams
¹/2 cup butter
1 egg
¹/3 cup milk

Alternate layers of cracker crumbs and clams in greased baking dish until all ingredients are used. Dot with butter. Beat egg with milk in bowl. Pour over layers, piercing layers with knife to absorb mixture well. Bake, covered, at 350 degrees for 30 minutes. Bake, uncovered, for 10 minutes longer or until brown.
Yield: 4 servings.

Approx Per Serving: Cal 481; Prot 19.9 g; T Fat 36.4 g; Chol 173 mg; Carbo 26.6 g; Sod 601 mg; Potas 469 mg.

Michael Wright
Ipswich, Massachusetts

Jeri Nelson of Springfield, South Dakota, dips fish fillets in flour, then in beaten egg, and then in cornflake crumbs. Arrange on a foil-lined baking pan and season to taste. Bake at 425 degrees for 15 minutes. Drizzle with melted butter and lemon juice. Bake at 375 degrees for 15 minutes longer.

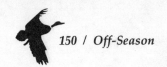

ITALIAN LINGUINE WITH CLAM SAUCE

2 onions, finely chopped
6 cloves of garlic, crushed
1 cup butter
1 bunch parsley, finely chopped
1/4 cup chopped oregano
8 cups chopped clams
with liquid
1 pound linguine
1/2 cup grated Romano cheese

Sauté onions and garlic in butter in saucepan until light brown. Add parsley and oregano. Sauté for 2 minutes. Add undrained clams. Season with salt and pepper to taste. Simmer for 30 minutes. Cook linguine according to package directions; drain. Place linguine in bowl. Top with clam sauce and cheese. Serve with tossed salad and garlic bread. Yield: 10 servings.

Approx Per Serving: Cal 400; Prot 14.1 g; T Fat 25.9 g; Chol 105 mg; Carbo 38.7 g; Sod 249 mg; Potas 287 mg.

Lorraine Matarese
Smyrna, Delaware

CRAB MEAT QUICHE

1 unbaked 10-inch deep-dish
pie shell
3 eggs
1 cup heavy cream
1 tablespoon tomato paste
1/2 teaspoon garlic salt
1/4 teaspoon red pepper
1/2 cup chopped green onions
1/2 cup chopped mushrooms
1/4 cup butter
1 1/2 cups fresh crab meat
2 tablespoons dry vermouth
1 cup shredded Cheddar cheese

Prick pie shell with fork. Bake at 425 degrees for 12 minutes. Beat eggs and cream in bowl. Add tomato paste, garlic salt and red pepper; mix well. Sauté green onions and mushrooms in butter in saucepan for 5 minutes. Add crab meat, vermouth and 1/2 cup cheese; mix well. Add crab meat mixture gradually to egg mixture, mixing well. Pour into pie shell. Bake at 375 degrees for 30 minutes. Sprinkle with remaining 1/2 cup cheese. Bake for 10 minutes or until knife inserted in center comes out clean.
Yield: 6 servings.

Approx Per Serving: Cal 431; Prot 18.1 g; T Fat 31.8 g; Chol 222 mg; Carbo 17 g; Sod 709 mg; Potas 319 mg.

W. N. Day
Norco, Louisiana

CRAB AND ARTICHOKE CASSEROLE

*1 14-ounce can artichoke
hearts
1 pound Blue crab meat
8 ounces fresh mushrooms,
sliced
6 tablespoons butter
3 tablespoons all-purpose flour
1¹/₂ cups milk
1 teaspoon Worcestershire
sauce
¹/₄ cup Sherry
¹/₂ teaspoon salt
Pepper to taste
¹/₄ cup Parmesan cheese
Paprika to taste*

Drain artichoke hearts and cut into quarters. Place in buttered shallow baking dish. Layer crab meat over artichokes. Sauté mushrooms in 3 tablespoons butter in skillet. Spoon over crab meat. Melt remaining 3 tablespoons butter in saucepan. Blend in flour. Add milk gradually. Cook over low heat until thickened, stirring constantly. Stir in Worcestershire sauce, Sherry, salt and pepper. Pour over casserole. Sprinkle with cheese and paprika. Bake at 375 degrees for 20 minutes. Yield: 6 servings.

Approx Per Serving: Cal 293; Prot 21.8 g; T Fat 15.8 g; Chol 109 mg; Carbo 14.6 g; Sod 669 mg; Potas 704 mg.

Coy Johnston

CRAB MEAT DRESSING

*8 slices French bread
1 large green bell pepper,
chopped
1 large onion, chopped
¹/₄ cup chopped celery
¹/₄ cup chopped parsley
2 tablespoons butter
Cayenne pepper to taste
1 pound crab meat
¹/₄ cup seasoned Italian
bread crumbs
2 tablespoons butter*

Toast French bread. Combine with water to just cover in bowl. Let soak for several minutes. Sauté green pepper, onion, celery and parsley in 2 tablespoons butter in skillet. Add cayenne pepper and salt to taste. Squeeze bread to remove moisture. Add bread and crab meat to vegetables; mix well. Place in baking dish. Top with bread crumbs. Dot with 2 tablespoons butter. Bake at 350 degrees for 40 minutes, stirring occasionally. Yield: 6 servings.

Nutritional information for this recipe is not available.

*Becky Fore
Wiggins, Mississippi*

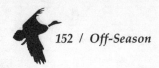
MOISE ISLAND CRAB CAKES

1 pound crab meat
1 pound potatoes, cooked,
mashed
3 eggs
1 medium onion, finely chopped
1 medium green bell pepper,
finely chopped
2 stalks celery, finely chopped
2¹/2 teaspoons cornstarch
¹/2 teaspoon salt
¹/2 teaspoon pepper
Corn oil for frying

Combine crab meat, potatoes, eggs, vegetables, cornstarch and seasonings in bowl; mix well. Shape into small patties. Fry in oil in skillet until light brown on both sides. Yield: 6 servings.

Approx Per Serving: Cal 196; Prot 20 g; T Fat 4.3 g; Chol 213 mg; Carbo 18.7 g; Sod 439 mg; Potas 629 mg. Nutritional information does not include oil for frying.

Ben Moise
Charleston, South Carolina

LASKY'S FRESH CRAB

¹/4 cup plus 2 tablespoons
olive oil
¹/2 teaspoon lemon juice
¹/2 cup chopped parsley
1 teaspoon garlic salt
¹/8 teaspoon pepper
1 fresh crab, cooked

Combine olive oil, lemon juice, parsley, garlic salt and pepper in bowl; mix well. Crack and disjoint crab, leaving in shell. Add to olive oil mixture. Marinate in refrigerator for 1¹/2 hours, stirring occasionally. Let stand at room temperature for 20 minutes. Serve with sourdough bread and white wine. Hunters at a duck club near Los Banos find that 1 crab is too much for 1 person and not enough for 2. Yield: 1¹/2 servings.

Approx Per Serving: Cal 604; Prot 20.7 g; T Fat 59 g; Chol 71.9 mg; Carbo 2.2 g; Sod 1765 mg; Potas 515 mg. Nutritional information includes all of marinade.

Fare Thee Well - Dolley

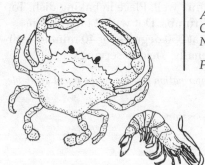

CRAB GRAVY

1 medium onion, finely chopped
2 tablespoons oregano
2 tablespoons chopped parsley
2 tablespoons basil
1¹/2 teaspoons minced garlic
¹/4 cup olive oil
2 28-ounce cans tomato purée
2 28-ounce cans water
15 crabs, cleaned

Sauté onion, oregano, parsley, basil and garlic in olive oil in saucepan until onion is tender. Add tomato purée and water; mix well. Simmer for several minutes. Add crabs. Simmer for 3 hours. Stir in salt to taste. Serve over cooked thin spaghetti. Yield: 15 servings.

Approx Per Serving: Cal 201; Prot 31.5 g; T Fat 7.3 g; Chol 108 mg; Carbo 6.5 g; Sod 679 mg; Potas 877 mg. Nutritional information does not include spaghetti.

Joe Bosco
Bay St. Louis, Mississippi

MAMMA'S PICKLED MUSSELS

¹/2 bushel mussels
2 tablespoons pickling spice
5 cups apple cider vinegar
3 medium onions, sliced
2 cups sugar
1 tablespoon salt

Cook mussels in boiling water in large saucepan until mussels open; drain. Remove mussel meat from shells, discarding shells and any unopened mussels. Fill hot sterilized jars ³/4 full with mussel meat. Tie each tablespoon pickling spice in cheesecloth bag. Combine with vinegar, onions, sugar and salt. Boil for 10 minutes. Strain, discarding cheesecloth bags. Spoon onions into jars. Fill with vinegar, leaving ¹/2 inch head space. Seal with 2-piece lids. Store for 2 to 3 days before using. Store in refrigerator after opening. Yield: 4 quarts.

Approx Per Quart: Cal 877; Prot 61.5 g; T Fat 143 g; Chol 340 mg; Carbo 127 g; Sod 3064 mg; Potas 2011 mg.

Lisa Laurence
Sullivan Harbor, Massachusetts

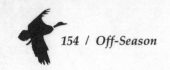

PANNED OYSTERS

1 dozen oysters
2 eggs
1/2 cup seasoned bread crumbs
2 tablespoons Parmesan cheese
1 teaspoon dillweed
Oil for frying

Drain oysters, reserving 2 tablespoons liquid. Beat eggs with reserved oyster liquid in bowl. Combine bread crumbs, cheese and dillweed in bowl. Add salt and pepper to taste. Dip oysters in egg mixture. Roll in crumb mixture, patting to coat well. Fry in 370-degree oil until golden brown. Drain on paper towel. Serve immediately. Yield: 2 servings.

Approx Per Serving: Cal 249; Prot 21.1 g; T Fat 11.8 g; Chol 371 mg; Carbo 12.9 g; Sod 411 mg; Potas 472 mg. Nutritional information does not include oil for frying.

W. N. Day
Norco, Louisiana

SCALLOP CASSEROLE

1 cup coarse fresh bread crumbs
1 cup butter cracker crumbs
1/2 cup melted unsalted butter
2 pounds scallops
1 1/2 cups whipping cream

Sauté bread crumbs and cracker crumbs in butter in saucepan until lightly toasted. Rinse scallops. Toss with crumbs, coating well. Place in 2-quart baking dish, leaving opening in center. Pour cream into center very gradually; rearrange scallops to fill center. Bake at 325 degrees for 30 to 40 minutes or until bubbly and liquid is nearly absorbed. Yield: 4 servings.

Approx Per Serving: Cal 846; Prot 42.6 g; T Fat 64.9 g; Chol 259 mg; Carbo 28.3 g; Sod 669 mg; Potas 845 mg.

Carolyn D. Connolly
Norwood, Massachusetts

BOURBON SUPREME SCALLOPS

1/2 cup Bourbon
1/4 cup soy sauce
1/4 cup packed brown sugar
1/4 cup minced onion
1/4 cup Dijon-style mustard
1 tablespoon Worcestershire
sauce
1 teaspoon salt
Pepper to taste
10 bacon slices, cut into thirds
15 large scallops, cut
into halves

Combine Bourbon, soy sauce, brown sugar, onion, mustard, Worcestershire sauce, salt and pepper in bowl; mix well. Cut scallops into halves. Add to marinade; mix well. Marinate for 1 to 2 hours, stirring occasionally; drain. Cut bacon slices into thirds. Wrap 1 piece bacon around each scallop half; secure with toothpick. Grill 4 inches from hot coals for 10 to 15 minutes or until bacon is crisp. May place on skewers or in hinged basket if preferred. Yield: 4 servings.

Nutritional information for this recipe is not available.

Norman Smith
Memphis, Tennessee

JEFF'S DRUNKEN SHRIMP WIGGLE

21/2 to 3 pounds large shrimp
1 to 2 ounces Old Bay
seasoning
3 16-ounce cans cheap beer

Sprinkle shrimp with seasoning. Combine with beer in saucepan. Bring to a boil. Cook until shrimp is no longer pink; drain. Yield: 4 servings.

Nutritional information for this recipe is not available.

Lisa Laurence
Sullivan Harbor, Massachusetts

Frances Szczesniah of Rosemount, Minnesota marinates salmon or trout in Italian salad dressing for 4 to 6 hours before grilling.

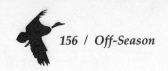

SHRIMP ROSEMARY

3 pounds unpeeled shrimp,
heads removed
1 cup melted butter
2 tablespoons Worcestershire
sauce
2 tablespoons lemon juice
Rosemary to taste
2 teaspoons coarsely
ground pepper

Place shrimp in large baking pan. Drizzle with mixture of butter, Worcestershire sauce and lemon juice. Sprinkle with rosemary and pepper. Broil for 20 minutes; do not overcook.
Yield: 6 servings.

Approx Per Serving: Cal 516; Prot 46.5 g; T Fat 34.6 g; Chol 428 mg; Carbo 3.3 g; Sod 644 mg; Potas 475 mg.

Markel R. Wyatt
Mobile, Alabama

SEAFOOD SUPREME

1 pound fresh mushrooms,
sliced
1/4 cup butter
1 can cream of shrimp soup
11/3 cups sour half and half
1/2 cup shredded Cheddar cheese
1/2 cup mayonnaise
2 cups uncooked thin
noodles, crushed
8 ounces cooked shrimp
1   8-ounce can crab meat
1   31/2-ounce can sliced
water chestnuts

Sauté mushrooms in butter in skillet. Combine with soup, half and half, cheese and mayonnaise in bowl; mix well. Fold in noodles, shrimp, crab meat and water chestnuts. Spoon into buttered baking dish. Bake, covered, at 325 degrees for 30 to 40 minutes. Bake, uncovered, for 10 minutes longer. Garnish with chopped black olives and parsley. Yield: 8 servings.

Approx Per Serving: Cal 542; Prot 24 g; T Fat 26.9 g; Chol 132 mg; Carbo 51.3 g; Sod 624 mg; Potas 572 mg.

Mrs. John F. Kaiser
Sun Prairie, Wisconsin

For a tangy mustard sauce to serve with poached fish, W.N. Day of Norco, Louisana, sautés 1/2 cup mushrooms in 2 tablespoons of butter. Add 1 tablespoon of flour, 1/2 cup of light cream, 2 tablespoons of lemon juice, 8 drops of Tabasco sauce, 2 tablespoons of Dijon mustard, garlic salt and salt and pepper to taste. Cook for 1 minute, stirring constantly.

Feeding Calls

Vegetables, Side Dishes and Breads

First Snow–Pheasants

Jim Killen

PHEASANT SANS SOUCI

1 pheasant, cut up
Butter
2 cans chicken broth
1 cup sliced mushrooms
Several sprigs of parsley
1 cup white wine

Brown pheasant in a small amount of butter in skillet. Place in 9x13-inch baking dish. Add broth to pan drippings; mix well. Add mushrooms, parsley and wine. Pour over pheasant. Bake, tightly covered with foil, at 325 degrees for 3 hours or until very tender. Serve with wild rice and fresh spinach salad. This recipe keeps the pheasant moist and is excellent for older bird. Yield: 4 servings.

Karen Killen

ANNE'S ARTICHOKE CASSEROLE

4 16-ounce cans artichoke
hearts
1/2 loaf stale French bread
1/4 cup butter
1/4 cup extra-virgin olive oil
1 clove of garlic, minced
1/4 cup sliced black olives
1/4 cup sliced stuffed
green olives
3 tablespoons green olive liquid
1/2 teaspoon salt
1/2 cup seasoned bread crumbs

Drain artichoke hearts, reserving liquid. Cut artichokes into quarters. Set aside artichokes and 1/2 cup reserved liquid. Combine French bread with remaining artichoke liquid in bowl, adding water if necessary to soak bread well. Melt butter in skillet. Add olive oil and garlic. Sauté garlic until tender. Squeeze liquid out of soaked bread. Crumble into skillet. Add olives, olive liquid, salt, artichoke hearts and reserved 1/2 cup artichoke liquid; mix well. Cook over low heat until heated through. Spoon into baking dish. Top with seasoned bread crumbs. Bake at 350 degrees until browned and bubbly.
Yield: 10 servings.

Approx Per Serving: Cal 291; Prot 7.9 g; T Fat 13.9 g; Chol 12.4 mg; Carbo 37.8 g; Sod 658 mg; Potas 519 mg.

Anne Babin
Houma, Louisiana

CALICO BEANS

1 pound ground venison
6 ounces bacon, chopped
1 medium onion, chopped
1 16-ounce can kidney beans
1 16-ounce can butter beans
1 28-ounce can pork and beans
1/2 cup packed brown sugar
1/2 cup catsup
2 tablespoons vinegar
1/2 teaspoon salt

Brown venison, bacon and onion in skillet, stirring until venison is crumbly; drain. Drain kidney beans and butter beans, reserving liquid. Add drained beans and pork and beans to skillet; mix well. Spoon into 9x13-inch baking dish. Combine brown sugar, catsup, vinegar and salt in bowl; mix well. Pour over bean mixture. Bake at 350 degrees for 1 hour, adding a small amount of the reserved bean liquid if mixture becomes too dry. Yield: 12 servings.

Approx Per Serving: Cal 319; Prot 23.1 g; T Fat 9 g; Chol 41 mg; Carbo 37.3 g; Sod 944 mg; Potas 633 mg.

Julie and Dale Thornburg
Beatrice, Nebraska

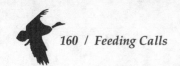

BROCCOLI AND CREAM CHEESE CASSEROLE

1 medium onion, chopped
6 tablespoons margarine
2 tablespoons all-purpose flour
1 cup milk
8 ounces cream cheese, chopped
2 10-ounce packages frozen
chopped broccoli, thawed
3/4 cup seasoned bread crumbs

Sauté onion in margarine in skillet over medium heat. Stir in flour. Add milk all at once, stirring constantly. Add cream cheese. Cook until cheese is melted and mixture is bubbly, stirring constantly. Place broccoli in 2-quart baking dish. Pour cream cheese sauce over top. Stir in 1/2 cup bread crumbs. Bake at 350 degrees for 40 minutes. Sprinkle with remaining 1/4 cup bread crumbs. Bake for 5 minutes longer.
Yield: 8 servings.

Approx Per Serving: Cal 233; Prot 5.9 g; T Fat 19.9 g; Chol 35.1 mg; Carbo 9.7 g; Sod 252 mg; Potas 323 mg.

Janet L. Franke
Decatur, Illinois

MARINATED CARROTS

5 cups sliced carrots
1 can tomato soup
1/2 cup vegetable oil
3/4 cup white vinegar
1 cup sugar
1 tablespoon prepared mustard
1 teaspoon salt
1 teaspoon pepper
1 medium onion, chopped
1 small green bell pepper,
chopped

Cook carrots in salted water to cover in saucepan just until tender. Drain and cool carrots. Combine soup, oil, vinegar, sugar, mustard, salt, pepper, onion and green pepper in airtight container; mix well. Add carrots. Marinate in refrigerator for 12 hours to 2 weeks. Drain and serve. May reserve dressing to use on other salads. Yield: 10 servings.

Approx Per Serving: Cal 213; Prot 1 g; T Fat 11.3 g; Chol 0 mg; Carbo 29.1 g; Sod 354 mg; Potas 243 mg.

Kathy Meyer
Medford, Oregon

CORN CASSEROLE

1 5-ounce package saffron rice
¹/₂ cup margarine
1 can cream of celery soup
1 16-ounce can Mexicorn
1 cup shredded Velveeta cheese

Cook rice according to package directions. Stir in margarine until melted. Add soup, corn and cheese; mix well. Spoon into baking dish. Bake at 350 degrees for 30 minutes. Yield: 6 servings.

Approx Per Serving: Cal 375; Prot 8.7 g; T Fat 23.4 g; Chol 22.7 mg; Carbo 35.1 g; Sod 681 mg; Potas 187 mg.

Mrs. Bill Purvis
Pelahatchie, Mississippi

FRESH MUSHROOM CASSEROLE

2 pounds fresh mushrooms, sliced
1 tablespoon butter
2 cups shredded Cheddar cheese
1 4-ounce can sliced black olives, drained
1 tablespoon all-purpose flour
1 tablespoon butter
1 cup bread crumbs
1 tablespoon butter
Pinch of thyme

Sauté mushrooms in 1 tablespoon butter in skillet until mushrooms render their juice. Layer half the mushrooms, cheese, olives and flour in baking dish. Dot with 1 tablespoon butter. Repeat layers of mushrooms, cheese, olives and flour. Top with bread crumbs, remaining 1 tablespoon butter and thyme. Bake at 350 degrees for 1 hour. Yield: 6 servings.

Approx Per Serving: Cal 296; Prot 13.5 g; T Fat 23.4 g; Chol 55.2 mg; Carbo 12.6 g; Sod 469 mg; Potas 614 mg.

Shirley Flinn
Lacombe, Alberta, Canada

For a delicious broccoli casserole, Karen Lane of North Pole, Alaska, combines 2 packages of frozen chopped broccoli, 1 cup of mayonnaise, 1 can of cream of mushroom soup and 1 chopped onion in casserole. Top with 1 cup of shredded Cheddar cheese and 20 crushed butter crackers; dot with butter. Bake, covered, at 350 degrees for 1 hour. Bake, uncovered, for 15 minutes longer.

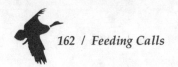

SWEET AND SOUR ONIONS

4 large sweet onions, sliced
1/4 cup butter
1/4 cup water
1/4 cup sugar
1/4 cup vinegar
1 teaspoon salt
1/8 teaspoon pepper

Place onions in buttered baking dish. Melt butter in saucepan. Stir in water, sugar, vinegar, salt and pepper. Pour over onions. Bake at 350 degrees for 1 hour. Yield: 8 servings.

Approx Per Serving: Cal 89; Prot 0.5 g; T Fat 5.9 g; Chol 15.5 mg; Carbo 9.6 g; Sod 316 mg; Potas 72.1 mg.

Dorothy Larsen
Southworth, Washington

ONION CASSEROLE

4 cups thinly sliced onions
4 medium tomatoes,
peeled, sliced
1 teaspoon salt
1/4 teaspoon pepper
1/2 teaspoon basil
6 slices American cheese, cut
into halves
1 can cream of mushroom soup
1/4 cup Sherry
1/2 cup bread crumbs
3 tablespoons melted butter

Cook onions in water to cover in saucepan for 10 minutes; drain. Layer onions, tomatoes, seasonings and cheese 1/2 at a time in 1 1/2-quart baking dish. Blend soup and Sherry in bowl. Pour over layers. Toss crumbs with butter. Sprinkle over casserole. Bake at 350 degrees for 35 minutes. Yield: 10 servings.

Approx Per Serving: Cal 149; Prot 5.2 g; T Fat 10.1 g; Chol 25.7 mg; Carbo 8.5 g; Sod 622 mg; Potas 224 mg.

Donna O'Brien
Salt Lake City, Utah

George Robinson of Jackson, Mississippi, remembers his mother's recipe for greens which combines 3 bundles of well washed greens, 1 sliced onion, a ham hock, 1 1/2 cups of sugar, 1 quart of water, lots of pepper, a dash of salt and 1/4 cup butter. Cook in a heavy saucepan over medium heat for 1 to 1 1/2 hours.

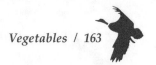

ITALIAN POTATO AND TOMATO CASSEROLE

1 tablespoon salad oil
4 large russet potatoes, peeled,
sliced 1/4 inch thick
3 medium tomatoes,
peeled, sliced
1 large sweet Spanish onion,
thinly sliced
1/4 cup Parmesan cheese
1/2 cup shredded provolone
cheese
1/2 teaspoon oregano
Pepper to taste
3 tablespoons margarine

Oil shallow baking dish with salad oil. Layer potatoes, tomatoes, onion, cheeses and seasonings in prepared baking dish until all ingredients are used. Dot with margarine. Bake at 400 degrees for 50 minutes or until vegetables are tender and top is brown. Yield: 6 servings.

Approx Per Serving: Cal 246; Prot 8.4 g; T Fat 14.3 g; Chol 15.9 mg; Carbo 22.1 g; Sod 314 mg; Potas 473 mg.

Barbara Ludwig
Reno, Nevada

POTATO AND CAULIFLOWER PURÉE

1 1/4 pounds cauliflowerets
1 medium potato, peeled,
chopped
1/2 cup whipping cream
1/2 cup freshly grated
Parmesan cheese
3 tablespoons unsalted butter
1/8 teaspoon freshly ground
white pepper
Large pinch of freshly
grated nutmeg

Steam cauliflower and potatoes in saucepan for 12 minutes or just until tender. Place in food processor container. Add cream, Parmesan cheese, butter, pepper and nutmeg. Process until smooth. Serve immediately or reheat in double boiler over hot water at serving time.
Yield: 8 servings.

Approx Per Serving: Cal 144; Prot 4.2 g; T Fat 11.5 g; Chol 36 mg; Carbo 7.5 g; Sod 147 mg; Potas 326 mg.

Jean Auchterionie
Birmingham, Michigan

ITALIAN SPINACH

1 28-ounce can spinach
6 cloves of garlic, minced
1/2 medium onion, chopped
2/3 cup olive oil
1 28-ounce can tomatoes

Drain spinach and press to remove excess moisture. Sauté garlic and onion in olive oil in 10-inch iron skillet. Add spinach and tomatoes. Simmer for 10 to 15 minutes, stirring occasionally. Spoon into serving bowl. Serve with freshly grated Parmesan cheese. Yield: 8 servings.

Approx Per Serving: Cal 204; Prot 3.9 g; T Fat 18.6 g; Chol 0 mg; Carbo 8.5 g; Sod 478 mg; Potas 573 mg.

Henry M. Jones
Memphis, Tennessee

LAYERED SPINACH SUPREME

1 cup buttermilk baking mix
1/4 cup milk
2 eggs
1/4 cup chopped onion
1 10-ounce package chopped spinach, thawed, drained
1/2 cup Parmesan cheese
4 ounces Monterey Jack cheese, cut into 1/2-inch cubes
12 ounces creamed cottage cheese
2 cloves of garlic, crushed
1/2 teaspoon salt

Combine baking mix, milk, eggs and onion in mixer bowl; mix well. Spoon into greased 8x12-inch baking dish. Combine spinach, cheeses, garlic and salt in bowl; mix well. Spoon evenly over batter in baking dish. Bake at 375 degrees for 30 minutes or until set. Let stand for 5 minutes before serving. Yield: 8 servings.

Approx Per Serving: Cal 291; Prot 16 g; T Fat 13.9 g; Chol 92.7 mg; Carbo 24.8 g; Sod 921 mg; Potas 333 mg.

Stephanie Connolly
Barrington, Illinois

Ann Dissell of Freeport, Maine, serves apple and cinnamon-flavored rice with duck. Sauté the slices of 1 apple in 1/4 cup butter. Stir in 2 cups cooked rice, 1/2 cup cooked wild rice and 1/8 teaspoon cinnamon.

ORANGE SWEET POTATOES

1¹/2 pounds sweet potatoes
1 tablespoon margarine
¹/4 cup orange juice
¹/8 teaspoon salt
¹/4 teaspoon pepper
¹/4 teaspoon ginger
3 oranges, peeled, chopped
¹/4 cup toasted slivered almonds

Pierce potatoes with fork. Bake at 400 degrees for 30 minutes or until tender. Peel potatoes. Mash pulp with margarine, orange juice, salt, pepper and ginger in bowl. Stir in oranges. Spoon into baking dish. Bake at 400 degrees for 45 minutes or until heated through. Top with almonds. Bake for 15 minutes longer if desired. Yield: 6 servings.

Approx Per Serving: Cal 219; Prot 3.5 g; T Fat 5.3 g; Chol 0 mg; Carbo 41.1 g; Sod 85.8 mg; Potas 449.1 mg.

Sarah Ann Rogers
Anchorage, Alaska

MIXED VEGETABLE CASSEROLE

4 large carrots
2 10-ounce packages frozen Italian green beans
1 16-ounce can stewed tomatoes
1¹/4 teaspoons minced onion
1 19-ounce can whole mushrooms, drained
1¹/4 teaspoons salt
³/4 teaspoon rosemary
3 tablespoons butter

Cook carrots in boiling water to cover for 10 minutes or until tender-crisp; drain. Cook green beans according to package directions; drain. Drain tomatoes, reserving juice. Combine tomatoes with onion, mushrooms, salt and rosemary in bowl. Add enough reserved tomato juice to make of desired consistency. Alternate layers of carrots, beans and tomato mixture in 2-quart baking dish until all ingredients are used. Dot with butter. Bake at 350 degrees for 30 minutes. Yield: 8 servings.

Approx Per Serving: Cal 100; Prot 3.2 g; T Fat 4.8 g; Chol 11.6 mg; Carbo 13.9 g; Sod 1169 mg; Potas 412 mg.

Susan Algard
Helena, Montana

RICE CASSEROLE

1 cup uncooked rice
¹/₂ cup butter
1 can consommé
1 consommé can water
1 4-ounce can whole
mushrooms, drained
2 tablespoons chopped parsley
³/₄ cup seedless grapes

Sauté rice in butter in saucepan for 5 minutes. Stir in consommé and water. Pour into baking dish. Bake at 350 degrees for 50 minutes. Add mushrooms, parsley and grapes; mix gently with fork. Bake for 10 minutes longer.
Yield: 6 servings.

Approx Per Serving: Cal 206; Prot 2.5 g; T Fat 11.8 g; Chol 31.2 mg; Carbo 23.2 g; Sod 274 mg; Potas 107 mg.

Lynn M. Carr
Pensacola, Florida

BROCCOLI AND RICE CASSEROLE

1 cup chopped onion
1 cup chopped celery
¹/₂ cup margarine
2 10-ounce packages frozen
chopped broccoli, thawed
2 cups minute rice
2 cans mushroom soup
1 8-ounce jar Cheez Whiz

Sauté onion and celery in margarine in saucepan. Stir in broccoli, rice, soup and Cheez Whiz. Spoon into baking dish. Bake, covered with foil, at 350 degrees for 1 hour. Yield: 8 servings.

Approx Per Serving: Cal 384; Prot 11.1 g; T Fat 24 g; Chol 18.8 mg; Carbo 32.8 g; Sod 1094 mg; Potas 375 mg.

Peggy Arvin
Caldwell, Idaho

WILD GAME CASSEROLE

1 cup wild rice
1 4-ounce can mushroom
pieces, drained
¹/₂ package Knorr dry vegetable
soup mix
2 tablespoons chopped chives
1 duck breast, chopped
2¹/₂ cups chicken broth

Combine rice, mushrooms, dry soup mix, chives and duck in bowl; mix well. Stir in chicken broth. Spoon into baking dish. Bake, covered, at 325 degrees for 1¹/₂ hours or until liquid is absorbed. Yield: 6 servings.

Approx Per Serving: Cal 139; Prot 9.8 g; T Fat 1.8 g; Chol 14.1 mg; Carbo 20.7 g; Sod 448 mg; Potas 222 mg.

Jon Sandholm
Minnetrista, Minnesota

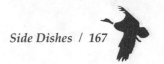

WILD RICE CASSEROLE

3 cups boiling water
1 cup wild rice
1¹/₂ pounds ground beef
6 tablespoons chopped onion
¹/₄ cup oil
1 can beef consommé
1 consommé can water
2 4-ounce cans sliced
mushrooms
2 cans cream of chicken soup
1 cup chopped celery
¹/₂ cup chopped almonds
2 sprigs of parsley, chopped
1 bay leaf, crumbled
1¹/₂ teaspoons salt
¹/₄ teaspoon onion salt
¹/₄ teaspoon garlic salt
¹/₄ teaspoon paprika
¹/₄ teaspoon Accent
¹/₄ teaspoon poultry seasoning
¹/₈ teaspoon thyme

Pour 3 cups boiling water over rice in bowl. Let stand for 15 minutes. Brown ground beef with onion in oil in skillet, stirring until ground beef is crumbly; drain. Drain rice. Add consommé, 1 can water, undrained mushrooms, soup, celery, almonds, parsley, seasonings and ground beef to rice; mix well. Spoon into 9x13-inch baking dish. Refrigerate overnight. Bake, covered, at 350 degrees for 2¹/₂ hours. Bake, uncovered, for 30 minutes longer. Yield: 10 servings.

Approx Per Serving: Cal 394; Prot 23 g; T Fat 25.3 g; Chol 63.8 mg; Carbo 19.8 g; Sod 1238 mg; Potas 478 mg.

Frances Szczesniak
Rosemount, Minnesota

VINAIGRETTE ON WILD RICE

1¹/₂ cups chopped carrots
1¹/₂ cups chopped celery
1 cup finely chopped parsley
8 cups cooked wild rice
¹/₂ cup coarsely broken pecans
1 cup salad oil
1 cup olive oil
²/₃ cup Sherry wine vinegar
1¹/₂ tablespoons Dijon-style
mustard
1¹/₂ tablespoons finely
chopped shallots
2 teaspoons salt
1 teaspoon pepper

Blanch carrots and celery in water in saucepan; drain. Combine with parsley, wild rice and pecans in large bowl. Combine salad oil, olive oil, vinegar, mustard, shallots, salt and pepper in bowl; mix well. Add to rice mixture; toss to mix well. Serve at room temperature over salad greens. Yield: 20 servings.

Approx Per Serving: Cal 320; Prot 4 g; T Fat 24.2 g; Chol 0 mg; Carbo 21.3 g; Sod 310 mg; Potas 281 mg. Nutritional information does not include salad greens.

Mary Jane Waltemate
Steeleville, Illinois

WILD RICE DISH

1 6-ounce can mushrooms,
drained
1 small onion, chopped
1 cup chopped celery
1/2 cup slivered almonds
1/2 cup margarine
1 cup wild rice
3 cups chicken broth

Sauté mushrooms, onion, celery and almonds in margarine in saucepan until tender. Stir in rice, broth and salt to taste. Spoon into baking dish. Bake, covered, at 350 degrees for 1 hour. Bake, uncovered, for 30 minutes longer.
Yield: 8 servings.

Approx Per Serving: Cal 198; Prot 5.1 g; T Fat 16.5 g; Chol 0.4 mg; Carbo 8.9 g; Sod 549 mg; Potas 237 mg.

Darla Glawe
Vergas, Minnesota

SAUSAGE AND WILD RICE CASSEROLE

8 ounces wild rice
1 1/2 pounds mild bulk sausage
2 cups chopped celery
1 medium onion, chopped
1 tablespoon butter
1 can cream of celery soup
1 can cream of mushroom soup
1 1/2 soup cans milk

Pour enough boiling water over rice in bowl to cover well. Let stand overnight. Drain rice. Cook rice according to package directions for 30 minutes or until most rice grains have opened. Drain and cool. Brown sausage in skillet, stirring until sausage is crumbly; drain. Sauté celery and onion in butter in skillet for 5 to 8 minutes. Combine soups and milk in saucepan; mix well. Cook until heated through. Add sausage and rice; mix well. Spoon into 3-quart baking dish. Bake at 350 degrees for 45 minutes. May cook in Crock•Pot on Low for 5 hours if preferred.
Yield: 20 servings.

Nutritional information for this recipe is not available.

Judy Tomke
Midland, Michigan

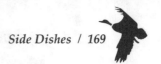

APPLE DRESSING FOR GAME BIRDS

2 tart apples, peeled, sliced
1/2 cup raisins
2 tablespoons butter
2 tablespoons currant jelly
2 tablespoons sugar
1/2 cup water
1 1/2 cups bread crumbs
1 egg yolk

Combine apples, raisins, butter, jelly, sugar and water in saucepan. Simmer until apples are tender; remove from heat. Stir in bread crumbs and egg yolk. Stuff into duck or goose. Roast as desired. May bake in baking dish at 350 degrees for 30 minutes to 1 hour if preferred.
Yield: 2 servings.

Approx Per Serving: Cal 756; Prot 13.3 g; T Fat 19.7 g; Chol 167 mg; Carbo 137 g; Sod 747 mg; Potas 619 mg.

Meredith Sterling
Thompson Falls, Montana

CORN BREAD DRESSING

2 8 1/2-ounce packages corn muffin mix
2/3 cup milk
2 eggs
2 13-ounce cans chicken broth
2 cups chopped celery
1 large onion, chopped

Combine corn muffin mix, milk and eggs in bowl. Mix just until moistened; batter will be lumpy. Pour into greased 10-inch cast-iron skillet. Bake at 400 degrees for 15 to 20 minutes or until golden brown. Cool until corn bread can be easily handled. Combine chicken broth, celery and onion in saucepan. Simmer until vegetables are tender. Alternate layers of crumbled corn bread and chicken broth mixture in baking dish until all ingredients are used. Bake at 350 degrees for 30 minutes or until golden brown.
Yield: 8 servings.

Approx Per Serving: Cal 173; Prot 5.4 g; T Fat 5.9 g; Chol 71.6 mg; Carbo 24.8 g; Sod 614 mg; Potas 250 mg.

Jan and Bill Gilliand
Chicopee, Massachusetts

BOB'S SASKATOON MALLARD STUFFING

2 cups bread crumbs
1 cup coarsely chopped celery
1 cup coarsely chopped onion
1 cup coarsely chopped parsley
1/4 teaspoon sage
1/4 teaspoon rosemary
1/4 teaspoon thyme
1/4 teaspoon marjoram
1/2 cup melted butter

Combine bread crumbs, celery, onion, parsley and seasonings in bowl; mix well. Drizzle with melted butter; mix well. Stuff into 2 large mallards. Roast in covered roaster at 325 to 350 degrees as desired, uncovering for last few minutes to brown well. Yield: 4 servings.

Approx Per Serving: Cal 287; Prot 3.1 g; T Fat 24.1 g; Chol 62.1 mg; Carbo 16.2 g; Sod 342 mg; Potas 262 mg.

Bob Rogers
Saskatoon, Saskatchewan, Canada

CRANBERRY CHUTNEY

1 12-ounce package cranberries
2 cups packed brown sugar
1 cup chopped celery
1 small onion, chopped
2 medium apples, peeled, chopped
1 cup raisins
1 cup chopped walnuts
1/2 cup lemon juice
1 cup water
1/2 teaspoon ginger
1/2 teaspoon cloves

Combine cranberries with brown sugar, celery, onion, apples, raisins, walnuts, lemon juice, water and spices in large heavy saucepan. Bring to a boil; reduce heat. Simmer for 20 minutes, stirring frequently. Spoon into 1/2-pint jars, leaving 1/2 inch headspace. Seal with 2-piece lids. Store in cool place. Yield: 7 cups.

Approx Per Cup: Cal 469; Prot 5.6 g; T Fat 10.6 g; Chol 0 mg; Carbo 95.9 g; Sod 51.7 mg; Potas 645 mg.

Irene Smith
Sprucedale, Ontario, Canada

Judy Bayless of Billings, Montana, makes salsa by combining 1 pound of sliced onions, 5 pounds of peeled tomatoes, 1 1/2 pounds of thinly sliced green bell peppers, 1/2 pound of hot peppers, 1/3 cup of lemon juice, 2 teaspoons of salt and 1/2 teaspoon of freshly ground pepper. Simmer to desired consistency.

SALSA

5 quarts tomatoes, peeled,
chopped
3 cups chopped onions
2 cups chopped green
bell peppers
4 dried red peppers, crushed
2 cloves of garlic, minced
1/4 cup sugar
1 tablespoon cumin
3 tablespoons salt
1 tablespoon pepper
1/2 cup cornstarch

Combine tomatoes, onions, green peppers, red peppers, garlic, sugar and seasonings in large heavy saucepan. Blend cornstarch with enough water to form a thin paste. Stir into tomato mixture. Cook over low heat for 1 hour, stirring frequently. Spoon into 1-pint jars, leaving 1/2 inch headspace. Seal with 2-piece lids. Store in cool place. Yield: 8 pints.

Approx Per Pint: Cal 177; Prot 5.3 g; T Fat 1.5 g; Chol 0 mg; Carbo 40.7 g; Sod 2439 mg; Potas 1148 mg.

Peggy D. Kuck
Aberdeen, South Dakota

APPLE BREAD

1 cup margarine, softened
2 cups sugar
4 eggs
4 cups all-purpose flour
2 teaspoons soda
1 tablespoon cinnamon
1 teaspoon salt
1/4 cup milk
2 teaspoons vinegar
31/2 cups chopped apples
1/4 cup sugar
1 teaspoon cinnamon

Cream margarine and 2 cups sugar in mixer bowl until light and fluffy. Blend in eggs. Combine flour, soda, 1 tablespoon cinnamon and salt in bowl. Mix milk and vinegar in small bowl. Add dry ingredients to creamed mixture alternately with milk mixture, beginning and ending with dry ingredients. Stir in apples. Spoon into 2 greased loaf pans. Mix 1/4 cup sugar and 1 teaspoon cinnamon in small bowl. Sprinkle over batter. Bake at 350 degrees for 1 hour. Remove to wire rack to cool. Yield: 24 servings.

Approx Per Serving: Cal 240; Prot 3.4 g; T Fat 8.9 g; Chol 46 mg; Carbo 37.3 g; Sod 260 mg; Potas 57.5 mg.

Janet L. Franke
Decatur, Illinois

EASY GARLIC BREAD

1/2 cup melted butter
1 teaspoon garlic salt
2 sprigs fresh parsley, chopped
1   14-ounce loaf frozen bread dough, thawed

Combine butter, garlic salt and parsley in small bowl; mix well. Shape bread dough into 1-inch balls. Dip each ball in butter mixture. Place in loaf pan. Drizzle with remaining butter mixture. Let rise, covered, for 3 to 4 hours. Bake at 350 degrees for 20 minutes. Invert onto serving plate. Pull apart to serve. Yield: 12 servings.

Approx Per Serving: Cal 171; Prot 3.6 g; T Fat 9.1 g; Chol 20.7 mg; Carbo 18.4 g; Sod 449 mg; Potas 88.2 mg.

Judy Nugent
Waupun, Wisconsin

ELLEN'S LIMPA

1/2 cup packed dark brown sugar
1/2 cup dark molasses
1/4 cup margarine
2 cups water
1 tablespoon grated orange rind
1/4 teaspoon cardamom
1 teaspoon aniseed
1 teaspoon salt
1 package dry yeast
21/2 cups all-purpose flour
3 cups rye flour
1/2 to 11/2 cups all-purpose flour
1 egg white, beaten
1/2 teaspoon crushed aniseed

Combine brown sugar, molasses, margarine, water, orange rind, cardamom, aniseed and salt in saucepan. Boil for 3 minutes. Cool mixture to 105 to 115 degrees. Combine with yeast in bowl; mix well. Add 21/2 cups all-purpose flour; beat until smooth. Add rye flour and enough all-purpose flour to form a soft dough; mix well. Let rest, covered with bowl, on lightly floured surface for 10 minutes. Knead until smooth and elastic. Place in greased bowl, turning to grease surface. Let rise, covered with plastic wrap and hot damp towel, until doubled in bulk. Punch dough down. Let rise for 30 minutes. Shape into 2 loaves. Place in greased loaf pans. Brush with beaten egg white. Sprinkle with crushed aniseed. Bake at 375 degrees for 40 minutes or until loaves test done. Remove to wire rack to cool. Yield: 24 servings.

Approx Per Serving: Cal 175; Prot 4.1 g; T Fat 2.4 g; Chol 0 mg; Carbo 34.8 g; Sod 125 mg; Potas 278 mg.

Ellen Olson
DePere, Wisconsin

MEXICAN CORN BREAD

1 cup self-rising cornmeal
1/2 teaspoon soda
1 teaspoon salt
2 eggs
1 cup buttermilk
1/3 cup oil
1 medium onion, chopped
2 jalapeño peppers,
  finely chopped
1 1/2 cups shredded
  Cheddar cheese
1 8 1/2-ounce can cream-
  style corn

Combine cornmeal, soda, salt, eggs, buttermilk and oil in large bowl. Add onion, peppers, cheese and corn; mix well. Pour into large greased iron skillet. Bake at 400 degrees for 30 minutes or until golden brown. Yield: 6 servings.

Approx Per Serving: Cal 792; Prot 34.4 g; T Fat 49.7 g; Chol 202 mg; Carbo 39 g; Sod 1720 mg; Potas 485 mg.

Mrs. Bill Purvis
Pelahatchie, Mississippi

BLUEBERRY MUFFINS

1/2 cup butter, softened
1 cup sugar
2 eggs
1 teaspoon vanilla extract
1/2 cup milk
2 cups all-purpose flour
2 teaspoons baking powder
1/4 teaspoon salt
2 cups blueberries

Cream butter and sugar in mixer bowl until light and fluffy. Blend in eggs and vanilla. Add milk, flour, baking powder and salt; mix well. Fold in blueberries. Spoon into paper-lined muffin cups. Bake at 375 degrees for 20 minutes.
Yield: 12 servings.

Approx Per Serving: Cal 242; Prot 3.8 g; T Fat 9.2 g; Chol 67.7 mg; Carbo 36.6 g; Sod 182 mg; Potas 69.7 mg.

Heather Bayless
Mt. Pleasant, South Carolina

Linda Heinke of Madison, Wisconsin, serves her Yugoslavian grand-mother's Polenta recipe with game birds. Gradually stir a mixture of 1 cup of cornmeal, 1 cup of cold water and 1 teaspoon of salt into 4 cups of hot water in double boiler. Cook for 15 minutes, stirring frequently.

ZUCCHINI MUFFINS

4 eggs
4 cups grated zucchini
4 teaspoons vanilla extract
1 teaspoon salt
6 packets Sweet 'N Low
4½ ounces dry cream of wheat
1 teaspoon soda
1½ cups nonfat dry
milk powder
3 cups crushed pineapple
2½ teaspoons pumpkin
pie spice
1½ teaspoons cinnamon
1½ teaspoons allspice
1¼ teaspoons nutmeg

Beat eggs in mixer bowl. Add zucchini, vanilla, salt, Sweet 'N Low, cream of wheat, soda, dry milk powder, pineapple and spices; mix well. Fill greased muffin cups ¾ full. Bake at 400 degrees for 20 minutes. Yield: 12 servings.

Approx Per Serving: Cal 198; Prot 14.7 g; T Fat 2.5 g; Chol 96.8 mg; Carbo 29.7 g; Sod 524 mg; Potas 717 mg.

Joan Marsh
Humboldt, Tennessee

MAINE RYE PANCAKES

1 cup rye flour
1 cup all-purpose flour
1 egg
1 cup buttermilk
1 teaspoon soda
6 tablespoons molasses
Oil for deep frying

Sift rye flour and all-purpose flour together. Beat egg in mixer bowl. Mix buttermilk and soda in small bowl. Add buttermilk and molasses to egg; mix well. Add sifted flours; mix well. Batter will be stiff. Drop by teaspoonfuls into hot oil. Deep-fry until golden brown. Serve with maple syrup. Yield: 6 servings.

Approx Per Serving: Cal 222; Prot 6.7 g; T Fat 2.8 g; Chol 51.2 mg; Carbo 43 g; Sod 185 mg; Potas 721 mg. Nutritional information does not include oil for deep frying.

Barbara Kamman
Old Lyme, Connecticut

After Hours

Desserts and Beverages

The Wary Ones

Jim Killen

FRIED WILD TURKEY BREAST

1 wild turkey breast
2 cups milk
3 cups Bisquick
1 can beer
2 tablespoons sugar
3 cups peanut oil

Skin turkey breast; remove breast from bone. Cut breast into 1-inch cubes. Marinate in milk for 30 to 45 minutes. Combine Bisquick, beer and sugar in bowl to make a thick batter. Heat oil in electric skillet to 375 degrees. Remove turkey from milk; dip into batter. Fry until golden brown. Drain on paper towels. Serve with toothpicks. Yield: 4 servings.

Karen Killen

BEJEWELLED CHRISTMAS CHARLOTTE

2 8-ounce packages
ladyfingers
1 egg white, beaten
1 cup unsalted butter, softened
5 ounces sifted confectioners'
sugar
1 ounce liqueur
5 egg yolks
2 ounces glacéed cherries,
coarsely chopped
2 ounces glacéed pineapple,
coarsely chopped
5 ounces walnuts,
finely chopped
2 ounces walnuts, coarsely
broken
2 ounces toasted hazelnuts,
coarsely broken
1 cup whipping cream
1 ounce confectioners' sugar
1 ounce liqueur

Brush ladyfingers with egg white. Line Charlotte mold with lady fingers. Cream butter and 5 ounces confectioners' sugar in mixer bowl until light and fluffy. Add 1 ounce liqueur and egg yolks; beat until smooth. Stir in fruit and nuts. Spoon into prepared mold. Chill or freeze overnight. Unmold on serving plate. Whip cream in mixer bowl until soft peaks form. Add 1 ounce confectioners' sugar and 1 ounce liqueur. Decorate Charlotte with whipped cream as desired. Garnish with crystallized rose petals and violets or glacéed fruits and nuts. Cut with knife dipped in hot water. Yield: 16 servings.

Approx Per Serving: Cal 553; Prot 7.2 g; T Fat 30.2 g; Chol 238 mg; Carbo 65.1 g; Sod 46.3 mg; Potas 138 mg.

Jill Probert
England

CHOCOLATE CHIP MINT DESSERT

26 Oreo cookies, crushed
1/2 gallon chocolate chip mint
ice cream, softened
1 12-ounce can chocolate
syrup
8 ounces whipped topping

Reserve 1/2 cup cookie crumbs. Sprinkle remaining crumbs in 9x13-inch dish. Spread ice cream in prepared dish. Freeze for 20 minutes. Drizzle chocolate syrup over ice cream. Freeze for 20 minutes. Top with whipped topping. Sprinkle with reserved crumbs. Freeze for up to several weeks. Yield: 12 servings.

Approx Per Serving: Cal 409; Prot 5.4 g; T Fat 19 g; Chol 39.3 mg; Carbo 57.8 g; Sod 208 mg; Potas 275 mg.

Colleen Seifert
Pelican Rapids, Minnesota

PINEAPPLE CHEESECAKE

1¹/2 cups graham cracker
crumbs
3 tablespoons sugar
¹/4 cup melted butter
¹/4 teaspoon cinnamon
16 ounces cottage cheese
4 eggs
24 ounces cream cheese,
softened
2 tablespoons all-purpose flour
1 cup sugar
1¹/4 teaspoons vanilla extract
¹/4 teaspoon salt
2 8-ounce cans crushed
pineapple, well drained
1 pint sour cream
3 tablespoons sugar
1 teaspoon vanilla extract

Combine cracker crumbs, 3 tablespoons sugar, butter and cinnamon in bowl; mix well. Press over bottom and 1¹/2 inches up side of 10-inch springform pan. Bake at 300 degrees for 10 minutes. Cool. Place cottage cheese and eggs in blender container; process until smooth. Combine with cream cheese, flour, 1 cup sugar, 1¹/4 teaspoons vanilla and salt in mixer bowl. Beat until smooth. Fold in pineapple gently. Spoon into baked crust. Bake at 300 degrees for 1¹/2 hours. Turn off oven. Let stand in oven with door ajar for 1 hour. Blend sour cream, 3 tablespoons sugar and 1 teaspoon vanilla in bowl. Spread over cheesecake. Bake at 350 degrees for 10 minutes. Cool. Store in refrigerator. Yield: 12 servings.

Approx Per Serving: Cal 555; Prot 13.6 g; T Fat 36.8 g; Chol 186 mg; Carbo 44.4 g; Sod 534 mg; Potas 261 mg.

Mary Jane Waltemate
Steeleville, Illinois

BURNT SUGAR DUMPLINGS

¹/2 cup sugar
2 tablespoons butter
¹/8 teaspoon salt
1 cup sugar
2 cups hot water
1¹/2 cups all-purpose flour
2¹/2 teaspoons baking powder
3 tablespoons sugar
¹/4 teaspoon salt
3 tablespoons butter
¹/2 cup chopped walnuts
³/4 cup milk

Sprinkle ¹/2 cup sugar in heavy skillet. Heat until sugar melts and forms a golden brown syrup. Add 2 tablespoons butter, ¹/8 teaspoon salt and 1 cup sugar. Stir in hot water gradually. Bring to a boil. Cook for 10 minutes or until sugar is dissolved, stirring constantly. Pour into 9-inch saucepan. Combine flour, baking powder, 3 tablespoons sugar and ¹/4 teaspoon salt in bowl. Cut in 3 tablespoons butter with pastry blender. Add walnuts. Add milk all at once, stirring just until moistened. Drop by tablespoons into simmering syrup. Simmer, tightly covered, for 15 minutes. Yield: 10 servings.

Approx Per Serving: Cal 295; Prot 3.3 g; T Fat 10.2 g; Chol 18 mg; Carbo 48.9 g; Sod 220 mg; Potas 75.3 mg.

Marie Day
Sandy, Utah

CURRIED FRUIT

1/4 cup melted margarine
1 cup packed brown sugar
1 teaspoon curry powder
1 11-ounce can mandarin
oranges
1 16-ounce can peach halves
1 16-ounce can pear halves
1 16-ounce can pineapple
chunks

Blend melted margarine, brown sugar and curry powder in bowl. Drain mandarin oranges, peaches, pears and pineapple. Add to brown sugar mixture; mix well. Spoon into baking dish. Bake at 350 degrees for 1 hour. Yield: 10 servings.

Approx Per Serving: Cal 245; Prot 0.7 g; T Fat 4.8 g; Chol 0 mg; Carbo 53.3 g; Sod 78.5 mg; Potas 224 mg.

Sandra Polkinghorn
Britton, South Dakota

SUMMER FRUIT FAVORITE

4 cups 100% bran flakes,
crushed
1/4 cup melted butter
2 cups sugar
3/4 cup butter, softened
2 eggs, beaten
1 quart strawberries, sliced
3 bananas, sliced
1 pint whipping cream
2 tablespoons sugar

Reserve 1/3 cup cereal. Mix remaining cereal with 1/4 cup melted butter. Press into 9x13-inch dish. Cream 2 cups sugar and 3/4 cup butter in mixer bowl until light and fluffy. Blend in eggs. Pour into prepared dish. Top with strawberries and bananas. Whip cream in mixer bowl until soft peaks form. Add 2 tablespoons sugar. Spread over fruit. Top with reserved cereal crumbs. Chill until serving time. Yield: 12 servings.

Approx Per Serving: Cal 483; Prot 5.7 g; T Fat 32.5 g; Chol 141 mg; Carbo 52.1 g; Sod 310 mg; Potas 598 mg.

Margie Knoblauch
Minnetonka, Minnesota

MOLASSES TAFFY ICE CREAM

1/4 cup sugar
2 tablespoons cornstarch
1/4 teaspoon salt
1/4 cup molasses
1 egg
2 cups half and half
2 teaspoons vanilla extract
1 cup whipping cream, whipped

Mix sugar, cornstarch and salt in saucepan. Add molasses and egg; mix well. Stir in half and half. Cook until thickened over low heat, stirring constantly; do not boil. Stir in vanilla. Chill, covered, in refrigerator. Beat until smooth. Fold in whipped cream gently. Pour into freezer container. Freeze until firm. Yield: 6 servings.

Approx Per Serving: Cal 325; Prot 4.2 g; T Fat 24.9 g; Chol 130 mg; Carbo 22.6 g; Sod 161 mg; Potas 536 mg.

Dorothy Larsen
Southworth, Washington

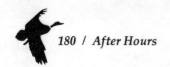

OVERNIGHT FRUIT DESSERT

1 11-ounce can mandarin
oranges
1 20-ounce can pineapple
chunks
1 16-ounce can sliced peaches
1 16-ounce can grapes
1 cup chilled cooked rice
1 cup flaked coconut
1 cup miniature marshmallows
1 large package vanilla instant
pudding mix
1/2 cup milk
16 ounces whipped topping
1 banana, sliced

Drain mandarin oranges, pineapple, peaches and grapes. Chop peach slices. Combine fruit with rice, coconut and marshmallows in large bowl. Mix pudding mix with milk and whipped topping in bowl. Fold into fruit. Chill overnight. Fold banana into mixture at serving time. Spoon into dessert dishes. Yield: 12 servings.

Approx Per Serving: Cal 443; Prot 2.8 g; T Fat 16.9 g; Chol 53.2 mg; Carbo 75.2 g; Sod 201 mg; Potas 254 mg.

Sandra Polkinghorn
Britton, South Dakota

BANANA PUDDING

1 small package vanilla
instant pudding mix
2 cups milk
1 14-ounce can sweetened
condensed milk
8 ounces whipped topping
1 12-ounce package
vanilla wafers
6 bananas, sliced

Blend pudding mix and milk in large bowl. Fold in sweetened condensed milk and whipped topping. Alternate layers of vanilla wafers, pudding and bananas in 9x13-inch dish. Chill until serving time. Yield: 12 servings.

Approx Per Serving: Cal 419; Prot 6.2 g; T Fat 14.3 g; Chol 34.5 mg; Carbo 69.2 g; Sod 250 mg; Potas 442 mg.

Becky Fore
Wiggins, Mississippi

SANDI'S BREAD PUDDING

4 cups dry bread cubes
1/2 cup sugar
1/2 cup packed brown sugar
1 cup raisins
11/2 teaspoons cinnamon
41/2 cups milk
4 eggs, slightly beaten
2 teaspoons vanilla extract

Place bread cubes in greased 9x13-inch baking dish. Sprinkle with sugar, brown sugar, raisins and cinnamon. Mix milk, eggs and vanilla in bowl. Pour over layers. Set dish in large pan with 1 inch hot water. Bake at 350 degrees for 1 hour or until set. Yield: 10 servings.

Approx Per Serving: Cal 240; Prot 7.6 g; T Fat 6.5 g; Chol 124 mg; Carbo 39.9 g; Sod 140 mg; Potas 331 mg.

Sandra Polkinghorn
Britton, South Dakota

PERSIMMON PUDDING

1 quart wild persimmons *1 quart milk* *3 eggs* *1/4 cup butter, softened* *4 cups all-purpose flour* *1 teaspoon soda* *2 cups sugar*	Combine persimmons and milk in bowl. Press through sieve. Combine pulp mixture with eggs and butter in mixer bowl; mix well. Add sifted flour, soda and sugar; mix well. Spoon into large buttered crock. Bake at 300 to 325 degrees for 2½ hours or until set. May bake in 2 buttered 2-quart baking dishes for 1 hour if preferred. Yield: 16 servings.

Approx Per Serving: Cal 349; Prot 8.4 g; T Fat 8.4 g; Chol 75.6 mg; Carbo 60.9 g; Sod 141 mg; Potas 283 mg.

Sarah Ann Rogers
Anchorage, Alaska

PUPPY CHOW CHOCOLATE SNACK

1 cup chunky peanut butter *1/2 cup margarine* *2 cups milk chocolate chips* *1 12-ounce package Crispix* *1 cup confectioners' sugar*	Melt peanut butter, margarine and chocolate chips in saucepan over low heat; mix well. Pour over Crispix in bowl; stir to coat well. Place confectioners' sugar in paper bag. Add Crispix. Shake until well coated. Spread on baking sheet. Let stand until cool and chocolate is firm. Yield: 10 servings.

Approx Per Serving: Cal 577; Prot 11.2 g; T Fat 34.7 g; Chol 0 mg; Carbo 63.3 g; Sod 556 mg; Potas 328 mg.

Kari Jo Kuck
Aberdeen, South Dakota

BRENDA'S CHOCOLATE CAKE

3 cups all-purpose flour *5 tablespoons unsweetened* *baking cocoa* *2 cups sugar* *2 teaspoons soda* *1 teaspoon salt* *3/4 cup plus 2 tablespoons oil* *1 tablespoon vinegar* *1 tablespoon vanilla extract* *2 cups water*	Mix flour, cocoa, sugar, soda and salt in bowl. Combine oil, vinegar and vanilla in bowl. Add to dry ingredients; mix well. Mix in water. Pour into greased and floured 9x13-inch cake pan. Bake at 350 degrees for 35 to 40 minutes or until cake tests done. Yield: 12 servings.

Approx Per Serving: Cal 389; Prot 3.7 g; T Fat 16.6 g; Chol 0 mg; Carbo 58.1 g; Sod 316 mg; Potas 58.5 mg.

Brenda E. Stauffer
Ephrata, Pennsylvania

EASY BAKE CAKE

1   21-ounce can cherry
pie filling
1   2-layer package chocolate
cake mix
1/2 cup water
1/4 cup oil
3 eggs
2/3 cup chopped pecans
2/3 cup chocolate chips

Stir pie filling into cake mix in bowl. Combine water, oil and eggs in bowl; beat until smooth. Add to cake mixture; mix well with spoon. Stir in pecans and chocolate chips. Spoon into greased 10-inch bundt pan. Bake at 350 degrees for 55 minutes. Cool in pan for 15 minutes. Remove to wire rack to cool completely. May bake in 9x13-inch cake pan if preferred. Yield: 16 servings.

Approx Per Serving: Cal 310; Prot 3.8 g; T Fat 14.9 g; Chol 51.4 mg; Carbo 42.6 g; Sod 275 mg; Potas 95.9 mg.

Jane Queal
Pratt, Kansas

ITALIAN CREAM CAKE

1/2 cup shortening
1/2 cup butter, softened
12/3 cups sugar
6 egg yolks
2 cups all-purpose flour
3/4 teaspoon soda
1/2 teaspoon salt
1 cup buttermilk
3/4 teaspoon vanilla extract
1/4 teaspoon butter flavoring
1/2 cup chopped pecans
2 cups coconut
1/2 cup chopped maraschino
cherries
6 egg whites
1/4 teaspoon cream of tartar
1/2 cup butter, softened
6 ounces cream cheese, softened
3/4 teaspoon vanilla extract
1/4 teaspoon butter flavoring
4 cups confectioners' sugar

Cream shortening, 1/2 cup butter and sugar in mixer bowl until light and fluffy. Add egg yolks 1 at a time, mixing well after each addition. Combine flour, soda and salt. Add to batter alternately with buttermilk, mixing well after each addition and ending with dry ingredients. Stir in 3/4 teaspoon vanilla, 1/4 teaspoon butter flavoring, pecans, coconut and cherries. Beat egg whites with cream of tartar in mixer bowl until stiff peaks form. Fold gently into batter. Spoon into 3 greased and floured 9-inch cake pans. Bake at 350 degrees for 30 to 40 minutes or until layers test done. Cool in pans for 10 minutes. Remove to wire rack to cool completely. Combine 1/2 cup butter, cream cheese, 3/4 teaspoon vanilla, and 1/4 teaspoon butter flavoring in mixer bowl; mix well. Add confectioners' sugar; beat until smooth. Spread between layers and over top and side of cake. Store in refrigerator. Yield: 16 servings.

Approx Per Serving: Cal 581; Prot 6 g; T Fat 36.3 g; Chol 145 mg; Carbo 60.7 g; Sod 262 mg; Potas 131 mg.

Carol Lochrie
Holladay, Utah

OLD-FASHIONED NUT CAKE

4 4-ounce cans walnuts
3¹/2 cups sifted all-purpose
flour
2 teaspoons baking powder
¹/2 teaspoon salt
1¹/2 cups butter, softened
2 cups sugar
6 eggs
³/4 cup milk
¹/4 cup rum

Place walnuts in bowl. Sift flour, baking powder and salt over walnuts; mix to coat well. Cream butter and sugar in mixer bowl until light and fluffy. Beat in eggs 1 at a time, beating at high speed until very light. Mix milk and rum in small bowl. Add flour mixture to batter alternately with milk mixture, mixing well after each addition and beginning and ending with dry ingredients. Pour into greased 10-inch tube pan. Bake at 275 degrees for 2¹/2 hours. Remove to wire rack to cool. Garnish with confectioners' sugar. Yield: 16 servings.

Approx Per Serving: Cal 566; Prot 12.6 g; T Fat 36 g; Chol 151 mg; Carbo 50 g; Sod 218 mg; Potas 221 mg.

Stephanie Connolly
Barrington, Illinois

PISTACHIO CAKE

1 2-layer package white
cake mix
1 small package pistachio
instant pudding mix
3 eggs
1 cup water
³/4 cup oil
¹/2 cup chopped pecans
1 small package pistachio
instant pudding mix
1 cup milk
12 ounces whipped topping

Combine cake mix, 1 package pudding mix, eggs, water, oil and pecans in mixer bowl. Beat until smooth. Line bottoms of 2 greased and floured 9-inch cake pans with waxed paper. Spoon batter into prepared pans. Bake at 350 degrees for 30 minutes. Remove to wire rack to cool. Combine 1 package pudding mix, milk and whipped topping in bowl; mix well. Chill until mixture begins to set. Spread between layers and over top and side of cake. Garnish with addiional pecans if desired. Yield: 16 servings.

Approx Per Serving: Cal 368; Prot 3.4 g; T Fat 22.1 g; Chol 53.4 mg; Carbo 40.2 g; Sod 270 mg; Potas 51.9 mg.

Gaylan Lang
Aberdeen, South Dakota

SUMMER LAUREN'S STRAWBERRY JAM CAKE

1 cup sugar
1 cup strawberry jam
2 cups all-purpose flour
3/4 cup butter, softened
1/2 cup buttermilk
1 teaspoon soda
3 eggs
2 cups sugar
1 cup milk
1 16-ounce can crushed
pineapple, drained
1 orange, peeled, ground
1/4 apple, chopped
1 31/2-ounce can coconut
1 cup chopped pecans

Combine 1 cup sugar, jam, flour, butter, butter-milk, soda and eggs in mixer bowl; mix well. Spoon into 2 greased and floured 9-inch cake pans. Bake at 325 degrees for 40 minutes. Remove to wire rack to cool. Mix 2 cups sugar and milk in saucepan. Cook until thickened, stirring constantly. Remove from heat. Stir in fruit, coconut and pecans. Spread warm filling between cake layers. Store in refrigerator. Yield: 16 servings.

Approx Per Serving: Cal 440; Prot 4.5 g; T Fat 17.7 g; Chol 77 mg; Carbo 69.4 g; Sod 158 mg; Potas 180 mg.

Joan Marsh
Humboldt, Tennessee

PUMPKIN CAKE RING

1 2-layer package yellow
cake mix
2 teaspoons cinnamon
1/2 teaspoon ginger
1/2 teaspoon nutmeg
2 eggs
1 cup solid-pack pumpkin
1 cup chopped pecans

Combine cake mix and spices in bowl. Reduce amount of water called for in package directions by 1/2 cup. Add remaining water, eggs and pumpkin to cake mix; mix well. Stir in pecans. Spoon into greased 10-inch tube pan. Bake at 350 degrees for 40 to 45 minutes or until cake tests done. Remove to wire rack to cool. Glaze with favorite lemon glaze if desired. Yield: 16 servings.

Approx Per Serving: Cal 188; Prot 2.8 g; T Fat 8.1 g; Chol 34.2 mg; Carbo 26.8 g; Sod 184 mg; Potas 71 mg. Nutritional information does not include lemon glaze.

Stephanie Connolly
Barrington, Illinois

BLUEBERRY COFFEE CAKE

2 packages Duncan Hines
blueberry muffin mix
1 cup sour cream
2 eggs
1 cup water
1 cup packed brown sugar
2/3 cup all-purpose flour
1 teaspoon cinnamon
1/2 cup margarine, softened
8 ounces cream cheese

Remove and rinse blueberries from mixes. Combine sour cream and eggs in mixer bowl; beat until smooth. Stir in water gradually. Add muffin mix. Stir just until moistened. Mix brown sugar, flour, cinnamon and margarine in bowl until crumbly. Layer half the batter, half the blueberries and half the crumb mixture in greased 9x13-inch baking dish. Slice cream cheese over layers. Top with remaining batter, blueberries and crumb mixture. Bake at 400 degrees for 30 minutes or until golden brown. Serve warm. Yield: 12 servings.

Approx Per Serving: Cal 420; Prot 5.9 g; T Fat 23 g; Chol 74.8 mg; Carbo 48.3 g; Sod 394 mg; Potas 177 mg.

Mary Dale Wesley
Barrington, Illinois

FILLED COFFEE CAKE

1 1/2 cups sifted all-purpose
flour
1 tablespoon baking powder
3/4 cup sugar
1/4 teaspoon salt
1/4 cup shortening
1 egg
1/2 cup milk
1 teaspoon vanilla extract
1/2 cup packed brown sugar
2 tablespoons all-purpose flour
2 teaspoons cinnamon
2 tablespoons melted butter
1/2 cup chopped pecans

Sift 1 1/2 cups flour, baking powder, sugar and salt into bowl. Cut in shortening until crumbly. Mix egg, milk and vanilla in bowl. Add to crumb mixture; mix well. Combine brown sugar, 2 tablespoons flour and cinnamon in small bowl. Add butter and pecans; mix well. Layer batter and pecan mixture 1/2 at a time in greased loaf pan. Bake at 375 degrees for 25 to 30 minutes or until coffee cake tests done. Remove to wire rack to cool. Yield: 10 servings.

Approx Per Serving: Cal 296; Prot 3.6 g; T Fat 12.6 g; Chol 35.3 mg; Carbo 43.3 g; Sod 189 mg; Potas 108 mg.

Carolyn D. Connolly
Norwood, Massachusetts

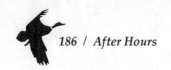

ANGEL FOOD BARS

1 package 1-step angel food
cake mix
1   21-ounce can lemon
pie filling
1 cup coconut
2 cups confectioners' sugar,
sifted
Juice of 1 lemon
1 tablespoon milk

Combine dry cake mix and pie filling in mixer bowl; beat for 5 minutes. Stir in coconut. Spread in greased and floured 9x13-inch baking pan. Bake at 350 degrees for 20 to 25 minutes or until light brown. Cool. Mix confectioners' sugar and lemon juice in bowl. Add enough milk 1 teaspoon at a time to make a thin glaze. Drizzle over cooled layer. Cut into bars.
Yield: 36 servings.

Approx Per Serving: Cal 93; Prot 1.2 g; T Fat 1.8 g; Chol 0.1 mg; Carbo 18.8 g; Sod 103 mg; Potas 43.9 mg.

Margie Knoblauch
Minnetonka, Minnesota

MIKE'S APPLE SQUARES

1/2 cup shortening
2 cups all-purpose flour
1 tablespoon lemon juice
2 egg yolks
7 or 8 tablespoons cold water
2 cups sliced peeled apples
1 cup sugar
4 1/2 tablespoons all-purpose
flour
1/8 teaspoon nutmeg
1/4 teaspoon cinnamon

Cut shortening into 2 cups flour in bowl. Add lemon juice, egg yolks and cold water; mix to form dough. Divide into 2 portions. Roll 1 portion on floured surface to fit 9x13-inch baking pan. Fit into pan. Combine apples, sugar, 4 1/2 tablespoons flour, nutmeg and cinnamon in bowl; toss to mix well. Spoon into prepared pan. Top with remaining pastry. Bake at 400 degrees for 40 minutes or until light brown. Glaze with confectioners' sugar glaze if desired.
Yield: 10 servings.

Approx Per Serving: Cal 310; Prot 3.7 g; T Fat 11.8 g; Chol 54.4 mg; Carbo 48.3 g; Sod 3.3 mg; Potas 81.8 mg. Nutritional information does not include confectioners' sugar glaze.

Marilyn A. Barkley
Greenup, Illinois

MOM'S BROWNIES

1 cup butter
4 1-ounce squares unsweetened chocolate
2 cups sugar
1¹/₃ cups all-purpose flour
4 eggs
2 teaspoons vanilla extract
2 cups chopped pecans
¹/₄ cup butter
1 1-ounce square unsweetened chocolate
¹/₄ cup milk
4 cups (about) confectioners' sugar

Combine 1 cup butter and 4 squares chocolate in 2-quart saucepan. Heat over low heat until melted; mix well. Remove from heat. Stir in sugar, flour, eggs and vanilla. Mix in pecans. Spread in greased and floured 10x15-inch baking pan. Bake at 350 degrees for 20 to 25 minutes or until brownies test done. Melt ¹/₄ cup butter and 1 square chocolate in saucepan; remove from heat. Stir in milk and enough confectioners' sugar to make of spreading consistency. Spread over warm brownies. Cool. Cut into squares. Yield: 36 servings.

Approx Per Serving: Cal 233; Prot 2.3 g; T Fat 13.7 g; Chol 47.9 mg; Carbo 28 g; Sod 63 mg; Potas 75.2 mg.

Susan Bumbaca
West Yellowstone, Montana

FUDGE BARS

¹/₂ cup margarine, softened
1 cup sugar
2 eggs, beaten
¹/₄ cup unsweetened baking cocoa
³/₄ cup all-purpose flour
1 teaspoon vanilla extract
³/₄ cup coarsely broken pecans

Cream margarine and sugar in mixer bowl until light and fluffy. Blend in eggs. Add cocoa, flour and vanilla; mix well. Stir in pecans. Batter will be stiff. Spread in greased 7x11-inch baking pan. Place in cold oven. Set oven temperature at 350 degrees. Bake for 25 minutes. Cool. Cut into bars. Yield: 24 servings.

Approx Per Serving: Cal 114; Prot 1.4 g; T Fat 7 g; Chol 22.8 mg; Carbo 12.4 g; Sod 57.2 mg; Potas 36.2 mg.

Mrs. John Henry Smith
Forsyth, Montana

MOLASSES COOKIES

1 cup molasses
1 cup bacon drippings
1 cup sugar
1 cup buttermilk
2 teaspoons soda
1 teaspoon salt
1 teaspoon ginger
1 teaspoon cinnamon
1 teaspoon nutmeg
1/8 teaspoon allspice
7 cups (about) all-purpose flour

Combine molasses, bacon drippings, sugar, buttermilk, soda, salt and spices in bowl; mix well. Add enough flour to form a soft dough. Knead in enough remaining flour on floured surface to make stiff dough. Roll in small portions to desired thickness. Cut as desired. Place on baking sheet. Bake at 375 degrees for 10 minutes. Cool on wire rack. Yield: 100 cookies.

Approx Per Cookie: Cal 65; Prot 1 g; T Fat 2.4 g;
Chol 13.5 mg; Carbo 10.1 g; Sod 56.1 mg; Potas 106 mg.

Sarah Ann Rogers
Anchorage, Alaska

NETE'S CUSTARD PIE

1/2 cup sugar
2 cups half and half
4 eggs, slightly beaten
1/4 teaspoon salt
1 teaspoon vanilla extract
1 unbaked pie shell
1/8 teaspoon cinnamon
1/8 teaspoon nutmeg

Combine first 5 ingredients in mixer bowl; mix well. Pour into pie shell. Sprinkle with spices. Bake at 350 degrees for 40 minutes or until almost set; do not overbake. Yield: 6 servings.

Approx Per Serving: Cal 372; Prot 8.3 g; T Fat 23 g;
Chol 212 mg; Carbo 33.7 g; Sod 351 mg; Potas 164 mg.

Marilyn A. Barkley
Greenup, Illinois

ZUCCHINI PIE

6 cups sliced peeled zucchini
1 cup sugar
2 teaspoons margarine
1/4 cup lemon juice
2 teaspoons cinnamon
1/4 teaspoon salt
1 tablespoon cornstarch
1 recipe 2-crust pie pastry

Combine zucchini, sugar, margarine, lemon juice, cinnamon and salt in saucepan. Bring to a boil. Blend cornstarch with a small amount of water. Stir into zucchini mixture. Cook until thickened. Cool. Spoon zucchini mixture into pastry-lined pie plate. Top with remaining pastry. Flute edges; cut steam vents. Bake at 400 degrees for 45 minutes. Yield: 6 servings.

Approx Per Serving: Cal 499; Prot 4.9 g; T Fat 19 g;
Chol 0 mg; Carbo 62.9 g; Sod 475 mg; Potas 372 mg.

Jan Hamen
Fairbanks, Alaska

BLACKBERRY CORDIAL

4 quarts blackberries
4 cups water
3 cups sugar
4 cups Brandy

Combine blackberries and water in saucepan. Bring to a boil. Cook for 5 minutes. Strain into bowl. Measure 8 cups blackberry juice. Combine with sugar in saucepan. Bring to a boil. Cook for 7 minutes. Cool. Combine 1 cup Brandy with every 2 cups blackberry syrup. Serve as an after-dinner drink. Yield: 24 cups.

Nutritional information for this recipe is not available.

Mrs. Donald E. Fultz
Bullhead City, Arizona

BOURBON SLUSH

2 cups sugar
9 cups water
3 tea bags
2 6-ounce cans frozen
lemonade concentrate
2 6-ounce cans frozen orange
juice concentrate
1 cup Bourbon

Combine sugar and 7 cups water in saucepan. Heat until sugar is dissolved. Cool. Bring 2 cups water to a boil in saucepan. Add tea bags. Let steep for several minutes. Discard tea bags. Combine sugar syrup, tea, juice concentrates and Bourbon in 5-quart container; mix well. Freeze until slushy. Yield: 14 cups.

Nutritional information for this recipe is not available.

Barbara Ludwig
Reno, Nevada

CRANBERRY LIQUEUR

2 cups fresh cranberries,
chopped
1²/₃ cups sugar
1 cup gin
¹/₂ teaspoon vanilla extract

Combine cranberries, sugar, gin and vanilla in large wide-mouth jar; mix well. Let stand at room temperature for 3 weeks, stirring gently at least once a week. Strain into decanter. Store in cool dark place. Yield: 4 cups.

Nutritional information for this recipe is not available.

Irene Smith
Sprucedale, Ontario, Canada

RHUBARB PUNCH

8 cups chopped rhubarb
8 cups water
2 cups sugar
1 3-ounce package strawberry
gelatin
3¹/₂ quarts lemon-lime
carbonated soda

Combine rhubarb with water in saucepan. Cook until tender; remove from heat. Stir in sugar and gelatin. Place in blender container. Process until smooth. Spoon into 1-quart refrigerator containers. Freeze until firm. Combine 1 quart thawed rhubarb mixture with 1 quart lemon-lime soda to serve; mix gently.
Yield: 56 ¹/₂-cup servings.

Nutritional information for this recipe is not available.

Joan Peabody
Alexandria, Minnesota

ROSE RED SLUSH

1 16-ounce can frozen
cranberry juice
concentrate
1 16-ounce bottle of
Reunite Rosato
1 quart 7-Up

Combine thawed cranberry juice concentrate and wine in freezer container. Freeze until slushy. Fill glasses ¹/₂ full with slush mixture. Fill glasses with 7-Up. Yield: 8 servings.

Nutritional information for this recipe is not available.

Jacquelyn Ann Miller
Castalia, Ohio

WHITE SANGRIA

1 bottle of dry white wine,
chilled
1¹/₂ cups Cointreau, chilled
¹/₄ cup sugar
1 10-ounce bottle of club soda,
chilled
1 orange, sliced
1 lemon, sliced
2 limes, cut into wedges

Combine wine, Cointreau and sugar in pitcher. Add ice cubes and club soda; mix gently. Add orange and lemon slices and lime wedges. Serve immediately. Yield: 4 servings.

Nutritional information for this recipe is not available.

Billy Joe Cross
Clinton, Mississippi

Food from the Field

Handling your game meats from field to table

More than many other food, wild game is the most misunderstood.

"It tastes strong...It tastes gamey...It's too tough...It's too greasy...."

I've heard every complaint under the sun—but never from someone who's eaten in my kitchen. After over 50 years of hunting and cooking, I've come to learn a little about wild meats. And the biggest thing I've learned is that those who complain the most know the least about wild game, let alone how to process and prepare it.

Such folks are not to blame for their misconceptions. Our super-civilized culture is the culprit. We've taken the idea of "food" out of the realm of woods and fields and placed it in a cold, sterile setting. There it lies in state, under fluorescent lights, in a sanitized chrome and stainless steel sarcophagus, mummified in cellophane, date-stamped with an epitaph: "to insure freshness." God help us should we ever eat *expired* food.

Preconceived notions are bound to rise from such a mindset, and those of us who appreciate wild game must do our level best to do away with them. The best way I've found is to invite your non-hunting friends over for dinner. You can tell your friends that game meats are more healthful than supermarket fare, with far less fat and chemicals. You can show them charts explaining that it is higher in protein and minerals. But a mouthful of a gourmet game feast best explains the true nature of nature's harvest. And it does so much more eloquently than a mouthful of words ever will.

The key to any successful meal, game or domestic, is *preparation*. When you buy meat from the supermarket, a few folks have already begun your preparation. Ranchers, truckers, packing house personnel, federal graders, boners, butchers, meat managers and stock boys are all involved. And they've saved you one hell of a lot of time, certainly. But how well (or poorly) each has done his job is a mystery.

Hunting is an important part of wild game preparation. How you handle your game from the field to the table determines what your meal will taste like. True, the hunter or game chef undertakes much more work than those who simply visit the supermarket. But the advantage is that *you are in control through every step of the process*. Nothing is a mystery. And if you know how to handle your game meats from field to dining table, you'll never hear those tired old complaints from family and friends again.

Let's get started.

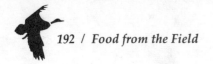

In the Field—Big Game

The smart cook thinks like a cook in the field as well as in the kitchen. *Handle your game with care.* For the big game hunter, this begins the moment the shot is placed. If you pick your shot wisely, you'll not ruin any choice cuts from backstrap or hindquarter. You'll also avoid gut shots, which can puncture the digestive system and release acidic juices that taint the meat. A heart or neck shot will put the animal down for keeps, and this is what you want. A wounded animal or one that's been pushed hard by hunters and dogs will have a high level of adrenalin, and that makes meat tough and strong tasting.

The infamous "gamey" flavor you've heard so many complaints over stems from improper handling of wild meats. The main point to remember here is that the quicker you get what's inside the animal outside of it, the better your meat will be. After field dressing, prop the cavity open and let the animal cool. Do not be rough in dragging the animal, and transport it in an open pickup bed or tied onto the roof of your car. Engine heat has ruined many a deer riding on the hood. Remember, outside the kitchen, heat and meat do not mix.

In the South, where it is not uncommon to hunt deer in 70-degree weather, a hunter especially needs to bleed and eviscerate the animal as soon as possible to dissipate body heat. You must do this because bacteria form and spread very quickly in warmth. You could never hang a deer in 60- or 70-degree weather, for example, because bacteria would destroy it.

But what about aged meat? Proper aging makes meat properly tender, and gives it that unique flavor you find in prime rib or well-aged steaks. Bacteria do the work in aging, it's true. But the thing to remember in aging is to make the bacteria work under *controlled* conditions. That means cold. You should hang your venison in a cooler at 35 to 40 degrees, skin on, for ten to twelve days. The hide protects the meat and keeps it from drying out. If you do not have access to a walk-in cooler, and if the weather is not right for outdoor hanging, you can quarter the carcass and age it in an ice chest or refrigerator.

Aging is not necessary if the meat is to be ground. If you do not intend to age your meat, remember that the same rule holds for immediate bleeding and evisceration in the field.

A warm deer skins more easily than a frozen one. In skinning, remember to keep your knives sharp, and try to do more peeling than cutting to keep "butcher nicks" out of the hide. After skinning, trim as much fat as possible off the carcass. Fat is to blame for a lot of "strong taste" people complain about. Use a hacksaw to quarter the deer, then "muscle it out," making steaks from the larger pieces. Set small trimmings aside for burger, and larger ones for stew. Use odd shaped pieces—especially long ones—to make rolled roasts for the smoker or grill. Always use white cotton string when tying meat, never a synthetic, which could melt.

Wrap your steaks, roasts and trimmings well before freezing. A double wrapping with freezer paper is usually sufficient, but you can go a step further and cover the meat in heavy-duty plastic wrap, being careful to squeeze all the air from it. Air dries meat out—that's called freezer burn. The best way to prevent freezer burn is to keep air off the meat with good wrapping. Larger pieces of meat are less likely to dry out than smaller ones, and if you'd like to freeze, say, a hindquarter of venison, double wrap the meat with heavy-duty plastic wrap. Push the air out as you wrap. Cover with freezer paper and tape with freezer tape. Date and mark your packages with waterproof pen. Use different color inks to denote different years or types of game.

A Bird in the Field

Most of the same rules that apply to big game should be followed when handling ducks, geese and other game birds. Waterfowl should be drawn as quickly as possible, in the field, preferably. (Eat your lunch early so you can use a plastic sandwich bag for the giblets.)

Picking feathers in the field is a good pastime between flights, so bring a bag for that, too. Not only does it save you a lot of drudge work late at night after a long day, but a warm bird is easier to pluck than a cold one. Make sure to leave at least one wing intact and attached for the wardens. *Always* pick your game birds, never skin them. Skinning is a

common sin committed by lazy hunters late at night. Ducks, geese, turkey, quail, grouse—name the game and the skin should stay on it. Game birds are dry. The fat is located right under the skin, and both these layers will help you in the kitchen later on. By skinning a bird you limit yourself as a cook, because only certain recipes will keep skinned meat moist. The sole time you should skin a bird is after a failed attempt at plucking due to thin skin, as, say, on a ruffed grouse.

You can make your plucking easier with hot paraffin, though this operation is easier done at home than in the field. Heat broken pieces of the wax in boiling water. Let cool a bit then dip your ducks. Coat them well. When the wax cools, peel the feathers away.

If you intend to age the ducks, leave the feathers on. Place the dressed ducks in a paper bag in the refrigerator. A normal refrigerator temperature of 38 to 40 degrees for three or four days is all you need. If you are in hunting camp and have a few birds that you wish to save for a another day, clean them completely, put them in Ziplock bags, add water and freeze. The water keeps dangerous dry air off the meat. You can also place the birds in bags alone, then freeze in a waxed milk carton filled with water. Crimp the carton top down and seal with freezer tape. The square and rectangular cartons make easier stacking in your freezer. Other handy stackables are cottage cheese cartons, large plastic margarine tubs and coffee cans. Later on, after you thaw the ducks, you can age them in the fridge for three or four days.

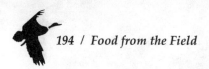

Use separate containers for giblets. You'll accumulate these at different times during the season. Keep a separate container for gizzards and hearts, and another for livers. Start with your opening-day entrails at the bottom of the containers, and freeze them with just enough water to cover. Add to these as the season progresses, working your way toward the top. When you have enough for a good batch of dirty rice or goose liver pâté, just thaw out a block.

Quick Tips for Game Bird Cleaning

- Use tin snips to cut the backbone out of small ducks, doves, woodcock or quail. Removal of entrails is much easier and you still have the option of stuffing the bird. Close up the back with picks or skewers.

- When forced to skin birds, roast with bacon over breasts, or use recipes calling for cream sauces or cream soups to keep meat moist. Oven bags are another option. Soups, stews and gumbos are also good ways to use skinless birds.

- Remove pesky leg tendons in pheasants by cutting all the way around the dark skin at the base of the "drumstick." Take care not to cut the tendons. Move the foot back and forth several times at this joint. Pull the foot off and the tendons will come with it.

- If a recipe calls for breast fillets from any game bird, freeze the rest of the carcass for soup stock.

- Never soak any game meat in salt water. Salt toughens meat.

- Never rinse waterfowl in a sink equipped with a garbage disposer. A steel BB might mean one *mean* repair bill.

From Bank to Banquet

The care, cleaning and cooking of your catch

For me, the year would not be complete without the all-too-few mornings I get to spend on the duck marshes. And if you're like me, a 30-day duck season just isn't enough time to get out and enjoy wild things and wild places. That's why they invented fishing.

Here, in Mississippi, I can fish from spring right through until fall, and believe me, I do. While I don't run into many trout, salmon or walleye where I live, it is not uncommon to haul in dozens of crappies in the two-pound range inside of an hour. And bass are even bigger. Throw in some channel cats and a bucketful of bream, and I wouldn't trade you any other place in the world to go fishing.

But no matter where you go to catch fish, from Canada to the Caymans, the care, cleaning and cooking of your catch is all about the same. While the fish flesh differs, the major kitchen methods really do not.

On Boat and Banquet

Fish, and all seafood for that matter, is the most perishable of foodstuffs. For this reason your catch requires care and attention—even more than game.

Whether on the bank or in a boat, the best way to keep your fish fresh is to keep it alive as long as possible. The old handy stringer is one method, as are mesh collapsible fish baskets, live boxes that sit in the water at dockside, or oxygen-bubbling live wells in boats.

The best way, however, is to immediately remove the gills and guts and get your fish on ice. A large cooler is best for this purpose. Try and keep the water drained so the fish do not soak.

The last choice is to clean the fish and keep it cool in a creel. Creels work because they keep that nice brook trout shaded, but more importantly, they allow air to circulate around the fish. Never hinder air circulation when holding just-caught fish. Smart old-timers always laid some streamside vegetation inside their creels for a little insulation.

Mr. Clean

You cannot clean fish without a good knife. Period.

Unless you pay someone else to do this job for you, your fish knife is just as important as hook and line. The all-around choice is, of course, the fillet knife. The springy, "flexi-thin" blade is built for just what this knife's name says it will do. Pick up several fillet knives of different sizes. They also come in handy for taking the breast meat off ducks, geese and other game birds. Beyond filleting, these knives can also be used for most general fish cleaning purposes, but you will need something heavier like a French chef's knife for breaking the bones on big fish like salmon or trout.

Most beginners are afraid to fillet fish, for they feel it is an obscure and complex art practiced by people named Pierre at streamside in Ontario. You don't have to be a guide to fillet fish. It is a simple operation, nothing more than slicing a slab of meat off a fish's side.

The advantage of filleted fish is obvious—no bones. This makes convenient eating and is great for feeding children. The downside is that when you remove bones, you also remove a lot of good flavor from the flesh. Save the bones in your freezer for making stocks and chowders.

The bigger and thicker the fish, the better the fish for making fillets. The basic idea is to use your springy knife blade to feel your way as you cut through the fish. Lay the fish flat on a cutting board. Salted hands or paper towels help keep the fish from slipping. You can also find cutting boards equipped with a heavy clip for this purpose. Hold the head with one hand and place your blade behind the pectoral fin, at the gill. Angle the knife toward the head, and cut down to the center bone. Turn the knife and gently saw your way toward the tail. Continue right on through. Lay this slab of meat skin-side down on your board, and trim away any belly fat and the rib cage. Now remove the skin by cutting into the meat at the tail. Stop your knife at the skin without cutting through. Turn your knife toward the front of the fillet. Now grasp the skin and

pull, while again working your knife with a gentle, sawing motion.

Another tool to consider is the electric knife. For me, and for most of the fisherman I know, this is the most important invention since the landing net. Let's say you've taken the kids fishing, stumbled onto a honey hole of bluegill or crappie, and have come home with about 147 of 'em. Kids generally suffer a disease that results in a miraculous loss of fishing interest at this point. If you've let them make their escape, there you sit, right? Not hardly. Get out the power tools.

I can fillet five panfish in a minute with my electric knife. With practice, so can you. Take the fish in one hand, thumb in mouth, index finger behind the gill. Angle your blade down into the meat behind the gill, again, feeling for the center bone. Once you hit the bone, run your blade down to the tail. Leave the fillet attached to the tail. Now run the knife down the other side of the fillet, peeling off the skin. A small part of the ribcage will be left, and again, these are easily flicked out with a fillet knife and should be saved for your next fish chowder or gumbo,

You can fillet big salmon or trout, but you don't really need to. These fish have large bones and the meat easily flakes away from them after cooking, so they really are not a hindrance during dining. There's no need, then, to sacrifice flavor by removing the bones. You can broil, bake, grill or poach these fish whole. Or, you can "steak them out." To do this, dress the fish, trim off the belly fat, and cross cut it every two inches or so. Try salmon steaks on the grill, basted with lemon, butter and garlic.

The Fish Fry

In recent years, fried foods have earned a bad name. And I'm not going to argue with your cardiologist. Instead, I'd like to invite him over next Friday night. A plateful of crappie and hush puppies might not change his mind about what's good for you—but I'll bet he asks for seconds.

For health and all-around flavor, the best oil to use is peanut oil. While it does add some fat to your diet, this oil has no cholesterol. And it imparts no "off" flavor to your fish, letting the true taste come through.

The best way to fry fish, by far, is to do it *outside*. Nothing smells finer than fish as it fries. And nothing smells worse than your house will for the next week. The splatters, too, are no fun later on. If you must cook inside, allow for ventilation, cover your fryer, and use fresh fish, not frozen, which tend to throw a stronger aroma when they fry.

For outdoor cookery, use a propane stove, camp stove, or gas grill as a heat source. Because of the high temperatures involved, you want a fairly substantial pan—no light alloys, aluminum or plastic handles. A deep, cast-iron pot or skillet is just the ticket. For smaller jobs, an electric frypan can work, too. The advantage with one of these is the built-in thermostat to help you gauge oil temperature. Whatever you cook in, you'll also need a wire basket or big, serrated metal spoon to pull the fish out after you drop it in. Regular panfish fillets are the perfect size for frying. Small fish (such as smelt) can be cooked whole, bones and all. These give the fish a crispy crunch, with a rich sort of nutty flavor. Rinse the fish in water, pat dry, then dust well with a mix of self-rising cornmeal or corn flour, a little black pepper and seasoned salt. Heat the oil to around 375 degrees. Drop a crumb of meal or batter in to test, and if it doesn't sizzle, wait a bit. Once hot, the oil will seal the coating immediately, and your fish flesh will turn out moist and flaky. Figure three to five minutes for good-sized panfish fillets. Give the oil a minute or two to get hot again between batches of fish.

In the Oven

In baking and broiling your fish, the key is to keep the fillets from drying. Baste liberally with butter or flavored butters—simply add lemon juice and any herb or spice you like. Make sure to oil the pan or rack you're broiling or baking on and your fish won't stick. Nothing is more frustrating than trying to pull a pretty speckled trout from the oven, only to have half of it tear away as you try to remove it. You can cook whole fish or fish steaks as well as you can fillets with these methods. In baking you needn't worry about turning your fish. But do plan to turn fish in the broiler. Broiling is a fast browning process which employs very high heat. For this reason you should use a thick piece of fish, preferably trout, salmon, swordfish or shark. Other good ones are amberjack, Spanish mackerel or lemonfish. These are heavier and more oily than panfish so they stand up to heat better without drying. Keep a watchful eye on broiling fish, making sure to turn the fish quickly when browned to prevent burning.

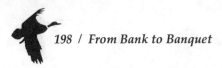

The Poached Approach

Poaching is a wonderful cooking process for many reasons. It is forgiving—you'll never make a good piece of fish dust dry through overcooking. It is healthful—you use no fats or oils. And it gives you firm control over the flavors that you wish to impart to your fresh fish flesh. The process is simply the immersion of a fish, or fish parts, in a simmering liquid. The liquid ensures you will never dry out your fish, as might easily happen under the broiler.

You should equip yourself with a fish poacher—a two-foot long covered roasting pan with a rack to lower the fish into, and raise it out of, the bubbling broth. A regular roasting pan will work, too. Substitute cheesecloth for the rack. The "cooking liquor" you choose can be as basic as a vegetable broth, or as ambitious as a classic "court bouillon" (or "short broth"). Here is a basic court bouillon: 8 cups water, 2 carrots, cut in chunks, 1 chopped onion, 3 lemon or lime slices with seeds, 3 peppercorns, pinch of tarragon, 1 tablespoon parsley, 1 bay leaf. Simmer together for 45 minutes before adding fish. Cook about 10 minutes per inch of thickness, measured across the fish's back. Remember, poaching is forgiving, so a few minutes more will not overcook your fish.

Great Grilling

Once again, substantial, oily fish such as salmon work best over the open fire. Cook whole fish with heavy-duty aluminum foil. Oil the foil and lay fish across it. Salt and pepper inside the cavity and stuff with lemon wedges. Baste liberally with lemon butter. Wrap in foil and put on hot fire. Cooking times will vary with fish size and fire size, but a good rule of thumb is about 20 minutes per side for a fish in the 8 to 10-pound class. Cook smaller fish less. Well wrapped, your fish will not dry out. Do not be afraid to pull the foil back and fork test near the backbone—it is done when it flakes.

For superb salmon steaks, break out the foil once again. Wrap 2-inch steaks with a strip of bacon. Cover with diced onion and green pepper. Wrap in foil, and onto the grill with them, cooking approximately 6 minutes per side. Serve with wild rice and almonds and a nice spinach salad with French Dressing.

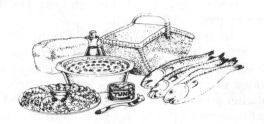

Putting It All Together

*Some tips on kitchen gear and cooking methods for
the well-equipped wild game chef*

No one becomes a master crafts-man without the tools of his trade. And the success of your game meals in many ways depends upon how well you use the cooking tools at your disposal.

You don't need to be elaborately equipped like Julia Child or Jeff Smith...TV stations foot the bills for the big kitchens these cooks work in. No, you don't have to break the bank to be a good game chef, and in fact, you probably are doing just fine with the kitchen gear you have already. But believe me, it is wise to take stock of your kitchen tool situation from time to time. It is far easier to assess a need and fill it, than to be caught short in the middle of some elaborate culinary preparation with company on the way over. In this chapter, I'd like to let you know about some of the items that I find indispensable in my kitchen. They may be of help in yours.

The Cutting Edge

Behind every good cook is a good set of knives. There isn't a kitchen in the world that is not equipped with a drawer full, so the lack of them, it seems, is never a problem. But the quality and condition of those knives is a different proposition.

Whether you plan to cook super-market turkeys or a big mess of opening-day ducks, good knives are essential in the kitchen. At the very least, you need a pair of good, sharp knives—a big one and a little one. But let's assume your cooking gets a little more ambitious than roast carving and potato quartering. A basic knife set for any kitchen should include a paring knife, for peeling vegetables; a carving knife, for large meats; a cleaver, for breaking big bones; and a straight-bladed chopper, or French chef's knife.

Any knife is only as good as its steel, and for my money, I'll choose one of carbon steel every time. Carbon steel will take and hold an edge better than other metals. Unlike blades made of stainless steel, your carbon steel knives may stain with years of use. But that is a small price to pay for having good, sharp knives all the time. Remember, "S" is for sharp and safe; "D" is for dull and very dangerous.

Beyond kitchen duty, the basic knife set above will also work well to clean and butcher game animals, big and small. You may wish to consider adding a short boning knife to your arsenal as well as the fillet knife and electric knife.

Remember to care for your tools. Rub wooden knife handles with cooking oil to prevent drying and cracking. Use a good sharpening steel on your blades often, a honing

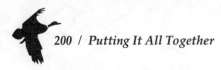

stone sparingly, and your act in the kitchen will look sharp for many years to come.

Wok this Way

You can use this wonderful oriental pan for virtually any kind of stove-top cooking, from steaming to boiling to deep frying. But the most popular and best use of the wok is stir-fry dishes.

Stir-frying is simply a fast fry over high heat. Your vegetables come out very crispy, your game meats, very tender. You can use *any* game meat or fish in a stir-fry. Heat a couple tablespoons of peanut oil, quickly fry your fish or meat and set aside. Now fry the veggies adding the hardest and most fibrous first so that they cook the longest. Stir the meat back in; serve over rice.

I prefer an electric wok over the rolled-steel type that sits on a ring above a stove burner. My electric pan sits squarely anywhere. This is handy, since I like to cook oriental dishes right at the table. The non-stick interior of the pan is a bonus as are the even, constant temperatures that come with a built-in thermostat.

Back in the Black

There are as many kinds of cookware on the market today as stores you can stumble into. But I submit that no new cookware is anywhere near as good as the old stuff that your grandmother used. I know, because I still use the black cast-iron pots and pans that once belonged to my grandmother.

Black cast-iron...everyone has seen it, but darn few know how to use it anymore. You will find no cookware more durable, and for this reason, cast-iron pots and pans are the best all-around cookware for any purpose. Whether in a modern kitchen or over a campfire, you won't be let down. In the outdoors, a heavy cast-iron pan or Dutch oven will hold heat a long time, even if your campfire starts to ebb on you. And carbon blackening is obviously no problem.

Those who did not grow up with cast-iron cookware generally make the same mistake in caring for it. I burn hotter than a tinderbox when a friend volunteers to help with dishes, then plunges my cast-iron skillet into sudsy dishwater. Detergent ruins your pan's "seasoning." That is, a thin layer of built-up oil adhering to the iron surface. Wash that away, and your pan will stick like the devil. When this happens, re-season your pan by scrubbing it well and oiling it. Bake it in an oven at 225 degrees for two or three hours and let cool. Future washings should consist of clear water and a good wiping. No detergents.

From the Inside Out

Outdoor cookery can be a fine change of pace, and an even finer change of *taste*. I know of no wild game meat or fish that is not enhanced through one method of outdoor cookery or another.

First, and most common, is the barbecue grill. Everyone has one, and I will not go into lengthy explanations, except to say that you should not be afraid to experiment. Add water-soaked fruitwood or hardwood chips to your charcoal to lend a different flavor to your meats. As I already discussed, the charcoal grill is a great way to cook fish—primarily the more oily ones such as salmon or big trout. Your white-fleshed fish tend to be less fatty, and thus, drier. For this reason you should keep them off the grill—but that does not mean that you cannot enjoy panfish with a wonderful, smokey flavor.

The backyard smoker is an indispensable tool for any sportsman. Ducks, geese, pheasants, quail, deer, elk, fish—name it, and it will do well in your backyard smoker.

Now You're Smoking

You can build your own smoker, using anything from an old refrigerator to a cardboard box, but for the novice, the best idea is to head for a department store or sport shop to purchase a ready-made one. You'll have two choices—a dry smoker or water smoker. A dry smoker employs a very hot fire, and its main advantage over a wet smoker is shorter cooking time. But you must pay constant attention and be quick with the basting brush. With a water smoker you do not have to worry about drying your meat out—there is a pan of liquid bètween the meat and the heat, which makes the smokey heat moist. For this reason you do not have to worry much about drying out those panfish, or any other piece of meat, for that matter. You can flavor your meats by adding herbs or spices to your water pan. Try beer, wine or bouillon. Also, don't be afraid to marinate your game meats before you smoke them. Again, fruitwoods

or hardwoods are the best to use in a smoker.

Dutch Oven Cooking

A Dutch oven is a heavy cast-iron pot with three legs, a heavy metal bail, and an iron lid with a 1-inch rim. An empty 12-inch oven and lid weigh about 20 pounds. These ovens can be used on a coal or wood range, in your electric or gas oven, outdoors placed on coals with coals on the lid, buried in the ground with coals, or hung over the fire.

Use charcoal briquets when practical, and light briquets 30 minutes prior to cooking. When using wood, always use hardwood coals which are not flaming, and have an extra supply of heated coals on hand to supplement while cooking.

Be sure to preheat the oven and lid and to be careful when lifting lid so that you do not spill ashes into the food. Prepare a place to lay the lid while inspecting food such as two sticks, a clean flat rock, or aluminum foil. Purchase or make a lid lifter. A fire poker is good or use a forked stick 18 inches long.

Be sure your Dutch oven is level and placed in an area without a draft. If it is windy and you cannot protect your Dutch oven, turn the oven one-quarter turn every fifteen minutes.

The general rule for the number of briquets for moderate heat for your oven is equal to two times the diameter of the oven. For high heat, use coals equal to three times the diameter of the oven. Most cooking will require more coals on the lid than on the ground. Spread coals

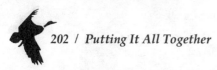

evenly on the ground. On the lid, use more coals around the edge and fewer in the middle. Dutch ovens may be stacked to save coals. Generally, for most meats, figure on 45 minutes to 1 hour for cooking.

Almost any food, such as stews, Swiss steak, pot roast, beans and vegetables can be done in a Dutch oven outdoors with approximately the same time and same results as at home. See pages 18 to 24 for menus and recipes.

Kitchen Essentials

Whether you cook inside or outside, you'll need to use some of the same things to bring your game meal to a successful conclusion. I've gone through my own kitchen and taken stock of the things I find essential in the cooking of wild game and fish. Consider these for your kitchen, if you haven't already.

- **Garlic Press**—Costs a little, gives you a lot—fresh garlic is better than processed powders.
- **Pepper Mill**—Again, inexpensive fresh peppercorns have a much sharper, more alive flavor than factory-ground powder.
- **Wire Whisk**—Couldn't make gravy or sauces without it. Get a big one and a little one.
- **Butter Clarifier**—Essential for gourmet dishes. A device that settles out and removes the cloudy, fatty solids from heated butter. Clarified butter does not burn as easily, and it looks nice.
- **Melon Scoop**—A number-10 melon baller is the best for dipping hush puppy batter. Makes pretty butter, melon or sherbet balls.

- **Wire Baskets**—For deep frying.
- **Electric Chopper**—My electric "mini chop," and my small manual chopper are great for chopping onion, pepper and celery very fine. Far easier to clean than a big Cuisinart.
- **Grinder**—The old-fashioned, hand-crank number. If you hunt deer or other big game, you need this for hash, sausage or ground meat. (For burger, chili, and spaghetti, add 30 percent fat.)
- **Scales**—A small set of accurate kitchen scales is a must, especially for recipes to feed a crowd.
- **Wooden Spoons**—Long and short handles—a complete set. Cheap, easy on cookware, won't melt, tarnish or flavor your food.
- **Basting Brushes**—A big one for the grill; a little one for inside.
- **Fondue Pot**—Electric is best—good for small amounts of soup and stew. Indispensable for hot dips or hot hors d'oeuvres.
- **Meat Thermometers**—You'll never overcook a roast.
- **Roaster**—A big one, with racks. Ducks, geese, venison—you'll be ready for them all. You can poach fish in it, too.
- **Pressure Cooker**—Good for fast cooking and tenderizing.
- **Slow Cooker**—For soups, stews, gumbos, chili, hot hors d'oeuvres. Cooks duck halves well, too.
- **Square Mesh Grill**—The hand-held type that everyone takes camping to do burgers and wieners over the fire. Great for steak or fish steaks.
- **Spatulas**—A set of durable metal ones—long and short handles.

Index

   for Tomatoes, 52
Fruit
   Fresh à la Mexico, 49
   Pink Champagne, 48
Pasta House
      Company, 49
Slaw
   with Class, 51
   Confetti, 50
   Hog Roost, 50
Spinach, Fresh, 51
Vinaigrette on Wild Rice, 167
SHELLFISH
Clam
   Casserole, Shep's, 149
   Italian Linguine with, Sauce, 150
Crab
   Cakes, Moise Island, 152
   Casserole, and Artichoke, 151
   Dressing, 151
   Gravy, 153
   Lasky's Fresh, 152
   Louis Appetizer, 12
   Quiche, 150
   Soup, 39
Lobster Hors d'Oeuvres, 33
Mussels, Mamma's Pickled, 153
Oysters, Panned, 154
Scallops
   Bourbon Supreme, 155
   Casserole, 154
Shrimp
   Dip, 32
   Jeff's Drunken, Wiggle, 155
   Rosemary, 156
Supreme, 156
SIDE DISHES
Chutney, Cranberry, 170
Dressing
   Apple, for Game Birds, 169
   Corn Bread, 169
Fruit, Hot Curried, 13, 179
Marinades, 60, 102
Rice
   Apple and Cinnamon, 164
   Broccoli and, Casserole, 166
   Casserole, 166
Salsa, 170, 171
Sauce
   Barbecue, 130
   Blender Basting, for Beef, 126
   Cranberry, Fresh, 16
   Fruited, for Duck, 57
   Lemon, 21
   Mustard, for Duck, 56

Stuffing
   Bob's Saskatoon Mallard, 170
   Oyster, 17
Wild Rice
   Casserole, 167
      Sausage and, 168
      Wild Game, 166
   Chowder, Minnesota, 46
   Dish, 168
   Soup, 47
      Cheese and Potato, 46
   Vinaigrette on, 167
SOUP
Arizona Red, 41
Autumn Game, 40
Bean, Keefer's Pink, 39
Booyah Belgian, 40
Chowder
   Barefield's, 41
   Fish, Maine Indian, 42
   Minnesota Wild Rice, 46
Crab, 39
Duck, Grandma, 42
Fish, Maine Indian Chowder, 42
Onion, French, 43
Steak, Joan's, 44
Tomato
   Arizona Red, 41
   Winter Warmer, 44
Tuna, Cream of, 45
Venison Cabbage, 45
Wild Rice, 47
   Cheese and Potato, 26
   Chowder, Minnesota, 46
   and Pheasant, 43
Winter Warmer, 44
Zucchini, 47
TURKEY
Broccoli Casserole, 138
Deep-Fried, 139
Wild, Ashepoo, 16
Veal, Scalloppine al Carciofi, 127
VEGETABLES
Artichoke
   Casserole, 159
   Dip, Butter's, 31
Beans
   Calico, 159
   Celery, Bake, 20
   Dilly Green, 17
   Soup, Pink, 39
Broccoli
   Casserole, 161
   and Cream Cheese Casserole, 160
   and Rice Casserole, 166
Carrots, Marinated, 160

Great Gifts!

Got a favorite outdoors person on your gift list? Why not pick up an extra copy of *From Duck Country*? A warm wild game feast makes for the warmest of holidays.

Send $9.95 plus $1.50 shipping and handling for each book to:

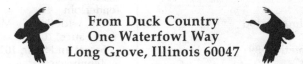

**From Duck Country
One Waterfowl Way
Long Grove, Illinois 60047**

Please send checks or money orders. For Visa and MasterCard orders call (312) 438-4300. Orders shipped UPS. Express shipping available on credit card orders at additional charge.